D0832173

UNFINISHED PEACE

REPORT OF THE INTERNATIONAL COMMISSION ON THE BALKANS

Leo Tindemans, Chairman
Lloyd Cutler
Bronislaw Geremek
John Roper
Theo Sommer
Simone Veil
David Anderson (ex officio)

ASPEN INSTITUTE BERLIN

CARNEGIE ENDOWMENT FOR INTERNATIONAL PEACE

© 1996 by the
Carnegie Endowment for International Peace
2400 N Street, N.W.
Washington, D.C. 20037
Tel. 202-862-7900
Fax. 202-862-2610

All rights reserved. Permission to reproduce parts of this Report for educational purposes (with full credit) will be liberally granted but must be obtained
in writing from Publications, Carnegie Endowment for International Peace.

Copies of this book can be obtained ($14.95/£ 11.75) from:

U.S. and International
(other than U.K. & Europe):
The Brookings Institution Press
Dept. 029, Washington, D.C. 20042-0029
Tel. 1-800-275-1447 or 202-797-6258.
Fax. 202-797-6004.

U.K. and Europe:
Plymbridge Distributors Ltd.
Plymbridge House, Estover Road
Plymouth PL6 7PZ, United
Kingdom
Tel. 44-1752-202301 or

Edited and produced by Valeriana Kallab.

Cover and book design: Paddy McLaughlin Concepts & Design.

Cover photo: © Nick Sharp, Reuters/Archive Photos.

Printed by Automatic Graphic Systems, Inc.

Library of Congress Cataloging-in-Publication Data
International Commission on the Balkans.
UNFINISHED PEACE: Report of the International Commission on the Balkans
Foreword by Leo Tindemans
p. 224
ISBN: 0-87003-118-X
   1. Balkan Peninsula—Politics and government—1989.
   2. Balkan Peninsula—Ethnic relations.
   3. National security—Balkan Peninsula.
   4. Yugoslav War. 1991-—Peace.   I. Title
   DR48.6.I58 1996   96-36352
   949.6'0559—DC20   CIP

The Carnegie Endowment for International Peace normally does not take
institutional positions on public policy issues. The views and recommendations
presented in this publication do not necessarily represent the views of the
Carnegie Endowment or the Aspen Institute Berlin, or of their officers,
trustees, or staff.

CONTENTS

FOREWORD, by Leo Tindemans   vii

SUMMARY OVERVIEW   xiii

INTRODUCTION   1

I.   THE BALKAN PREDICAMENT   13

THE ORIGINS OF THE WAR:
FALLACIES AND REALITIES   13
    Great Power Ambitions?   13
    Ancestral Hatreds?   14
    A Clash of Civilizations?   15

THE BREAKUP OF YUGOSLAVIA   22
    The Dual Legacy of Ethnic Nationalism
      and Communism   23
    The Failed Transition to Democracy   26

NATION-STATE BUILDING IN
A MULTI-ETHNIC ENVIRONMENT   28
    From Self-Determination to Secession   28
    Bosnia and Herzegovina—A Nation-State
      Without a Nation?   32

MAIN ISSUES TO BE ADDRESSED   35

II. THE WAR AND THE INTERNATIONAL RESPONSE   37

PRELUDE AND WAR   37

THE LOGIC OF PEACE PLANS   42
    Last Chances   43
    Croatia   45
    Bosnia and Herzegovina   47

TRANSATLANTIC STRAINS   55
    The European Response   56
    The United States   62
    Russia   65
    The United Nations   67
    Three Errors of Western Policy   68

CONCLUSIONS   74

III. COUNTRY CONDITIONS, TRENDS, AND PROPOSALS — 77

BOSNIA AND HERZEGOVINA — 77
  Republika Srpska — 79
  The Bosniak-Croat Federation — 81
  Trends in Bosniak Politics and Society — 84
  Conclusions and Recommendations — 84

CROATIA — 102
  The Opposition in Croatia — 104
  Conclusions and Recommendations — 106

SERBIA — 107
  Conclusions and Recommendations — 111

KOSOVO AND SERBIA'S TANGLED ETHNIC RELATIONS — 112
  Kosovo — 113
  Conclusions and Recommendations — 117

THE ALBANIANS — 119
  Albanians in Macedonia — 119
  Albanian Union? — 122
  Albania — 123
  Conclusions and Recommendations — 126

MACEDONIA — 127
  Conclusions and Recommendations — 129

BULGARIA, THE BULGARIAN TURKS, AND TURKEY — 130

GREECE AND TURKEY IN THE BALKANS — 132
  Minorities in Greece — 133
  Turkey's Role in the Balkans — 134
  Turkey's Ethnic Entanglements — 135

IV. **THE REGION: CONCLUSIONS
AND PROPOSALS**   **137**

BALKAN REGIONAL COOPERATION   140
     Economic Cooperation   142

RECONSTRUCTION AND DEVELOPMENT   144
     Developing the Economies of the Region   145

DEMOCRACY: CIVIL SOCIETY AND MEDIA   148
     Obstacles to Democracy   148
     Civil Society   150
     Independent Media   152

ETHNIC RELATIONS AND THE
TREATMENT OF MINORITIES   157

SECURITY   164
     Arms Control and Collective Security   165
     The Continuing Commitment of NATO   169

EPILOGUE   **173**

ANNEXES

     MAPS   175

     The Commission's Study Missions and Meetings   179

     About the Commission, its Members, Staff,
         and Consultants   191

     About Aspen Institute Berlin and
     the Carnegie Endowment for International Peace   194

     The 1913 Carnegie Endowment Commission's
         Report on the Balkans   198

FOREWORD

In 1914, the Carnegie Endowment for International Peace published the *Report of the International Commission to Inquire into the Causes and Conduct of the Balkan Wars* of 1912 and 1913. The drawing up of that document had been entrusted to a small International Commission, presided over by the French Senator Baron d'Estournelles de Constant, who had represented his country at the Peace Conferences of The Hague in 1899 and in 1907.

In his introduction to the Commission's Report, d'Estournelles de Constant stated that he would never forget the impression of sadness and astonishment that he carried away from his visits to the Balkan states. All this horror will not cease to exist, he wrote in 1914, as long as Europe continues to ignore it. And he added: "This is the state of things which the Americans wish to help in ending. Let them be thanked and honored for their generous initiative."

Regretting that the powers of Europe had over half a century spent "hundreds of billions" contributing to arsenals in the region instead of helping to provide the poor countries of the Balkans with roads, waterways, schools, laboratories, museums, hospitals, and public works, d'Estournelles de Constant recognized that a more suitable title for the Commission's Report would have been "Divided Europe and her Demoralizing Action in the Balkans." But "taking it all round," he wrote, this criticism "might have been unjust." He concluded that: "In reality there is no salvation, no way out either for small states or for great countries except by union and conciliation."

In 1995, in much the same spirit as prompted the formation of the 1913-14 inquiry, the Carnegie Endowment and the Aspen Institute—together with several European and American foundations (see complete listing, p. xii)—took the initiative to again create such an International Commission, giving it the mandate of drawing up a report on the situation in the Balkans and of formulating long-term measures to contribute to the establishment of a durable peace in that region. These special efforts led to a unique cooperation: American and European foundations worked together. It was a remarkable transatlantic achievement. The sponsoring institutions took the initiative because they were convinced that the existing difficulties and the domination mentality in the Balkans are a lasting menace to peace, a terrifying example of intolerance, and a shame for Europe. As our predecessors did in 1914, I wish to thank all those who were convinced that an effort of that kind could have positive results—notwithstanding the extremely difficult atmosphere reigning in Europe. They believed in the need for such an initiative, and they carried it through. We are grateful for their inspiration, which they supported so tenaciously and courageously.

It was a personal and intellectual pleasure for me to work with the team that was chosen to carry out the present task. The members of this International Commission were: Simone Veil, John Roper, Theo Sommer, Lloyd Cutler, Bronislaw Geremek, David Anderson (ex officio), and myself. The role of executive director was entrusted to Jacques Rupnik. Commission members were aware that—being totally independent and serving no particular interest—they had to speak their minds, without ambiguity. Their objective was peace, a durable one, to pave the way to democracy, prosperity, well-being, and a humane society. And they did not ignore that the persuasive power of their conclusions and proposals would depend on the correct analysis of the problems.

In 1993, the Carnegie Endowment reissued the 1914 Commission Report, with an introduction by George F. Kennan that "lifts our sights while lowering our expectations"—as Morton Abramowitz, Carnegie Endowment president, remarked in describing the new volume. Kennan underlined that the prevailing question remains how, in the years to come, relations should be organized among the Balkan states. Many of them violated the basic principles of the United Nations Charter. Some of them cherish territorial aspirations. Is this a matter of indifference for the international community? A territorial status quo must be obtained, with solemn recognition of the borders. Is it not inevitable that, to create the conditions of a durable peace, the rights and duties of sovereign states have to be clearly defined? Moreover, a minimum of military force must be available, and the conviction must exist that, if necessary, force will be used. This presupposes the building up of an efficient European security policy.

Although the military conflict seems over, at least for the present, the international community, and particularly the European Union, will remain confronted with a lasting challenge in this southeastern part of the European continent.

The present Commission's visits, interviews, meetings, comments, exchanges of views, and analyses not only helped deepen our knowledge of the problems, but also were conducive to the formation of a common opinion concerning the elements needed for peace. When I express my thanks to the members of the Commission and our staff, this is not just an expression of my personal feeling of gratitude; it is a public recognition and appreciation of their contribution to the common task.

Our task was not an easy one. We took it up when the Dayton Accords were not in sight. Then, part-way into our enterprise, we adapted out efforts to also address the challenges of anchoring and widening an unfinished peace. In our work, the most difficult problems of a modern society had to be examined and evaluated. Among these were: the relationship between nation and state; the conflicting expectations of ethnic and religious minorities; the development of nationalism, regionalism, confederalism, and federalism; the viability of a multi-ethnic state; the acceptance of cultural autonomy; the requirements of modern democracy and civil society; the role of political parties; employment; the transition to market economies; the activities and role of the media; and constitutional problems. Moreover, in the Balkans, where history so often shapes the attitudes of today, a good knowledge of the past was often a precondition for the success of our dialogues.

In 1914, Baron d'Estournelles Constant thought it necessary to mention that he expected the issuance of the Commission's Report to meet with criticism—because "it would give full satisfaction to none and would displease everybody more or less." We hope that the findings of this Commission, too, will prompt debate.

Our visits to the Balkan states, the considerable research effort, the preparation of the Report itself—all these were an exceptional political adventure during which we were looking for material to help build a peaceful society in the Balkans. Today we present the result of our endeavors. We can console ourselves with the Chinese saying: "If you wish to produce a perfect book, it will never be finished." Ours is completed now.

Let me conclude this presentation of our Report with the motto of Charles the Bold, Duke of Burgundy—a motto that sums up all our efforts and expresses our fervent hope and fondest wishes:

"I have undertaken it,

May good come of it."

Leo Tindemans, *Chairman*
International Commission on the Balkans

July 1996

THE INTERNATIONAL COMMISSION ON THE BALKANS

Leo Tindemans, Chairman
Member of the European Parliament,
and Former Prime Minister of Belgium

Lloyd Cutler
Partner, Wilmer, Cutler & Pickering,
and Former U.S. Presidential Counsel

Bronislaw Geremek
Historian, Chairman of the Foreign Affairs Committee
of the Polish Parliament, and Former Solidarity Advisor

John Roper
Fellow, Royal Institute of International Affairs, Former Director of the
Institute for Security Studies of the Western European Union,
and Former Member of the British Parliament

Theo Sommer
Publisher of Die Zeit, and Former Chief of Planning Staff,
Ministry of Defense, Federal Republic of Germany

Simone Veil
Former President of the European Parliament, and
Former French Minister of Health and Social Affairs

David Anderson (ex officio)
Director, Aspen Institute Berlin,
and Former U.S. Ambassador to Yugoslavia

SENIOR STAFF

Jacques Rupnik, *Executive Director*

Dana H. Allin, *Deputy Director*

James F. Brown, *Senior Analyst*

Mark Thompson, *Senior Analyst*

SUPPORTING EUROPEAN AND AMERICAN FOUNDATIONS

The Aspen Institute (Washington, D.C., and Berlin)

The Carnegie Endowment for International Peace (Washington, D.C.)

The King Baudouin Foundation (Brussels)

The Berghof Foundation for Conflict Research (Munich)

The Robert Bosch Foundation (Stuttgart)

The Carnegie Corporation (New York)

The European Cultural Foundation (Amsterdam)

The European Cooperation Fund (Brussels)

The Ford Foundation (New York)

The Koerber Foundation (Hamburg)

The Charles Stewart Mott Foundation (Flint, Michigan)

The Open Society Fund (New York)

The City of Berlin and Siemens, A.G., generously provided the Commission's staff with offices and equipment.

SUMMARY OVERVIEW

In the spring of 1914, the report of the first Carnegie International Commission on the Balkans asked: "Must we allow these Balkan wars to pass, without at least trying to draw some lesson from them, without knowing whether they have been a benefit or an evil, if they should begin again tomorrow and go on forever extending?" The Commission commented that "Europe and the great military powers . . . . could, in spite of everything, solve the problem if they were not determined to remain blind."

This Commission believes that turning a blind eye to the Balkans would be no less a recipe for disaster at the end of the twentieth century than it was at its outset. Outside guarantors, even enforcers, of the peace will have to remain in the region—first and foremost in Bosnia—for a considerable period of time.

Because the prospects for peace and stability in the region remain tenuous, the Commission believes it is imperative to muster the political will and the strategic consensus to do now what the world was unable to do in the midst of conflict. The lessons of the past few years are that the United Nations, torn by conflicting national perspectives, cannot organize international action in time, that the United States and Europe must work together if they want to affect a particular situation, and that diplomacy not backed by force is tantamount to hollow gesturing.

The disappearance of the likelihood of East-West conflict in Europe contributed to the dilatory nature of the West's response to the dissolution of Yugoslavia and to the war. At the same time, changed strategic considerations suggest that outside guarantors of the peace have room within which to work against older patterns of intra-regional conflict, and that these may be amenable to new approaches to establishing security, ensuring minority rights, and instilling democracy.

Three historical explanations have been offered concerning the origins of the recent Balkan war. The first, widely held in the Balkans, sees today's return of nationalist conflicts as reflecting ambitions of great powers to reestablish Balkan spheres of influence. The second, widely held in the West, emphasizes the "return of ancestral hatreds" or the "return of the suppressed nations." A third thesis looks for origins of the war in cultural and religious fault-lines—a "clash of civilizations."

There are elements of truth here, and no one should under-estimate the weight of history in the Balkans. But the main caus-es of the war lie in the sparks of aggressive nationalism fanned into flames by those political leaders of the dissolving Yugoslav federation who have invoked the "ancient hatreds" to pursue their respective nationalist agendas and have deliberately used their propaganda machines to justify the unjustifiable: the use of violence for territorial conquest, expulsion of 'other' peoples, and the perpetuation of authoritarian systems of power.

The stakes for the West in restraining aggressiveness in the Balkans remain high. Renewed fighting would doubtless entail more 'ethnic cleansing'—either requiring large-scale interven-tion to stop it, or occasioning another failure of the major pow-ers to intervene that could raise further questions about what values both sides of the Atlantic are willing to defend.

Worsened ethnic relations and deterioration in the treat-ment of minorities in the Balkans would have repercussions elsewhere in Eastern Europe and in the former Soviet Union, where demographics and political boundaries do not coincide. Moreover, the fate of the Muslims—their political integration or separateness—could become a touchstone of relations between Europe and the Islamic world.

REGIONAL RECOMMENDATIONS

Security

The Commission found in Southeastern Europe a potential for conflict much greater than that to be found anywhere else in Europe outside the former Soviet Union. There are two major epicenters of conflict in the Balkans today. The first, the north-ern tier, centers on Bosnia but involves more broadly the Serbo-Croatian relationship. Dayton stopped the fighting but not some of the sources of conflict in the region. The second, the southern tier, centers on Kosovo and directly concerns Serbia, Albania, and Macedonia; it also potentially involves Bulgaria, Greece, and Turkey.

Improved ethnic relations, democracy, and Balkan cooper-ation are necessary for lasting peace and security. But these will require a framework of peace and military security—arms-con-trol, confidence-building, and collective security measures within the region, and, more immediately, a continuing and coherent military engagement by NATO. The Dayton Accords set out measures for: (1) confidence and security-building in Bosnia and Herzegovina; (2) sub-regional arms control agreements covering all three republics; and (3) a longer-term objective of a regional arms-control agreement for the area in and around former Yugoslavia.

Many Americans argue that the internationally recognized Bosnian government cannot again be left defenseless; Europeans, on the other hand, maintain that whatever is provided to Sarajevo's forces could easily be countered by weapons from Russia and other sources—leading to an arms race and, ultimately, *less* security for the Sarajevo government. The Commission itself is divided on whether or not to arm and train the Bosnian army but believes that an international security presence—in particular, a follow-on mission to the Implementation Force (IFOR)—could help resolve the dilemma until progress is made in cooperation among the parties.

NATO's Partnership for Peace offers a way, short of membership, to respond to Balkan aspirations to join NATO without abandoning the Western Alliance's ability to influence the region. The Commission therefore recommends creation of a "Balkan Association of Partnership for Peace" to ensure through a coordination office that all NATO members keep a continuing active interest in the security of the region. But for the foreseeable future, the need for a NATO commitment that goes beyond Partnership for Peace will remain. The Contact Group, which could be expanded to include Italy, must be maintained as a mechanism for common decision-making—on Bosnia, but perhaps for Balkans policy in general. Given the credibility of American military power in the region, a military presence of the United States must be maintained.

The success of Dayton will depend on Americans and Europeans continuing to work together, and the question of a post-IFOR deployment is becoming a test-case both for a European common foreign and security policy (CSFP) and for a new division of roles within NATO. Fortunately, there is increased appreciation on both sides of the Atlantic that transatlantic unity and a European defense identity are not contradictory; development of policy on the Balkans must foster both.

Finally, NATO members should recognize that it may be necessary to demonstrate their will with military force. Another Bosnia in the Balkans, or Bosnia itself, might not directly threaten the West, but it would again corrode its sense of unity and purpose. And, as in the experience of early 1990s, intervention probably would occur—sooner or later.

The outside factors that made possible the mass slaughter at Srebrenica were numerous: the refusal of the leading international powers, until summer 1995, to exert a credible threat of force to impose a solution; the gap between the rhetoric and the willingness of the international powers to back their words with actions; the under-equipping of the U.N. forces; the inability of humanitarian intervention to substitute for a political strategy involving, if necessary, the use of force; the tendency of many U.N. officials to equate impartiality with neutrality between warring parties, even when one or more were violating Security Council mandates; and the tendency of the U.N. Secretariat—especially when faced with impracticable, unenforceable, and crucially ambiguous mandates, to "redefine" the mandates to minimize the risks of implementation. It must not be allowed to happen again.

Reconstruction and Development

In Bosnia, the immediate need is for reconstruction, but the entire region also requires removal of the obstacles to dismantling state socialism and reversal of the effects of war and sanctions. The needs include: a proper banking system, legal and fiscal rules, and a dismantling of trade barriers to foster regional cooperation. The Commission believes that small-scale capitalism—except in the urgent case of Bosnian infrastructure development—in industry, agriculture, and commerce and services, will be more important than large-scale projects for future prosperity and cooperation in the Balkans.

International assistance is indispensable: to improve market access for Balkan exports, especially those of the Yugoslav successor states; to provide quick financial assistance for rebuilding infrastructure and for settling refugees (necessary before private capital will flow); to provide, through the IMF, the World Bank, and other institutions, assistance for stabilization, market reform, and structural adjustment efforts, in Bosnia especially; and to help settle the claims of international banks, governments, and citizens on the Yugoslav successor states.

Democracy

Obstacles to effective democracy in the Balkans stem from the legacies of war, of communism, and of history. The obstacles include: the fragility of parliamentary democratic institutions; the absence of institutions independent of the state and of social forces capable of sustaining them; the weakness, or indeed, absence of an organized democratic opposition; and "apparat nationalism," or the legacy of attempts by Balkan communist leaders to assert autonomy vis-a-vis Moscow while sustaining domestic totalitarianism in the name of national unity.

Moreover, the adoption of presidential, rather than parliamentary, systems in some Balkan countries tends to reinforce centralized authoritarian features, as does the subordination of the state administration to ruling-party whims—normal practice in Romania, Serbia, Bulgaria, or Croatia. Meanwhile, control of the media, especially television and radio, by ruling parties leaves the opposition without a voice, while intense nationalism undermines the development of political pluralism.

The Commission recommends that public and private Western institutions adopt—as a long-term priority—the development and revival of the institutions of civil society, including independent cultural or professional associations, independent judiciaries, and free media. International NGOs should strive to identify *local* priorities and coordinate better to avoid duplication.

Independent media are a problem of vital importance for the prospects for democracy in the whole region. The ugly propaganda campaigns that nationalist media mounted to foment war in former Yugoslavia must not be overlooked or forgotten. Western governments and international institutions should place a high priority on freedom of the media in their dealings with the countries of the region.

Ethnic Relations and Treatment of Minorities

The 'ethnic cleansing' or forced assimiliation that has prevailed in much of the Balkans since the nineteenth century has been a response to the notion that one state should correspond to one nation, one culture, one religion. Some argue that ethno-nationalism can be defused politically by granting minorities cultural rights (language, religion, etc.) so that cultural autonomy will preempt demands for territorial autonomy.

This is unlikely to work in the Balkans: Minorities will not trust legal guarantees if they are not accompanied by territorial autonomy, while the major national groups fear that granting collective rights and autonomy will encourage disintegration and irredentism.

The Commission believes that: state constitutions should provide the protection of minority rights; that these rights should be specified and not left for interpretation by local officials; that proportional representation, despite its potential for fostering fragmentation, should be included in the electoral systems; and that decentralization and some degree of autonomy on the regional and municipal levels are essential in mixed territories. Above all, however, a "community of security" requires a civil society (in which ethnicity is not the exclusive organizing principle), the rule of law (guaranteeing human rights and minority rights), and institutional means of mediation and arbitration to settle disputes.

The Commission recommends the development of an international tribunal (the World Court or the European Commission and Court on Human Rights could be assigned the task) to deliberate on the limits of self-determination—in effect, helping to resolve the inherent tension between the right to self-determination expressed in the U.N. Charter and the international commitment to the inviolability of borders.

Regional Cooperation

The potential for further conflict in the Balkans has led to suggestions for some form of preemptive international conference. The Commission, however, questions the feasibility of either an International Conference on Security in the Balkans or an even more ambitious conference aimed at creating a South Balkans Confederation. Such an approach, because it would not be able to gain the necessary compromises by all parties from the outset, would be unlikely to succeed.

Instead, to begin the slow process toward Balkan cooperation, the Commission recommends the establishment—with the EU and the United States taking the diplomatic initiative—of a network of regional commissions to work on specific problems, including: ethnic and minority relations, religious reconciliation and cooperation, civil society, economic and infrastructural development, the environment, transnational crime, and relations with Western institutions.

Should some Balkan nations oppose participation in or even the establishment of these commissions—many in the region see any commitment to cooperation as only postponing the aim of joining Europe, not as preparing for it—it would probably be necessary for the West to use pressure, by taking advantage of the Balkan nations' eagerly sought "acceptance" by Europe. The EU could offer bilateral Trade and Cooperation Treaties to Croatia, Bosnia-Herzegovina, Serbia and Montenegro, Macedonia, and Albania; association agreements with several Balkan states already exist or have been promised.

A free trade area seems to the Commission the most politically realistic and economically expedient starting point; it would afford its members maximum economic and political sovereignty. Eventually such a free trade area might become part of the Central European Free Trade Area (CEFTA)—thereby lessening fears among the Balkan countries that regional cooperation is a prelude to re-establishing "Yugoslavia."

COUNTRY-BY-COUNTRY RECOMMENDATIONS

Bosnia and Herzegovina

With respect to Bosnia, the Dayton settlement is inherently contradictory: It accepts the status quo of ethnic territorial lines achieved by force, yet tries to protect and restore the multi-ethnic character of Bosnia. The latter is a very difficult task; with Bosnian Serbs gravitating toward Serbia and Bosnia Croats toward Croatia, the Bosniaks alone of the three constituent peoples will be left with a vital interest in preserving the new state. Indeed, a confederal arrangement—tending to undermine the new Bosnia from the start—is implied by the Dayton Accords' formulation that the entities have the right to establish "special parallel relations with neighboring states consistent with the sovereignty and territorial integrity of Bosnia and Herzegovina."

Of three scenarios for Bosnia—(1) restoration of multi-ethnic Bosnia; (2) peaceful coexistence of three communities within two entities, under a common roof; and (3) partition, first into two and then into three parts, possibly leading to *de facto* annexation by Croatia and Serbia, leaving some 30 per cent of Bosnia as a tiny rump state for Bosniaks—the third may be the most likely. Although some hold that such full, three-way partition is inevitable and thus should be accepted now, we believe that to leave an Islamic state sandwiched between a 'Greater Serbia' and a 'Greater Croatia' is a recipe for instability and would have decidedly negative effects on Islamic relations with Europe.

To prevent full partition and, over time, promote reintegration of a truly multi-ethnic Bosnia, the provisions of Dayton, now flouted with impunity, must be fully implemented. Moreover, the United States and Western Europe must be united in purpose. The Commission would base a transatlantic strategy for Bosnia on the following principles:

- A guarantee of long-term security—a guarantee that will require first of all an international military presence that continues for several years after December 1996;

- The preservation and strenthening of all the main common institutions of Bosnia and Herzegovina;

- Enforcement of the Dayton signatories' solemn commitment to cooperate in delivering indicted individuals to the U.N. War Crimes Tribunal; if they are not delivered, the Tribunal should try them "in absentia."

- Guaranteeing the existence of free and independent media and removing effective monopolies of the most influential media in Bosnia by the various party-regimes;

- The building of civil society—the nationally mixed institutions and social infrastructure destroyed in the war—with help from Western governments, foundations, and NGOs;

- Since the environment in which the September 1996 elections are scheduled to be held (before this Report is released) can hardly be described as being free and fair, international efforts should focus now on ensuring that new elections are held within two years under truly free and fair conditions;

- Reconstruction efforts should give priority to projects promoting Bosnia's economic integration;

- The civilian side of the Western presence must be rationalized and strengthened, including giving a long-term mandate to the High Representative and improving coordination between IFOR (and post-IFOR) troops and civilian components, to ensure military support for civilian tasks;

- The right of refugees to return must be preserved. If refugees, the prime (living) victims of the war, cannot go home if they wish, it is improper to speak of a just peace at all. The financial burden of the refugees should be shared among EU countries, which will also need to be more forthcoming on offering permanent visas to refugees and their families.

Croatia

With Croatia bent on "reintegration with Europe" (President Tudjman's words), European and American governments should raise the price for their friendship and support and make clear their expectations of improvement in the treatment of minorities, the return of refugee Serbs, freedom of the press, and the promotion of the local dimension of democracy. Above all, Zagreb should be expected to establish constructive relations with Bosnia and Herzegovina, help dissolve the 'Croat Republic of Herceg-Bosna,' promote the functioning of the Bosniak-Croat Federation, and take part in Bosnia's economic recovery. Sustained Western pressure will be needed.

Serbia

The West should not encourage the notion that implementing Dayton requires giving President Milosevic a free hand in Serbia and Kosovo. Serbia's quest for legitimization offers the West leverage, and Serbia's reintegration into the community of nations should be made contingent on its respect for the sovereignty of Bosnia and its compliance with Dayton—including its provisions relating to indicted war criminals. Belgrade should accept the draft treaty on the succession of former Yugoslavia, regulating the distribution of its debts and assets. And in light of the U.N. resolution stating that Yugoslavia has ceased to exist, Belgrade should be expected to reapply for admission to the United Nations and other international institutions; the West should coordinate its strategy for recognizing the new Yugoslavia.

Kosovo

The Serb minority in Kosovo has been dwindling, leading most Albanians in Kosovo to believe that "time and patience" will bring the province independence from Serbia and sovereignty. A stand-off has evolved between the official Serbian state and a "parallel" Albania state, but this reflects less a coexistence based on tolerance than an apartheid based on growing Albanian hatred of Serb maltreatment and humiliation and Serbian fear of being eventually overwhelmed. The longer a solution to the Kosovo problem is delayed, the greater the risk of a conflagration—one that might easily spread beyond Kosovo's borders.

The Commission suggests that:

- Serbia should lift martial law entirely, restore autonomy, and, before negotiations begin, gradually withdraw troops and police. A normal civil and cultural life should be restored to Kosovo through efforts by the Albanian leadership, Western foundations and NGOs, and the Serbs. Pristina University must be restored as an open and pluralistic institution.

- The Kosovo Albanian leadership should be ready to enter negotiations without preconditions, backing off from their refusal to talk about anything other than independence.

- A final outcome should take into account legitimate Serb concerns, including reliable guarantees of the rights of the Serbian minority in Kosovo, and also acknowledge the right of the Kosovo Albanians to self-government including, but not limited to, control of their own police and judiciary, and health, cultural, and educational institutions.

If no agreement can be reached within a reasonable period of time, say two years, the West should support a binding international arbitration to determine the future political structure of Kosovo, including, if the arbitrators so recommend, a Kosovo-wide referendum on the various options.

Albania

The Commission believes that the pro-Western orientation of Albania should continue to be encouraged, but that the Berisha government should not be allowed to interpret this as a license for undemocratic behavior; that Albania's infrastructure should be brought up to the level of its neighbors—a task especially for the EU and for Italy and Greece; and that Turkish and other Balkan ties should be encouraged over other Islamic ties. Albanians do not define their country in religious terms, and any move to do so would be a mistake.

Macedonia

Macedonia has proven to be one of the more stable successor states of former Yugoslavia, but much will depend on how it deals with the problem of its Albanian minority. The primary goal of outside influence should be to encourage an Albanian stake in Macedonian statehood—an approach that will require a high degree of decentralization in Macedonia and continued political restraint on both sides. The presence of UNPREDEP should be maintained pending substantial progress in resolving the Kosovo problem. The Macedonian government should take the lead in defusing the tense Tetovo University dispute. Restoring normal operations at Pristina University in Kosovo together with complete opening of the Kosovo-Macedonia border could help.

Bulgaria, the Bulgarian Turks, and Turkey

In Bulgaria, former President Zhivkov's successors reversed the brutal Turkish assimiliation policy of the 1980s, and many, perhaps half, of those in the Turkish minority who moved to Turkey returned. But many Bulgarians, even among liberals, are apprehensive of Turkey as a powerful and increasingly assertive neighbor and over Turkey's relations with Bulgaria's Turkish minority.

Greece and Turkey in the Balkans

Strained Greek-Turkish relations have been reflected throughout the Balkans, and Greeks, more than Turks, see their mutual rivalry as zero-sum. There is a dangerous arms buildup on both sides, and Cyprus is a worrying reminder that ethnic conflict can threaten regional stability.

The most direct form of Balkan intervention for either country so far was Greece's economic blockade of Macedonia between 1993 and 1995, and nothing has been less rational than the initial hysteria whipped up in Greece over Macedonia. But there has been movement toward a settlement with Macedonia; and Greece, as a member of EU and NATO, could yet prove to be Macedonia's political, commercial, and intellectual conduit to the world at large.

For Turkey, the Balkans are not an overwhelming strategic preoccupation—compared to the Caucasus and pipeline problems—but loom large emotionally—as a symbol of secular Islam's fate within Europe, as the birthplace of peoples sprinkled throughout Turkish society, and as the detritus of empire, leaving behind Turkish and Muslim communities whose fate cannot be ignored.

Within Turkey, long-standing minority communities of Bosnians and Albanians have pushed Ankara toward a more active policy in the Balkans. Recognition of historical if not ethnic kinship with Bosniaks has a religious dimension that encourages some Turks to see in the Bosnian carnage a Western disdain for Muslims. Even sophisticated Turks, however, see the failure of Bosnia's national experiment as casting a shadow over Turkey's survival as a pluralist Muslim community with aspirations to join Europe. And at bottom is the grievance that Western Europe cannot identify with a Muslim society, however secular. Meanwhile the Bosnia theme has been a potent weapon in the hands of Turkey's Islamists, who now hold the Prime Ministership and are making unprecedented advances on the domestic political scene.

The Balkans should not be seen solely through the prism of the Bosnian tragedy. Today they stand at the crossroads, confronted with the prospect of being marginalized once again or of overcoming the present crisis and creating the conditions for their integration into the European mainstream. The ultimate challenge, for both the West and the Balkan peoples themselves, is to create a framework that gives everyone a stake in peace. This applies especially to the former warring parties of ex-Yugoslavia. In order to avoid a new nationalistic eruption, it is not enough to propose technical solutions. Each side must feel it is gaining something in exchange for sacrificing something. The Western powers are unlikely to maintain their forces in the Balkans forever. Thus, each side must be made to see the cost of resuming war as higher than the cost of maintaining peace.

The peoples of the Balkans deserve the chance to leave their tragic past behind. The nations that have done so earlier owe it to their sense of humanity, their dignity, and peace of conscience to help the fragile nations in the region overcome their present predicament and transform the bloody Balkans of yesteryear into the Southeastern Europe of the future.

UNFINISHED PEACE
REPORT OF THE INTERNATIONAL
COMMISSION ON THE BALKANS

INTRODUCTION

When the guns of Europe fell silent on May 8, 1945—after five and a half years of death and destruction—the peoples of the Continent drew a deep breath. Exhausted and chastened, victors and vanquished alike swore to themselves: Never again! During the subsequent forty years of Cold War between East and West, the guns remained silent. In the end the Berlin Wall came down, the Iron Curtain crumbled, the Soviet Empire dissolved, and communist ideology landed on the ashheap of history. There was an unquestioned assumption that the spirit of peace and neighborliness would henceforth guide all the nations of Europe. Citizens of all the European nations enjoyed the comforting expectation that the much-touted 'peace dividend' would finally materialize. At long last, they thought, they could afford to concentrate on their other urgent problems.

And then, as all of Europe was geared to the pursuits of peace, war broke out in the Federal Republic of Yugoslavia. It crept up on the rest of Europe from behind—and not only on the Europeans, but on the Americans as well. For a short while, the major powers sought to keep the federation together, but they soon realized that this was a forlorn hope. The dissolution of Yugoslavia proceeded apace. What started with a series of skirmishes in Slovenia quickly evolved into a wider war encompassing Croatia and, from March 1992 on, Bosnia and Herzegovina. It was a war primarily caused and relentlessly driven by Belgrade's 'Greater Serbia' ambitions. Before long, it spread into the most violent and disruptive armed conflict Europe had seen since 1945.

The civilized world was shocked, then horrified, and soon outraged. At the same time, it was perplexed and divided.

The shock resulted from the sobering recognition that the scourge of war had survived the end of the confrontation between East and West. The threats and risks no longer lay in the possibility of an armed clash pitting the 'free world' against the 'communist empire.' Now they arose from the resurgence of the most archaic kind of conflict: internal war. In Yugoslavia, the first 'failing state' in post-Cold War Europe, what started as civil war soon took on some features of an armed conflict between sovereign states, but its origins clearly were intra-state and ethnic, not inter-state.

What horrified the world was the unspeakable cruelty with which the conflict was conducted, first and foremost by the Bosnian Serbs, but not only by them. Croats and Bosniaks (Muslims) clearly were the victims of Serb aggression and savagery. There is no denying the fact, however, that they, too, perpetrated war crimes and other crimes in defending themselves against the Serbian onslaught. The world rediscovered the sad truth noted eighty years earlier by the first Carnegie Endowment Commission on the Balkans: that the veneer of civilization is very thin indeed, and that "the unloosing of the human beast" is an ever-present possibility when outrage turns patriotism into crime and heroes into brutes. The sight of "millions of human beings systematically degraded by their own doing, corrupted by their own violence" was no less jolting in the 1990s than it had been in the years immediately preceding World War I. And this time the pictures of death and inhumanity—Vukovar, Dubrovnik, Omarska, Sarajevo, Srebrenica—were flashed to households around the world in real time. Moreover, it was not just the cruelty of the method but the very idea of 'ethnic cleansing' as an organizing principle of state and society that challenged the fundamental values of the pluralist democracies on both sides of the Atlantic.

The world's outrage had different roots. It was nourished by the inability—some would say unwillingness—of the major Western powers to prevent, mitigate, or terminate the bloodshed and destruction in its initial phases. No state, statesman, or international institution responded with glory to this challenge. The European Community, proclaiming the opportunity to stop the wars of Yugoslav dissolution "the hour of Europe," mediated an endless succession of truces. One by one, these were violated as the ink was still drying on the cease-fire documents. The Americans, under President Bill Clinton as under his predecessor George Bush, were content to leave the matter to the Europeans. Both Americans and Europeans meandered almost to the eve of the Dayton agreement. In the same vein, the United Nations revealed glaring deficiencies as the war widened. It also brokered one peace plan after another only to see each torn up by one or all of the warring parties of Bosnia and Herzegovina as soon as it had been agreed upon. The peacekeeping efforts of the U.N. Protection Force (UNPRO-

FOR), valiant though they were, remained pitifully inadequate to the task of stopping the fighting. True, the gigantic supply and support operation run by the U.N. High Commissioner for Refugees (UNHCR) alleviated the lot of millions caught between the hammer and the anvil, the besieged in Sarajevo, and the uprooted elsewhere. Yet these efforts could not put an end to the killing; often the relief programs were feeding those who were about to die.

By 1995, no one could any longer escape the obvious conclusion: To be successful, outside mediation required outside *force* to make the regional actors comply with any kind of settlement. By mid-1996, a second conclusion appeared equally compelling to most observers: A minimal ground force from outside would have to be deployed—and employed, if need be—to bring the various parties to observe the Dayton Accords. Without a continuing military commitment by the sponsor powers, peace appeared highly unlikely to last. How long that commitment should last remains an open and critically important issue at the time of writing. There was a certain logic to the argument that the pre-scheduled withdrawal date of the Implementation Force (IFOR)—December 20, 1996—should be adhered to, for only in this way could the Bosnian warring parties be expected to meet the various deadlines set in Dayton. The obverse argument gained strength, however, as the progress on the civilian side began to lag. Without an indefinite international military presence—IFOR II, or IFOR 'light'—the Dayton framework and the process of peace-building might fall apart as soon as the more obstreperous local actors felt free of the constraint inherent in the presence of foreign forces on the ground.

As the Commission traveled the length and breadth of the Balkans during the second half of 1995 and the first half of 1996, its members were often struck by parallels between their impressions and the insights of the first Carnegie Commission of 1913-14. The earlier Commission's haunting question is still pertinent: "Must we allow these Balkan wars to pass, without at least trying to draw some lesson from them, without knowing whether they have been a benefit or an evil, if they should begin again tomorrow and go on forever extending?" Equally relevant is the 1914 Report's incisive comment that this was "a dark prospect which, however, might become brighter if Europe and the great military powers so wished. They could, in spite of everything, solve the problem if they were not determined to remain blind."

It is the firm conviction of the present Commission that turning a blind eye to the Balkans is no less a recipe for disaster at the end of the twentieth century than it was at its outset. If the ghosts of the past are to be laid to rest for good, outside guarantors, even enforcers, of the peace will have to remain present in the region—first and foremost in Bosnia and Herzegovina—for a considerable period of time. If they are fully withdrawn because of domestic preoccupations, the intervening powers will soon again confront the same intolerable situation in which they found themselves from the spring of 1991 onward to late 1995. Without outside involvement, outside guidance, and outside support for some time to come, the peace process between the Adriatic and the Danube could quickly fall victim to the same disruptive forces of malignant nationalism, territorial ambition, and ethnic mania that precipitated the conflict in the first place.

If the years 1991 to 1995 hold one lesson for the West, it is clearly that the very ugly problems of the Balkans will not simply go away. The prospects for peace and stability in the region remain tenuous. This goes for Bosnia and Herzegovina, whose future as a unitary multi-ethnic state modeled on the Dayton pattern is clouded by uncertainty. Yet it is not only Bosnia that could create new problems. There are other flash-points, left virtually untouched by the Dayton agreement—especially Macedonia and Kosovo. They will have to be dealt with as part of a larger Balkan peace process if long-term stability is to be achieved in the region.

The central question is therefore the degree of commitment, resolve, and political will that the community of nations will be able to muster in the years ahead.

The Commission harbors no illusions on this score. It realizes that the term "international community" is a misnomer—at best a euphemism reflecting the hopes of the downtrodden and disadvantaged but not the reality of world politics. The history of the wars of Yugoslav dissolution teaches that there are clear limits to what may be expected from the international community. It is not a world policeman, not even a moral authority. It is a fictitious entity, appealed to by those who feel wronged, called upon by others to sanctify their wrongdoing, and used as an excuse for inaction by all states unwilling to get involved—or as a pretext for action by those eager to enter the fray.

Nor does the United Nations, the institutionalized international community, measure up to expectations when it comes to preventing war or restoring peace in Yugoslavia-type contingencies. The world organization can speechify and moralize, disapprove and condemn; it can pass resolutions and provide good offices; it can alleviate human suffering and deploy peace-keeping forces. It cannot, however, keep a peace that does not exist. Nor is it capable of providing the military sinews to create peace unless and until its more powerful member nations have interests of their own in providing the forces.

The European Union, then? It was still the European Community when the crisis erupted. Its leading troika[1] plunged into tireless diplomacy, but after three months it felt constrained to appeal to the United Nations. From October 1991 through July 1992, Lord Carrington and Cyrus Vance jointly organized peace conferences and the deployment of UNPROFOR in Croatia. In February 1992, Carrington created a special conference on Bosnia-Herzegovina, presided over by Jose Cutilheiro. The conference produced the first of many plans for partitioning Bosnia and Herzegovina along cantonal lines. Soon after, the initiative passed to the United Nations, and later to the Contact Group composed of Britain, France, Germany, the United States, and Russia. None of the peace plans drafted— Vance-Owen in January 1993, Owen-Stoltenberg in July 1993, the Contact Group Plan in July 1994—was able to secure the support of all the warring parties and the outside powers. The most promising of those plans, the one tabled by Vance and Owen in 1993, failed to win the support of the Clinton Administration and of the Izetbegovic government in Sarajevo.

All the while, the war kept intensifying. The siege of Sarajevo continued, the number of casualties incurred during almost uninterrupted shelling and sniper-firing rose from week to week. The world was stunned by the two market massacres in the Bosnian capital (February 5, 1994, and August 28, 1995). Then, one after the other, the "safe havens" proclaimed by the Security Council fell to Serb conquerors: Gorazde, Bihac, Zepa, and above all Srebrenica—names that will live in infamy—engraved themselves on the memory of mankind. But more was yet to come: U.N. soldiers were taken hostage and humiliated by the Serbs; and then U.N. contingents could be seen on the television screens standing by as several thousand Muslim men were marched away to certain death by Serb killers.

---

[1]In the European Community (and later the European Union) context, the "troika" signifies the member countries representing the present, preceding, and the next-in-succession presidencies of the EC/EU.

It was only then that the West shook off its earlier perplexity. Since the spring of 1994, NATO had occasionally used its airpower. Now the decision was taken to employ force far more robustly. In June 1995, the Allied Rapid Reaction Force was created, providing UNPROFOR with punch and power. In July, the London Conference authorized massive air strikes against the Serbs. In August, the Croat Army, with the tacit agreement of the Western powers, started its campaign to retake the Krajina region of Croatia and the northern part of Bosnia-Herzegovina. At the same time, the United States launched the diplomatic drive, energetically pushed forward by Assistant Secretary of State Richard Holbrooke, which led to the conclusion of the Dayton Accords on November 21, 1995. Three weeks later, the Accords were signed—in Paris, in symbolic recognition of the impetus that French President Jacques Chirac had injected into the stagnant process earlier in the year.

Dayton marked the end of the war but only the beginning of the peace. It is by no means a perfect agreement. The Commission realizes, however, that Dayton was not Versailles, where the victors imposed their conditions on the vanquished. Rather, it was the result of protracted negotiations and compromises necessary to reach a consensus. Under the circumstances, the agreement made at Wright-Patterson Air Base was the best that could be had. Despite its imperfections, it also has its merits. Above all, it provides a framework for peace in Bosnia-Herzegovina and a process through which this peace can gradually be reinforced, thus contributing to the wider peace of the region.

In the view of the Commission, it is imperative now to muster the political will and the strategic consensus to do what the world was unable to do while the fighting went on. This requires, above all, that the civilized world take to heart the lessons of the past few years.

The first lesson is that the United Nations, while it may confer legitimacy on international action, is much too torn by conflicting interests to organize such action in time. In addition, it lacks the military assets to ensure the success of any decisive operation. Moreover, its financial predicament undercuts its efficiency as a peace-keeping or peace-enforcing factor. Only when the interested parties become direct players can they have an influence on the course of events.

The second lesson is that the United States and Europe must work together if they want to affect a particular situation.

Proceeding separately invites stagnation or failure; working at cross-purposes means courting disaster. In contrast, cooperation between America and Europe offers the best hope for success—more particularly so because in the framework of NATO, well-established procedures, familiar lines of command (and, of course, the entire intelligence, communications, and logistics infrastructure of the Alliance) can be put to good use.

The third lesson—reluctantly grasped even by many staunch pacifists—is that diplomacy not backed by force is tantamount to hollow gesturing. It is the punch of power that lends conviction to the suasion of diplomats. Where it is lacking, the well-meaning are left to the mercy of the reckless, and brute force rather than reason sustained by might determines the outcome of conflict.

Bosnia would have been spared a great deal of death and destruction and the world much anxiety if these lessons had been learned. Neglect, hesitation, and procrastination exacted an extremely high price.

The people of Bosnia-Herzegovina—Bosniaks, Croats, and Serbs—paid the lion's share. Before the war, the population was 4.4 million; when the war ended, less than 3 million were left. In the course of the conflict, at least 145,000 have died, 174,000 have been injured, 2.5 million have been uprooted from their homes, and 1.1 million have gone abroad—among them a high proportion of the country's intelligentsia, including many scientists and skilled workers. Sixty percent of all housing and 28 percent of the roads have been badly damaged. The suffering of Sarajevo stands for the excruciating experience of the rest of the country: 10,500 of the city's people were killed and 60,000 wounded during the thousand-day siege; 150,000 left the city during the war or, like many Serbs, upon its conclusion. The killing fields of Bosnia and Herzegovina, the blown-up farm buildings all over, cities like Sarajevo or Mostar reduced to rubble all bear a chilling resemblance to Europe at the end of World War II.

But the rest of the world also paid a heavy price for the years of indecision. The humanitarian effort of the Office of the U.N. High Commissioner for Refugees (UNHCR) alone has cost more than US$ 1 billion during the period 1991-96. For this sum, 3.5 million people were provided with shelter, supplied with the basic necessities of life, and fed. Transport planes from 20 nations—mainly American, French, British, Canadian, and

German—flew over 12,950 relief missions into Sarajevo, starting in July 1992. All told, they delivered 630,000 metric tons of goods worth more than US$ 1 billion. Alongside UNHCR, other institutions, a number of foundations, and a great many private organizations were involved in the unprecedented relief effort. Between 1991 and 1996, the European Union budgeted US$ 865 million for this effort. Another burden assumed by the international community was the influx of 1.1 million refugees into various Western European nations. Germany took in the bulk— 410,000, of whom 320,000 came from Bosnia-Herzegovina. Austria accepted 80,000; Sweden, 50,000; Italy, 22,500; and Denmark, 20,000.[2] Germany alone is estimated to spend DM 8 billion (US$ 5 billion) on them every year.

Nor did the military missions during the four years of the post-Yugoslavia crisis come cheap. During this short span of time, soldiers from 42 countries took part in U.N. peacekeeping operations in Croatia and Bosnia-Herzegovina. These operations were the first to involve a European theater for the United Nations and were the largest it had mounted since the Congo Crisis. Of the 55,000 IFOR troops in Bosnia-Herzegovina, 28,000 came from European countries (not including Russia) and 18,000 from the United States.

The bill for the UNPROFOR operation ran to US$ 4.8 billion in the period 1992-96. In addition, NATO financed both the Airborne Warning and Control System (AWACS) surveillance missions and the naval patrol in the Adriatic through several years; the European and international police contingents had to be paid; and the European Union spent ECU 200 million (US$ 249 million) for its salvage operation in Mostar. The costs imposed upon the neighboring countries by the international sanctions regime against Yugoslavia—an estimated US$ 35 billion—have to be added to this tabulation.

The figures carry a clear message. Quite apart from all the human suffering that might have been prevented by earlier and more robust outside involvement, the financial cost of standing aside for so long has been staggering. Arguably, the costs of indecision turned out to be as high as the costs of intervention. It follows from this that never again should those powers which take a direct interest in the fate of the Balkan region hold back in feeble indecision. They must stay intimately involved if they

---

[2]Switzerland accepted 15,000 refugees; France, 14,500; and Great Britain, 6,500.

want to help transform the proverbially chaotic, bloody, and unpredictable Balkans of the past into a stable, peaceful, and dependable Southeastern Europe of the future.

This, the Commission feels, is the task. Dayton is but the point of departure, and the road leading beyond it is full of uncertainties. This Report points them out in detail. It analyzes the issues. It lays out the hard choices. Among these are: Does post-conflict reconciliation require that indicted war criminals be brought to trial forthwith, or should priority be given to the peace-building and nation-building process—*fiat justitia, pereat pax* or *fiat justitia floreat pax*? Should the Dayton provision for the return of refugees be implemented forthwith—or must the world resign itself to the fact that conditions will hardly be ripe for a wholesale return of minority members to ethnic majority areas? Can progress toward civil societies be best ensured by normal democratic processes—even if elections should confirm the old nationalist, authoritarian elites in power for the time being? Or is it more promising to postpone elections until new political forces have had a chance to organize?

These are important questions, and they merit serious discussion; the Commission's views are set out in the body of this Report. The Commission feels strongly that none of these questions will find a lasting answer unless and until the international aid program for the reconstruction of Bosnia-Herzegovina moves into higher gear. The rebuilding of the transport system, the telecommunications infrastructure, and the energy grid is the precondition of economic recovery; and economic recovery is a precondition of societal tranquility and communal peace. The recovery program would of course have to aim at interrelating the entities making up the state of Bosnia-Herzegovina; reconstruction should not promote their separateness or separatism. Sensible intra-Bosnian cooperation should be the *sine qua non* of outside support.

In the same vein, the Commission is convinced that a measure of economic cooperation among the successor states of Tito's federation is indispensable to the prosperity of the region. This should not be misconstrued as a plea for restoring the old Yugoslavia. It is nothing of the sort. But the principles of economic soundness should be heeded. Beyond that, the Commission feels that a wider regional framework for inter-Balkan cooperation should be constructed.

For the rest, the message of the Commission is simple and clear. The United States cannot remain indifferent to the Balkan situation; America's commitment remains of crucial importance. But the Balkan predicament, as George F. Kennan has pointed out, is primarily a problem for the Europeans: "And if they claim, as many of them do, that they lack the political unity to confront it successfully, the answer is perhaps that this is one of those instances, not uncommon in the lives of nations as of individuals, when one has to rise to the occasion." The point is well taken.

The answer to the Balkan predicament lies first and foremost in Europe. Cooperation within a wider Europe must complement cooperation within the region. And Europe, in this instance, is not only the European Union, which it is the ambition of all the Balkan nations to join sooner rather than later. It is also CEFTA, the Central European Free Trade Agreement. It is those formerly communist countries whose transformation into democracies and free-market societies holds valuable lessons for all post-Yugoslavia states. And Russia also has a significant part to play in bringing calm and stability to a region that for centuries has been the crucible of conflict among the European powers.

In 1913, Baron d'Estournelles de Constant, Chairman of the first Carnegie Commission on the Balkans, ended the introduction to its Report on an acrid note. "The most suitable title for this report," he wrote, "would have been, 'Europe Divided and her Demoralizing Action in the Balkans,' but taking it all round, this might have been unjust. The real culprits . . . are not the Balkan peoples. Here pity must conquer indignation. Do not let us condemn the victims. Nor are the European govern ments the real culprits. They at least tried to amend things, and certainly they wished for peace without knowing how to establish it." His conclusion rings as pertinent today as it was then: "In reality there is no salvation, no way out either for small states or for great countries except by union and conciliation."

High-minded words, noble and sound—but they went unheard. Four months after the publication of the first Carnegie Report on the Balkans, the assassination in Sarajevo triggered World War I. At least in this respect, the international community has learned its lesson: The Balkan conflict at the end of the twentieth century did not spark off a global conflagration. Yet many other lessons will have to be learned by us all before peace has a chance to prevail in Europe's tinderbox of two hundred years.

The international context in which this Report was written is different from that of 1913-14—as is the specific location where the wars occurred. But there are also similarities among the three Balkan wars. By far the most disturbing of them is the savagery with which the wars were conducted. Indeed, much of the 1914 Carnegie Commission Report was devoted to the meticulous detailing of some of the atrocities that occurred. And it is in that light that the Report is still remembered and read in the region. Today, with the gruesome immediacy of television and with the compilations of human rights violations made by the U.N. Commission for Human Rights and its special rapporteurs Tadeusz Mazowiecki and Elizabeth Rehn, as well as by non-governmental organizations such as Helsinki Watch, this is no longer necessary. But anyone studying the Balkan wars in the 1990s must be mindful of the continuity, and must be indebted to the Carnegie commissioners of 1914 for their conscientiousness and courage.

What can be the contribution of our own Report now that a peace agreement has been signed? First, there is a case for caution as to the viability of the peace settlement and certainly a need to look beyond the one-year horizon provided by the Dayton agreement. This Report argues for a *long-term* approach and for measures aimed at establishing a lasting peace in the region. Second, the violent break-up of Yugoslavia has sent shock-waves throughout the Balkans. The return of peace in the Balkan 'northern tier' (Bosnia-Herzegovina, Serbia, and Croatia) should not lead us to underestimate the threats to stability in the region's 'southern tier.' The Report highlights the two epicenters of tension with widespread regional implications: Bosnia (can a multi-ethnic concept of Bosnia-Herzegovina be saved?) and the South Balkans (involving Kosovo and Macedonia, but also Albania, Serbia, and Greece). The objective is to assess the existing or latent conflicts in a broader regional context and to suggest a process and a framework for defusing and overcoming them.

The aims of this Report are:

1. To inquire into the causes of instability and conflict in the Balkans (part I);

2. To assess the international response to the recent conflict and the lessons to be drawn from it (part II);

11

3. To outline the longer-term prospects for the Balkans, the dangers inherent in some of them, and the constructive potential in others (part III); and

4. To recommend measures that might, in the Commission's view, serve not only to avoid or mitigate future dangers, but also to encourage factors that might be conducive to reconstruction, stabilization, and cooperation (part IV).

The recommendations in this Report are presented for consideration by Western governments and non-governmental institutions, as well as by their counterparts in the region itself.

I. THE BALKAN PREDICAMENT

THE ORIGINS OF THE WAR: FALLACIES AND REALITIES

It is tempting, in searching for the origins of the recent war in former Yugoslavia, to look for historical analogies in the previous Balkan wars. The 1914 Commission Report points to "depressing evidences of similarity" in the nature of nationalist conflicts and the manner in which warfare has been waged. The temptation is all the stronger because other historical analogies frequently have been invoked by some of the protagonists of the Balkan conflict and by Western political leaders and observers.

Yet interpreting current Balkan politics by drawing historical analogies can also be misleading. Broadly speaking, three historical 'explanations' have been offered concerning the origins of the recent Balkan war: one held in the Balkans, one in the West, and one shared between them.

Great Power Ambitions?

The first view, widely held in the Balkans, finds continuity in the destabilizing role of external powers and events at the turn of the century, when rivalries between the Russian, Ottoman, and Habsburg Empires gave rise to competing Balkan nationalisms. Today's return of nationalist conflicts is seen by many in the Balkans as reflecting ambitions of the great powers to reestablish their Balkan spheres of influence in the post-Cold War reordering of the international balance of power ('evidence' cited includes German support for Croatia's independence and Turkey's support for the Muslims in Bosnia-Herzegovina). There is a marked tendency among Balkan political and intellectual elites to overestimate the region's strategic importance to the major powers and to blame the maneuvers of these powers for the failure of the Balkan peoples to achieve peaceful, multiethnic development of their societies.

The truth is that the Sarajevo of the 1990s is not the Sarajevo of 1914. The cause of the recent conflict was not greatpower manipulation of local nationalisms (as was the case in 1914), and no current power is going to start a World War III over Bosnia. The real novelty for the peoples of the Balkans after the Cold War is that, for the first time in modern history, they found themselves ignored and on their own. The causes of this war came from within the Balkans rather than from without.

What did play a role was not the direct involvement of outside powers but the changing international environment beyond the Balkans. The impact of this environment on the Yugoslav status quo was twofold. Tito had been remarkably skillful at using the external Soviet threat to enhance internal cohesion and implicit Western support. Most NATO crisis scenarios for East-West conflict started either in Berlin or in Yugoslavia. With the advent of Mikhail Gorbachev and the end of the Cold War, the strategic importance of Yugoslavia to the rivalry of the superpowers declined significantly.

The second factor was the collapse of the communist system. In 1989, a chain reaction swept away communist regimes from Central Europe to the Balkans. Yugoslavia had been the first and often most daring promoter of *reform* of the communist system; but it found itself the last in the *exit* from communism as a system of government. Suddenly, the Yugoslav brand of non-aligned, "self-management" socialism appeared quaintly obsolete and irrelevant from outside and almost intolerable to its more prosperous or more democratic components inside. In that respect the falling dominos of collapsing communism did not spare Yugoslavia. The questions then became: Would Yugoslavia disintegrate? And could this occur without affecting the stability of the entire region?

Ancestral Hatreds?

The second interpretation, widely held in the West, consists of variations on the themes of the "the return of ancestral hatreds" or the "return of the suppressed." In the 1914 Commission Report, there is an arresting metaphor concerning the Ottoman Empire: It had acted as a "vast refrigerator" preserving the Balkan nationalisms in "a condition of torpor"—the implication being that the decay of Ottoman rule helped bring these dormant nationalisms back to life. A similar metaphor has sometimes been used for East European communism: It "froze" nationalist ideologies and rifts that we now rediscover awesomely revived half a century later.

Certainly the end of communism and of the Cold War has given greater room for maneuver to local or regional actors with long-suppressed aspirations and old scores to settle. But it is a deceptive oversimplification for Western media and political leaders to interpret this as a post-communist resurgence of ancestral hatreds.

There are of course historic differences and animosities, and they have of course been exploited and abused by modern political leaders in the region. But there is little or no evidence, for instance, that such hatreds played a major role in the pre-twentieth century history of Serbo-Croatian relations. In this century, the political tensions of inter-war Yugoslavia culminated in unprecedented violence during World War II, when the Ustashe regime in Croatia massacred Serbs and Jews—a major trauma. The World War II conflicts between nationalists, or between communists and nationalists, did indeed cause more casualties than the struggle against German occupying forces. But here again the stereotype should be corrected. German occupation was opposed not just by Tito's communist partisans, in whose ranks Croats were relatively the most numerous, but also by Serbian forces loyal to the monarchy.

Similarly, in Bosnia-Herzegovina, although there has long been Serb and Croat resentment of an alleged "opportunist apostasy" on the part of the Bosnian Slavs who became Muslims after the Ottoman conquest in the fifteenth century, much of the pre-1990 hostility was due to socio-economic factors (predominantly Christian peasantry versus Muslim landowners, rural versus urban); to imperial rivalries (Habsburg versus Ottoman); and, more recently, Serb and Croat nationalist ambitions. After 1878, when Bosnia came under Austro-Hungarian rule, the three communities had lived together fairly peacefully. The two major occurrences of violence were related to the two world wars and were largely induced by causes outside Bosnia's borders.

A Clash of Civilizations?

The third thesis, shared by the Balkan protagonists as well as some observers in the West, looks for the origins of the war in cultural and religious fault-lines described as a "clash of civilizations." Yugoslavia in general, and Bosnia in particular, are located in a region of transition between Western Christianity, Eastern Greek Orthodoxy, and Islam; after being suppressed by the ideological tensions of the Cold War, the traditional fault-lines between cultures are once again becoming evident. The "third Balkan war," the argument goes, was thus rooted in fundamental cultural and religious incompatibility. This incompatibility is seen as all the more dramatic and compelling since the conflicting parties in Serbia, Croatia, and Bosnia-Herzegovina all belong to the Southern Slav group of nations and speak the same language. In this view, the primary difference among the three cultures is religion; it is pointed out that places of worship have been among the prime targets in the war. Significantly, the "clash of civilizations" is one of the rare themes on which there seems to be a thread of agreement linking Croatia's President Franjo Tudjman, the Bosnian Serb leader Radovan Karadzic, and the Islamists.

At a meeting with the Commission in April 1996, President Tudjman elaborated at length on the "clash of civilizations" theme: "The Yugoslav experience showed that cultural and geopolitical divides and constraints turned out to be decisive— so strong that the common state proved not viable. The current fault-line overlaps with those of the Roman Empire (Theodosian line) between Rome, Byzantium, and Islam, as well as with the border between the Ottoman and Habsburg empires. And the region where this divide of civilizations is most palpable, Bosnia-Herzegovina, produced one of the most powerful crises of today."

Radovan Karadzic has frequently spoken of the necessity of separating the peoples of Bosnia-Herzegovina along cultural/religious lines. He has recalled a "Greek-Turkish" precedent: "Between Greece and Turkey there were exchanges of territories and population on a large scale because it was a conflict between Orthodoxy and Islam." He has also said (to *Komsomolskaya Pravda*, quoted in *Oslobodjenje*, May 20, 1995): "We will never allow the return of Turkey in the Balkans." Karadzic has asserted, moreover, that "Serbs, Croats, and Muslims can no longer live together. Just as the Croats and Muslims didn't want to live in a united Yugoslavia, so we don't want to live in their states. You can't keep a dog and a cat in a box together. Either they would always be quarreling and fighting or they would have to stop being what they are."

The Islamists have their own version of the "clash of civilizations." Imam Mustafa Ceric, the head of Bosnia's Islamic Community, has described the war as "a kind of crusade against Islam," the purpose of which was "to eliminate Islam and Muslims in this part of the world." The fact that *Slavic* Muslims—the most secularized and integrated Muslims on the European continent—became the prime target of such a violent onslaught is seen as proof that it was precisely their religion that mattered. Granada 1492—seen as both precedent and analogy for Bosnia 1992.

Yet all this is far from being a religious war like those which wracked Europe in earlier centuries. Under Ottoman rule, the Balkan nations were identified by their religious communities (*millet*). The recent conflict, however, has occurred in largely secularized societies where religious practice had been declining steadily for half a century.

Certainly the churches and religious symbols have been used by nationalist politicians seeking to legitimize their intransigence, and some parts of the clergy have perhaps lent themselves more easily than others to this abuse. But it is also worth noting in this context that the thesis of the new "religious wars" is rejected by religious leaders in the region. In meetings with the Commission, both Patriarch Pavle, head of the Serbian Orthodox Church, and Cardinal Kuharic, the Croatian Catholic Primate in Zagreb, stressed the importance of religion for the cultural and national identities of their flocks, but repudiated the political misuse of religious differences for stirring up conflict. To quote Cardinal Kuharic: "The church does not create states. It does not combat states. It lives within states."

Bosnia-Herzegovina, especially some of its main cities, had generally been a land of religious coexistence. Sarajevo in particular was famous for the fact that the main places of worship of four religious communities (Muslim, Orthodox, Catholic, Jewish) were situated side by side within a few hundred yards of each other in the old city. Tito sought to give the Muslims a political identity by allowing their religion to also become a nationality. As in the rest of Yugoslavia, the Muslims in Bosnia fell roughly into three categories: (1) those Muslims who were connected with (and to the end very loyal to) the 'Titoist' system; (2) the non-practicing Muslims, representing the vast majority of the population; and (3) the practicing Muslims, of whom only a small "dissident" intellectual group had been influenced by fundamentalist Islamist teaching.[3]

---

[3]Interestingly, the Commission learned in Istanbul that Tito—to avoid reviving old Ottoman connections and using his "non-aligned" network—preferred that young religion students be sent to study Islam in Egypt rather than Turkey; thus, instead of connecting with the moderate Islam associated with the Turkish model, he inadvertently promoted the import of a more radical Islamic culture from the Middle East.

The breakup of the Yugoslav federation and the war in Bosnia destroyed the 'common roof' over the three main religious communities. For the Orthodox in Bosnia, this meant identifying as Serbs, and for the Catholics, identifying as Croats; but for the Bosnian Slavs who had become Muslims, the only thing to fall back on was their cultural identity of Islam. Feeling abandoned by Europe, some of them looked (with mixed results) for support in the Islamic world, including Iran. But their Islam is that of a people in distress who realize that if they really turned "Islamist" they would lose Western (and particularly American) support. They recognize that their economic future will depend mainly on the West. The last thing they want is to become a Muslim ghetto in Europe.

The Commission found little evidence to suggest that this revived emphasis on Muslim identity has made the Bosnian Muslims vulnerable to the call of Islamic radicalism. But the very fact that the question can now be seriously discussed means that in some way Karadzic and the aggressive Serb nationalism he represents have actually helped to create what they were purporting to dread.

It deserves mention in this context that the fate of Islam in Bosnia is of importance for three reasons going beyond the country or even the Balkans: (1) it has become a factor in the West's relations with the Islamic world; (2) it might become important for Turkey's relationship with Europe; and (3) it has implications for the Islamic communities of Western Europe. At a meeting with the Commission, Gilles Kepel, a leading expert on Islam, warned that the Bosnian issue (much like the Palestinian and the Afghan issues in the past) has become a prime focus for the mobilization of radical Islam in the Muslim communities of the Western metropolises. Bosnia has been presented by some of them as an illustration of the pointlessness of integration into what they see as the hostile, secular, democratic societies of Western Europe.

Neither the "clash of civilizations" nor the "new religious war" theory is a satisfactory explanation of the causes of the recent war. Indeed a simple answer would be to remember that, historically, the Orthodox have fought each other much more than they have fought other religious denominations, and that, for at least two centuries, the conflict between Orthodox Greece and Orthodox Bulgaria has been much fiercer than the relatively recent conflict between Orthodox Serbs and Roman Catholic Croats.

But do the realignments in the Balkans since the fall of Yugoslavia reflect the return of older, historical/cultural patterns? Many in the Balkans are convinced of it and try their hardest to convince others. There is no shortage of speculation about the "arcs of influence"—Catholic, Orthodox, or Muslim (known as "Green transversal")—in the Balkans. But a closer examination reveals the limitations of this kind of speculation.

A Northwest/Catholic Arc? "How many divisions has the Pope?" Stalin's famous quip became a serious obsession of Serbian propaganda in the early 1990s. It was usually combined with a revived specter of an alleged German threat. "Germany has attacked us for the third time in a century," declared General Veljko Kadijevic, the Yugoslav Minister of Defense (*Le Monde,* October 24, 1991). This and similar statements reflected the siege mentality that prevailed in Belgrade at the outbreak of the war—a mentality that the official propaganda machine deliberately induced. Slovenia and Croatia did seek the support of their 'Catholic' neighbors: Austria, Italy, Hungary. Such ties or sympathies were certainly there, but they proved of limited use.

Austria, in particular, appeared to welcome the return of Slovenia to the Central European club. Close relations between Vienna and Ljubljana soon developed; Slovenia had the best economic prospects and was least involved in the war—and thus was not seen by the Austrians as a potential security risk.

After a slow start, Italy came out in support of Slovene and Croat independence. But it was not long before it began formulating claims on issues such as property restitution in Istria and Dalmatia—issues considered to have been settled by the Osimo Treaty of 1976 between Italy and the former Yugoslavia. Thus Ljubljana discovered that Rome could be a hindrance rather than a help on the road to European Union. Zagreb, too, began complaining about an alleged pro-Serbian turn in Italy's Balkan policy. During the Berlusconi-Fini coalition, there were hints of a 'Balkanization' of Italy's policy toward the region—though not nearly on the same scale as the policy of Greece. This surprised and worried not only Slovenia and Croatia, but also some of Italy's European Union partners. The recent change of government in Italy has brought with it a more flexible attitude and the signing of an association agreement between Slovenia and the European Union during the Italian presidency of the EU in early 1996.

Hungary hesitated between two attitudes: sympathy for neighboring Croatia, which had been part of a Hungarian state from the twelfth century to 1918, and a more prudent concern for the situation of the Hungarian minority in the Vojvodina province of Serbia. The first attitude was illustrated by Prime Minister Jozsef Antall's statement (summer 1991) recalling that Vojvodina had been assigned to Yugoslavia, not to Serbia, after World War I. The implication was obvious. Hungary subsequently followed a more cautious policy, mainly out of concern for its image in the West as a success story of post-communist transition to democracy and a market economy. Historical and cultural sympathies thus had their limits.

A Southeast/Orthodox Arc? The Orthodox nations (Serbs, Bulgars, Greeks, Romanians, Macedonians, and Montenegrins) represent the dominant religion in the Balkans (50 million out of 70 million). They sometimes see themselves as "boxed in" between Catholics (Croats, Slovenes, Hungarians) in the northwest and the Muslims (including Turkey) in the southeast. Throughout the recent conflict, Serbia hoped for a meaningful "Orthodox axis" from the Balkans all the way to Moscow. But it never materialized.

Greece was the most forceful and consistent backer of Serbian policies. The main reason was shared opposition to Macedonian statehood and Skopje's alleged irredentist designs on Greek Macedonia. A second motive was shared hostility to a renewed Turkish role in the Balkans. It is debatable how much of the formidable nationalist mobilization that overran Greek politics between 1991 and 1995 (to the great benefit of the Socialist Party) was actually attributable to the influence of the Orthodox Church. According to the Eurobarometer Survey, 69 percent of Greeks believed that there were too many foreigners in the country, and 90 percent considered that the presence of foreigners in the country represented a "public danger." Eighty-nine percent declared an aversion to the Turks, and 76 percent to the Albanians. The same survey (conducted in 1993) showed that xenophobia was far stronger in Greece than in the other EU countries. It also suggested that intolerant nationalism in the Balkans is by no means just a consequence of post-communism.

Romania's reasons for support of Serbia were different: Romania's President Ion Iliescu, like Serbia's President Slobodan Milosevic, is a product of the communist apparatus, now combining authoritarian rule with nationalism. Both are concerned to leave as little as possible to their Hungarian minorities. But neither such affinities nor the alleged Romanian violations of the international embargo on Serbia can seriously be linked to the bonds of Orthodoxy.

From Russia there was rhetorical support for Serbia, but little more. True, there is an alliance of ultra-nationalists keen to see Moscow (the "Third Rome") as the protector of Orthodoxy in the Balkans: Vladimir Zhirinovsky got a hero's welcome from many Serbian nationalists in Belgrade; and in April 1996, Radovan Karadzic was awarded (by a Russian foundation) one of the most prestigious distinctions, the order of St. Andrei, "for his statesman-like qualities." But ever since the failed coup in Moscow in August 1991, there has been no chance whatsoever of direct Russian support for Belgrade.

As for Macedonia and Bulgaria, their improved relations with Turkey and the pro-Western orientation of their foreign policies in the first half of the 1990s hardly fitted into any "Orthodox axis."

A "Green Transversal"—linking Muslims in Bosnia, Sandjak, Kosovo, Albania, and Turkey? There is little evidence of close ties between Muslims in Bosnia and Kosovo (although there is some of increasing ties between Bosnia and Sandjak). Turkey has given support to Albania and Bosnia—but also to Macedonia. Thus there also is not much of a case for viewing religion as the key to the foreign policies of these countries.

Clearly there are limits to cultural determinism in Balkan politics. Yet cultural/religious fault-lines remain relevant to the way Balkan protagonists construct their national identity and their relationship to "Europe." Croats see their Europeanness as derived from their belonging to Western Christendom—i.e., precisely on what separates them from Orthodox Serbs or Muslims. The Serbs in turn speak of themselves as the last rampart of Christian Europe against the spread of Islamic influence. Much as in Central Europe—where Catholic "Europeanness" is often used to distinguish countries from the Orthodox East (mainly Russia)—among the Orthodox in the Balkans, Christian Europeanness tends to be defined against Turkey and Islam. Consequently, Europe itself is not defined *positively*, as representing the universal values of human rights or certain norms of the rule of law that one can identify with and strive to implement; it is defined *negatively*, as a divide. Clearly, in the Balkans more than elsewhere, identification with "Europe" takes on dif-

21

ferent forms and has different justifications, and one nation is always another nation's "barbarian."

The irony, of course, is that in the recent Balkan conflict it was precisely the Muslims who, despite their many shortcomings and lapses, came closest to defending a European ideal of a tolerant, open society against those who sought their eradication in the name of Christian Europe. The main causes of war have to be sought elsewhere: in the sparks of aggressive nationalism fanned into roaring flames by some of the political leaders of the dissolving Yugoslav federation.

The principal responsibility for the recent war in former Yugoslavia rests with those post-communist politicians throughout Yugoslavia who have invoked the "ancient hatreds" to pursue their respective nationalist agendas and deliberately used their propaganda machines to justify the unjustifiable: the use of violence for territorial conquest, the expulsion of "other" peoples, and the perpetuation of authoritarian systems of power. In that process, they manipulated fears through misinformation and incitement to hatred.

Here again it seems appropriate to quote d'Estournelles de Constant's introduction to the 1914 Commission Report:

> The true culprits are those who mislead public opinion and take advantage of the people's ignorance to raise disquieting rumors and sound the alarm bell, inciting their country and consequently other countries into enmity. The real culprits are those who by interest or inclination, declaring constantly that war is inevitable, end by making it so, asserting that they are powerless to prevent it. The real culprits are those who sacrifice the general interest to their own personal interest which they so little understand, and who hold up to their country a sterile policy of conflict and reprisals.

THE BREAKUP OF YUGOSLAVIA

It is fashionable to point to Yugoslavia itself as an artificial construction and to its breakup as inevitable. But one should beware of judging with hindsight. Yugoslavia emerged at the end of World War I as a voluntary association, not just a 'creation of Versailles.' Rather, it could be described as a Croat idea achieved through Serbian means.

Ever since Versailles, however, there have been ambiguities and differing interpretations of Yugoslav statehood. The national identities of Serbs, Croats, and Slovenes were already too separate to merge into a "Yugoslav nation." For Serbia, which saw itself as the Piedmont of the new state, Yugoslavia was a means to unite all the Serbs of the former Ottoman and Habsburg Empires. For the Croats (and the Slovenes), it was a means to gain independence from Austria-Hungary and, urgently, to avoid inroads from Italy. The fact that Yugoslavia disappointed their hopes can be ascribed to the centralized Serb concept that influenced it throughout, and not necessarily to Yugoslavia's very inception.

While the Titoist model of federalism could not survive the demise of communism, this did not necessarily mean that disintegration and war were inevitable. First, there was the option of transforming a communist federation into a democratic confederation (as advocated by Slovenia and Croatia in September 1990). Second, even when separation proved unavoidable, a negotiated separation for the other republics (a "velvet divorce," Czech-Slovak style) might have been possible, but it was never considered by the Belgrade leadership. To understand why both options were ruled out, one has to examine the way in which ethno-nationalism was combined with communist authoritarianism. The Serbian power system has been the most lethal combination of these two elements evidenced anywhere in the former communist world. This accounts for the failed transition to democracy and the violent *fuite en avant* that followed.

The Dual Legacy of Ethnic Nationalism and Communism

In Central Europe, the three main crises of the post–World War II era (Hungary 1956, Czechoslovakia 1968, Poland 1980) posed the question of democracy, involved the society, and divided the ruling elite, but they acquired a "national" dimension only when external suppression of the democratic goals became ominous. In the Balkans, on the other hand, the three main postwar crises all related to the autonomy of a national Communist Party machine vis-a-vis Moscow. Ethnic nationalism was explicitly used to legitimize the policy while, internally, the totalitarian features of the system were reinforced. Tito's Yugoslavia in 1948, Enver Hoxha's Albania in 1961, and then Nicolae Ceausescu's Romania were three examples of earlier

23

attempts of Balkan communist regimes using nationalism as a source of surrogate legitimacy.

The power of Tito's myth has sometimes obscured the complexities of the way he tried to resolve the national problems of Yugoslavia. The Titoist legacy can be summed up as follows:

—"Divide and rule": Serbia (especially) and Croatia were kept in check, while "nation-building" was encouraged for the Macedonians (to offset competing claims by Serbia, Bulgaria, and Greece) and for the Muslim "nation" in the 1960s (to balance Serb-Croat rivalry in Bosnia).

—All major attempts at reformulating the national problem in Yugoslavia through a democratic process were crushed. In 1971, there was the crackdown on the Croatian Spring reform movement and the purge of its leading figures. This killed the last chance to provide an answer to Croatia's national aspirations within democratized federal institutions. Then, in 1972, the liberal Serbian leadership was purged, preparing the ground for the eventual succession of a leader like Slobodan Milosevic.

—Yugoslavia's 1974 Constitution shifted considerable economic and political power from the federal center to the republics and the two autonomous regions of Serbia (Kosovo and Vojvodina). After Tito's death in 1980, the veto power that had been given to each of them meant always searching for the lowest common denominator and led to a paralysis of the political system. The Communist Party itself became 'federalized' and eventually succumbed to the disease it was meant to cure. Instead of being a unifying factor for Yugoslavia as a whole, it divided the federation along national lines. The only pluralism that was now allowed to exist was 'pluralism' along those national lines.

Milosevic was the first Yugoslav politician to capitalize on the consequences of Tito's death. There was a power void at the center that he proceeded to fill. His recentralization of power in Serbia at the expense of Kosovo and Vojvodina was seen as a prelude to a recentralization of the power of Serbia within the Yugoslav federation as a whole.

In this context, the Yugoslav People's Army (JNA) became the last centralized institution committed to the Yugoslav legacy out of conviction and/or self-interest (status and privileges). When, in the summer of 1991, the Army found itself overnight without a state, it fought a war in Croatia largely to safeguard its own material and institutional interests (i.e., what one might call a 'trade union' war). Milosevic made good use of this situation, eventually transforming the Yugoslav People's Army into the fighting arm of Serbian nationalism.

In his use of Serbian nationalism, Milosevic employed a two-pronged strategy. First he exploited the grievances of the Serbs of Kosovo to obtain the leadership of the Serbian Communist Party. He then abolished the autonomy of Kosovo and Vojvodina as a prelude to tightening the federation at the center. The means he used were mobilization of the population against local bureaucracies and the Titoist legacy, as well as his increasingly explicit endorsement of the nationalist program formulated with growing vigor by many Serb anti-communist intellectuals.

The clearest and best-known expression of this program is in the 1986 Memorandum of the Serbian Academy of Sciences and Arts. In effect, the thesis presented there marked the beginning of the end of Yugoslavia. The Memorandum asserted that, since 1981, the Kosovo Serbs had been subjected to an "Albanian war" and to "genocide." It then declared that: "The physical, political, legal and cultural genocide of the Serbian population in Kosovo and Metohija is the worst defeat in all the Serbian-led battles of liberation from Orasac in 1804 to the 1941 uprising." The Memorandum attributed responsibility for this humiliation to the Communist Party of Yugoslavia and to the Serbian Communists who had remained loyal to it.

Milosevic stole the program of the nationalist opposition in order to seize power in Serbia and leave the anti-communist opposition powerless and without a cause. His combination of nationalism and populism took a distinctly authoritarian turn through the use of force by the police and the army in Kosovo in 1988—a prelude to the use of force in Belgrade against the largest-ever demonstration for democratic change on March 9, 1991.

The connection between the use of force on the national question and the preservation of an authoritarian system of power became obvious precisely when, in 1989-90, the communist system started crumbling and the issue of democratic change became the order of the day. In an interview shortly after the celebration in June 1989 of the 600th anniversary of the battle of Kosovo, Milosevic described himself as "a communist by conviction." Asked about the prospects for a multi-party system, he answered that he preferred a "system without parties" (*Le Monde*, July 12, 1989). His policy certainly bore out this statement. Milosevic's brand of nationalist populism—unite the nation around its leader and protector—stunted any possible emergence of pluralist democracy in Serbia and reinforced the authoritarian features of the regime.

The rise of Serbian nationalism and Milosevic's attempt to tighten the federation (the latter was favored by the International Monetary Fund and other international financial institutions to increase Belgrade's control over the economic policies of the republics) set in motion a chain reaction that was to lead to the breakup of the federation itself. Whatever else was wrong with the Titoist solution of the national question, it was at least based on the concept that no nationality (no matter how politically frustrated or economically disadvantaged) felt its existence to be threatened. That changed in the second half of the 1980s when Serbian nationalists, and Milosevic personally, introduced the politics of fear into inter-ethnic relations. Serbs were proclaimed to be under threat in Kosovo; this was seen as justifying putting the province under a state of siege and thus making the Albanians feel collectively endangered. The use of force in Kosovo in 1987-89 (only scantily reported in the West) in turn persuaded other national groups—the Albanians in Kosovo, the Slovenes, later the Croats and by 1991 even the most committed "Yugoslavs" (the Macedonians and Bosnians)—that *they* were under threat in a Serbia-dominated state.

The Failed Transition to Democracy

Yugoslavia's breakup was brought about by the interaction between the decay and collapse of communism and the decay and collapse of the federal state. In the process, the idea of federalism became as discredited as the idea of socialism. (Here there are striking similarities between Yugoslavia and the Soviet Union.)

At no point did the democratic forces within the different nationalities form a coalition to provide an alternative to the decaying communist regime. While communism ceased to be an integrating force, democracy did not provide a new integrating multi-ethnic principle. If anything, the transition to democracy strengthened the secessionist forces within each of the federal republics.

What accounted for this nationalist 'hijacking' of the democratic process? Although Yugoslav communism had been in some respects more flexible and less repressive than that in the Soviet bloc, it did not allow for the emergence of real dissent or the emergence of a democratic opposition unified around the concepts of civil society and democratic freedoms. Whenever such concepts did emerge, they were mostly confined to a particular republic or subordinated to nationalist agendas.

The political fragmentation of the 1990s reflected a more general trend seen in the erosion of the Yugoslav common market, the nationalization of education systems (Serbs, Albanians, and Slovenes no longer used the same textbooks), and, finally, the nationalization of the media. The division of the media along republic lines released a tide of unabashed nationalist propaganda that sustained the war. (Sarajevo television was the last to relay both Serbian and Croatian TV and thus predictably became one of the first casualties of the war.) The disintegration of common public media contributed to the disintegration of the entire country.

The first free elections in Yugoslavia, held between April and December 1990, were a crucial moment in the link between the legitimization of the institutions and the territorial framework in which politics, the regime, and the state would exist. As shown by the Spanish case (and in the opposite sense by the Soviet case), the order in which regional and national elections take place is of utmost importance in the transition to democracy in a multi-national state. Thus, for example, it was essential for the survival of the Spanish state that the first free elections after Franco encompassed the *entire* country (even though this was followed by substantial transfers of power to Catalonia and the Basque regions). In contrast, the inability to organize the first democratic elections over the whole territory of the country sounded the death knell for Federal Yugoslavia. As soon as the first free elections took place in the republics (first in Slovenia and last in Serbia), the federal state had been delegitimized. Power and legitimacy shifted to the republics, which promptly opted for independence as a means to complete their democratic transition. While majorities in Slovenia and Croatia voted in non-communists, the elections in Serbia (and Montenegro) enabled the communists (renamed Socialists) to stay in power. The former thus came closer to the Central European pattern, where broadly based anti-communist coalitions took over, while Serbia fitted the Balkan pattern in which the ex-communists

27

won the first elections in Romania, Bulgaria, and Albania. In this way, for Slovenia and Croatia, the end of communism became identified with the exit from Yugoslavia.

The nation-state was declared the necessary precondition for democracy. It turned out not to be a sufficient one. Elections do not necessarily create democracies. Indeed (with the exception of Slovenia), none of the successor states to Yugoslavia can today be described as a liberal democracy, where the question is not who the ruler is, but rather how the ruler's power will be contained. Most of the successor states have moved from communist monopoly to nationalist hegemony.

NATION-STATE BUILDING IN A MULTI-ETHNIC ENVIRONMENT

From Self-Determination to Secession

Yugoslavia was born in 1918, upon the collapse of the Ottoman and Habsburg Empires, in the name of the principle of self-determination of nations. It died in 1991 in the name of the same principle—this time invoked by each of Yugoslavia's constituent Slav nations as it emerged from communism. This irony of history illustrates the changing face of self-determination—from the right to create a federal state to the right to secede from that federal state.

What, then, are the limits to self-determination? Wilsonian idealism identified the principle of self-determination with the principle of justice. But when one considers the plight of the national minorities in post-imperial nation-states, one more often sees simply a switching of the roles of oppressor and oppressed: Ethnic group A invokes self-determination in claiming independence from nation B, but in turn refuses it to ethnic group C—each time in the name of "national survival."

Hans Morgenthau (in 1957) defined the nationalist paradox with special reference to the Balkans:

> There are no inherent limits to the application of the principles of nationalism. If the peoples of Bulgaria, Greece, and Serbia could invoke those principles against Turkey, why could not the people of Macedonia invoke them against Bulgaria, Greece, and Serbia? . . . Thus yesterday's oppressed cannot help becoming the oppressors of today

because they are afraid lest they be again oppressed tomorrow. Hence, the process of national liberation must stop at some point, and that point is determined not by the logic of nationalism, but by the configuration of interest and power between the rulers and the ruled and between competing nations ("Paradoxes of Nationalism," *Yale Review*, June 1957, p. 485).

Beginning in the nineteenth century, Balkan nationalism saw a gradual shift from the revival of cultural identity to the creation of new political entities through the process of emancipation from the Ottoman Empire. The bids for national independence through state sovereignty resulted in secession (the separation of nations from a multi-national state) and irredentism (pressure for the incorporation into the new nation-states of ethnic relatives beyond their borders). From their inception, many of the newly created states saw their mission as annexation of the remaining "national territory." Hence the competing (but often also mutually incompatible) national ambitions for a Greater Greece, Greater Serbia, or Greater Bulgaria—referred to in the 1914 Carnegie Commission report as the "children of contemporary megalomania."

The post-Cold War situation (like that after the two World Wars) is marked by the fragility and the de-legitimization of existing borders. This is first of all due to the fact that most of these borders are *recent*. They were established in three phases: the Berlin Congress of 1878; the period between the first Balkan wars and the treaties of Versailles, Trianon, and Saint-Germain (1912-1920); and at the end of World War II. But the post-imperial *status quo* was never accepted in the Balkans as permanent; the borders had been established by the great powers and were considered imposed and changeable.

This non-correspondence of ethnic and political boundaries is of course the continuing challenge to nation-state building in the Balkans. Hence this is a classic situation of "one territory for two dreams"—with the same territory claimed by two or more nations as pivotal to their national identity. *Transylvania* has been a recurring object of controversy between Hungary and Romania. *Kosovo* is claimed on historical grounds by the Serbs as the cradle of the medieval Serbian kingdom, and by the Albanians on demographic grounds (90 percent of the population is Albanian). The Serbs claim it in the name of the past, the Albanians in the name of the present and the future. *Bosnia*, too, has seen rival claims based on dubious readings of history by Serbs, Croats, or Muslims. *Macedonia* has seen competing historic and demographic claims by Bulgarians, Greeks, Serbians, Albanians and, of course, Macedonians. The Bulgarians consider "Macedonian" to mean merely a dialect of the Bulgarian language. The Serbs have never forgiven Tito for what they view as his ethnic engineering with a "Macedonian" identity in what they called South Serbia. And the Greeks claim to have the copyright on the name Macedonia dating back to Philip and Alexander.

Borders are the focal points for the conflicting historical memories of nations. And in times of historic change in the Balkans, it is sometimes only one step from conflicting memories to actual conflict.

According to one approach, the recent conflicts should be seen as a part of the belated completion of the process of nation-state formation. From this perspective, the original creation of Yugoslavia was an answer to the fact that modern national consciousness developed at different speeds in the Balkans. It represented for its peoples a transition from empires to homogeneous nation-states that has been the dominant model for Balkan state-formation since the nineteenth century. The process is unpleasant and has made life in parts of the Balkans "nasty, brutish, and short." But the adherents of this school of thought argue that it is an inevitable stage of modernization; they therefore view the latest Balkan conflict not as a resurgence of ancestral hatreds, but rather as a stage on the road to 'modernity.'

The problem with this approach (leaving aside any moral reservations) is that the formation of ethnically homogeneous states is a practical impossibility in the Balkans. Ethnic groups are simply too numerous and too intertwined. Yugoslavia and other successors of the multi-national empires all claimed to be nation-states, but usually reproduced to some degree the multi-national structure of the former empires. Neither are their successors—Serbia, Bosnia-Herzegovina, and Macedonia—homogeneous nation-states. All the other Balkan states also have national minority problems: Bulgaria has its Turkish minority; Romania, its Hungarian minority; Greece, its Turkish and Slavic minorities; and Albania, its Greek minority.

To pursue the logic of ethnic homogeneity is to invite an unending process of 'ethnic cleansing'—whether violent or 'soft'—and the continuation of tensions and conflicts in the area.

The Balkans therefore remain trapped by the drive to combine an ethnic concept of the nation with a centralized concept of the state. The combination is a recipe for conflict.

Most states are constituted and governed by the ethnic group that has the largest percentage of the population. They grant themselves a status and privileges (for example, in language and education rights) that exclude or marginalize the minority national groups in the same state. Indeed, these privileges are likely to be structured against the interests of these minorities, who are compelled to respect 'civic' norms that they perceive as merely reflecting the superior status of the dominant community.

In a multi-ethnic environment, the creation of a "nation-state"—as in the cases of Croatia and Macedonia, for example— *de facto* divides citizens into two groups. This follows from the very definition of the state given by the Constitution, i.e., as the state of a given national group that ensures the equality of citizens and minority rights. Thus, for example, the Croatian Constitution of December 1990 refers to: "Croatia, the national state of the Croatian people and the state of members of other nationalities and minorities which are its citizens." Croatian independence consequently was perceived by the Serbian population on its territory as radically changing their status from being part of a "constituent nation" in Yugoslavia to being a minority in Croatia. (This, together with the loss of the power, status, safeguards, and privileges that they had enjoyed under Yugoslav conditions, fostered the resentment and separatism of the Krajina Serbs).

The very definition of citizenship in these nation-states introduces dual status. The Macedonian Constitution states: "Macedonia, the national state of the Macedonian people, which guarantees the complete civic equality and the permanent cohabitation of the Macedonian people with the Albanians, the Turks, the Roma, and other nationalities living there." The state is clearly that of the 'main' nation. No less important, the state symbols (flag, anthem, etc.) are those of the 'main' nation. The minorities perceive the state as a tool of the dominant national group and are thus unlikely to endorse a definition of citizenship ("nationality") marked by explicit references to the identity of the dominant national group. As long as this concept of statehood prevails (even including any rights granted to the minority), the state is unlikely to be accepted as legitimate by the minority (even without explicit encouragement from their 'mother nation'). The result is a persistent ethnicization of politics—a systematic escalation of demands on one side and a permanent suspicion of irredentism on the other—especially when the minority ethnic group is in the majority on the other side of the border. In the words of Vladimir Gligorov, son of the President of Macedonia: "Why should I be a minority in your state when you can be a minority in mine?"

Bosnia and Herzegovina—
A Nation-State Without a Nation?

The ultimate absurdity of building a homogeneous nation-state in a multi-ethnic environment is presented by the case of Bosnia and Herzegovina, where no ethnic group has a majority. It is a distinct entity whose borders are the oldest within the former Yugoslavia; it has also been a 'community of fate' resulting from the centuries of side-by-side coexistence of its three main components: Serb, Croat, and Muslim. It survived the process of nation-state building in the nineteenth century largely because it was part of three successive multi-national states: the Ottoman Empire; the Habsburg Empire, and, after 1918, Yugoslavia. Bosnia was sometimes called a "mini-Yugoslavia" because it was composed of Southern Slavs speaking the same language but classified into three main national groups (43.7 percent Muslims, 31.4 percent Serbs, 17.3 percent Croats, and 5.5 percent "Yugoslavs"—often the children of mixed marriages). As the federation started to disintegrate at the beginning of the 1990s, the dual challenge was: Could Bosnia and Herzegovina survive, as a multi-ethnic society *and* as a political entity, in the absence of a federated Yugoslavia?

Several specific features of Bosnian multi-ethnicity help to answer this question. The first concerns the nature of the society inherited from Ottoman days and from the Yugoslav period. This was based on the idea of the coexistence of distinct communities—the notion of *komsiluk* (a Bosnian word of Turkish origin), which refers to neighborly relations based on respect and reciprocity both between people belonging to different communities and between the communities themselves. Coexistence was based on living next to each other in the countryside and the actual mixing of populations in the cities, especially after World War II.

The Yugoslav communist system contributed to the political institutionalization of this community. Much as at the

Yugoslavia level, political power and patronage in Bosnia-Herzegovina was distributed according to a "national key." In a one-party state, the census became more important than the elections. This worked as long as the state of Yugoslavia provided a common roof and acted as referee. When that state started to disintegrate in a context of competing nationalisms, the Bosnian equilibrium came under severe strain from both within and outside. The strain within was expressed when, in the first free elections in November 1990, the undisputed victors were the three nationalist parties, which together accounted for 71 percent of the popular vote. Between 1990 and 1992, these three parties spared no effort to impose the structure of three separate communities in all spheres of social and political life. From outside, there were repercussions from the collapse of the federal state and the outbreak of the conflict in Croatia. It was this interaction between internal and external forces that made any attempt to draw a distinction between a war of aggression and a civil war a very tenuous one.

Two aspects of the breakdown of Bosnia-Herzegovina are relevant here—the question of the state and the question of democracy. As long as the common state existed, in both its republican and federal incarnations, the citizens were loyal to it; they saw it as the guarantor of security and of peaceful coexistence among the three communities. But once the state began to disintegrate, between 1990 and 1992, its citizens tended to seek security within their own separate communities. This falling back upon their respective communities in turn accelerated the process of disintegration, reinforcing separatism and consolidating an antagonistic, confrontational ethnic divide.

This was reflected in the changing attitude of the Bosnian population toward ethno-nationalism in the transition to democracy. A few months before the first free elections, a poll showed that 74 percent of Bosnians opposed the nationalist parties, which they felt should not even be allowed to participate in the election. Yet a few months later, the same proportion voted for the three nationalist parties. The democratic process accelerated the disintegration of Bosnia and Herzegovina by bringing to power three national elites that were allied on the issue of separatism and at the same time competing in all other ways—allied in the first election of November 1990 in their joint opposition to the so-called civic parties (denounced as a legacy of communism); divided and competing as to the future concept of Bosnia and Herzegovina in the context of Yugoslav dissolution.

The Bosnian Croats (HDZ) and later the Muslims (SDA) refused to stay in a Serbia-dominated rump-Yugoslavia that, since the summer of 1991, was involved in a war in neighboring Croatia; the Bosnian Serbs (SDS) insisted on either Bosnia-Herzegovina's staying in Yugoslavia or the separation of its Serbian component, which they had declared under the name of "Republika Srpska."

The total incompatibility of these different approaches became obvious on October 14, 1991, in the memorable exchange between the Serb leader Radovan Karadzic and the Muslim Bosniak leader Alija Izetbegovic in the Bosnian Assembly. Karadzic for the first time used the explicit threat of extermination: "Do not think that you will not lead Bosnia into hell, and do not think that you will not perhaps lead the Muslim people into annihilation, because the Muslims cannot defend themselves if there is war. How will you prevent everyone from being killed in Bosnia?"Izetbegovic replied: "His words and manner illustrate why others refuse to stay in Yugoslavia. Nobody else wants the kind of Yugoslavia that Mr. Karadzic wants any more. Nobody except perhaps the Serbs."

In such a context, it was quite obvious why Yugoslavia no longer existed, but could there still be a Bosnia? Whatever the correct answer to that question, it was naive to assume that a referendum could be the solution. The constitutional logic of the Arbitration Commission set up by the EC under the chairmanship of Robert Badinter seemed impeccable: Bosnia and Herzegovina is a republic, therefore a people in whose hands sovereignty rests; if the majority of the people democratically endorses independence, then the conditions are met for accepting a new state into the community of nations. As the outcome demonstrated, majoritarian democracy in a setting of three ethnic groups (with one of the three ethnic components opposed to the other two) does not provide a solution; it only highlights the conflict.

Indeed the dissolution of Yugoslavia and the consequent process of nation-state building along ethnic lines illustrates the tension—sometimes the contradiction—between legal norms and social realities, between law and politics. The independence of Slovenia and Croatia, declared in June 1991, showed that an attempted solution can be politically 'right' (independence was achieved through the democratic process involving the vote of a democratically elected parliament confirmed through a referendum of the whole population), yet legally 'wrong' (from the point of view of international law, recognition of independence came only in January 1992). The Bosnian case shows the opposite: a solution can be legally 'right' (the referendum complied with the request, and norms of the international community seemed to give a clear mandate for independence only), yet politically 'wrong' (independence approved by a majority of voters but rejected by one of the three ethnic groups was bound to lead to conflict).

Questions of democracy and statehood continue to be important for the future of post-Dayton Bosnia: Will the elections in Bosnia and Herzegovina simply legitimize the power of nationalist elites that have destroyed the country, or can the democratic process help put together what it earlier helped undo?

MAIN ISSUES TO BE ADDRESSED

The Commission considers the following issues important in the search for ingredients that might help defuse ethnic conflict and the logic of exclusion in the Balkans:

• The wars of Yugoslav dissolution have brought into the open the **unresolved conflict between self-determination and the sanctity of state borders.** The United Nations Charter upholds the "self-determination" of "peoples" without defining whether self-determination means "sovereignty" or what a "people" is. The Charter also upholds the borders of member nation-states and bars other members from intervening in the internal affairs of other members, including their civil wars. The Charter does not explicitly recognize the right of all ethnic groups to form their own nation-states by force, or with the aid of a neighboring state in which their nationality forms a majority. The right to self-determination should not be equated with sovereign statehood. The overwhelming majority of the states in the world are not ethnically homogeneous nation-states. To imply or to make policy on the premise that self-determination into new nation-states is part of 'modernity,' or 'normalcy,' with which the Balkans are simply catching up is an invitation to endless armed conflict. The granting of complete sovereignty to each community cannot succeed in the long run. There is a need to relinquish the dream of complete sovereignty for all in exchange for security and enhanced self-government.

• The post-Yugoslav nation-state building of Serbia and Croatia implied the destruction of Bosnian society. *To survive, a*

35

multi-ethnic society must strive to become a 'civil society' in which cross-cutting ties and solidarities in the society can develop as a counterweight to the ties offered by nationalism. But no less importantly, the society also needs to be a state capable of enforcing the rule of law.

• Some argue that a 'Greater Serbia,' 'Greater Croatia'—or, tomorrow, a 'Greater Albania'—are the most likely outcomes in the post-Yugoslavia Balkans. Is this the cost of a new stability that might emerge from the present turmoil? Such a scenario might prevail, but it would be unlikely to bring stability for at least two reasons. First, it implies the disappearance of Bosnia-Herzegovina and Macedonia, two multi-ethnic 'mini-Yugoslavias' that are unlikely to go down peacefully. Second, it both implies the creation of new minorities within the borders of each 'Greater' state and threatens new conflicts within and among such 'Greater' states.

• How can feasible solutions be devised that avoid rhetorical posturing (such as: only multi-ethnicity in the Balkans is acceptable) and dangerous cynicism (such as: partition of Bosnia-Herzegovina is regrettable but unavoidable)? And can a degree of pragmatism in international affairs be combined with a rejection of 'ethnic cleansing' and respect for human rights? Yugoslavia has demonstrated that this is far more difficult than it might at first have appeared. But the quest for such a balance has to continue.

II. THE WAR AND
THE INTERNATIONAL RESPONSE

During the first half of the 1990s, the Balkan predicament became one of the most urgent of the international problems confronting the Western democracies. Part II of our Report examines the crisis from three angles. First, it describes the war itself. Second, it takes up the succession of peace plans that embodied the international effort to cope with the crisis. Finally, it assesses the transatlantic dimension: the nature of the challenge that the war in Yugoslavia posed to the cohesion of the Western democracies, and how and why they failed—and we hope will finally succeed—in meeting that challenge.

PRELUDE AND WAR

In 1990 and early 1991, Yugoslavia moved to the brink of war. Multi-party elections were held in all six republics, bringing to power governments with conflicting ambitions. Efforts to secure the future of the federation were in vain. Slovenia established a timetable for progress toward independence; Croatia followed suit. Serbia, already dominant within the federal organs of power, tried to engineer a general state of emergency and threatened to demand territory from other republics if the federation was to be reformed as a looser, confederal structure. Belgrade intensified its repression in the overwhelmingly Albanian-populated province of Kosovo, whose autonomy the Milosevic regime had revoked in 1989. In Croatia, tensions escalated between the government and Serb-majority areas. In Bosnia, the government was immobilized by antagonisms and suspicions among the three national parties sharing power.

On June 25, 1991, Slovenia and Croatia declared their independence. Two days later, Yugoslav Army tanks moved to regain control of Slovenia's borders with Italy, Austria, and Hungary. When Slovenian forces resisted, the Army seemed uncertain whether to escalate fighting or retreat. By the end of June, Belgrade agreed to a cease-fire. The troika of European Community foreign ministers brokered a preliminary settlement, known as the Brioni Accords (July 7, 1991). But clashes spread to Croatia and intensified. During July and August 1991, the EC brokered more cease-fires, which were all no sooner signed than violated, with the result that peace negotiations could not begin. The fighting worsened, with the Yugoslav Army involved alongside Serb irregular forces on the ground and assisting from the air. On August 26, the Croatian government announced a general mobilization for a "war of liberation." Although the federal authorities in Belgrade never declared war against Croatia, males of fighting age were drafted in Serbia and Montenegro.

In August 1991, the Croatian town of Vukovar, with 45,000 inhabitants, was shelled by Yugoslav Army artillery. It was the start of a savage three-month siege—from land, air, and the Danube river—a siege that took the lives of more than 2,000 people and reduced the town to rubble. By September, Serb forces, backed by the Yugoslav Army, controlled some 30 percent of Croatian territory, spread across the south, center, and east of the country. In October, Yugoslav forces began to bombard the ancient coastal city of Dubrovnik.

After Vukovar fell in mid-November, Serb forces controlled Croatia's eastern marches—the only part of the republic of direct strategic and economic value to Serbia. The Serbian government now sought a cease-fire. On November 23, Cyrus Vance, Special Envoy of the U.N. Secretary-General, brokered a truce between Croatia and the Yugoslav Army as a precondition for deploying U.N. peacekeepers. In December 1991, EC ministers established a mechanism for granting recognition to separate republics by mid-January 1992. The Serb-controlled areas in Croatia responded by declaring the establishment of a 'Republic of Serb Krajina.' A cease-fire signed on January 2 proved lasting. Under pressure from Belgrade, the local Serb leadership in the Krajina accepted the deployment of a U.N. peacekeeping mission (the Vance Plan). By this time, some 247,000 people had become refugees from Serb-held territory in Croatia.

It was now only a matter of time before the conflict would spread to the neighboring republic of Bosnia and Herzegovina. The elected government there was composed of three nationalist parties and headed by a collective presidency under Alija Izetbegovic, leader of the Bosniak nationalist party, the SDA (*Stranka Demokratske Akcije*, or Party of Democratic Action). These authorities agreed that Bosnia-Herzegovina should remain neutral during the war in Croatia. But the Serb Democratic Party (SDS) in Bosnia, which had gained the great majority of Serb votes in the 1990 elections, was working with the Serbian regime and the Yugoslav Army, especially the garrison in Banja Luka, to arm the self-proclaimed 'Serb Autonomous Regions' in northern and eastern Bosnia-Herzegovina. Meanwhile, the compact Croat communities in southwestern Bosnia were consolidating ties with Zagreb.

Warning that war could spread to Bosnia, Izetbegovic pressed for the European Community to extend its monitoring mission from Croatia to Bosnia-Herzegovina. In October 1991, a member of the Bosnian collective presidency asked for 2,000 U.N. peacekeeping troops; the reply was negative. In November and December, Izetbegovic appealed for immediate deployment of peacekeepers to Bosnia, including along its border with Serbia. The United Nations offered only observers—to be deployed in those parts of Bosnia-Herzegovina adjacent to Croatia.

Nevertheless, as the likelihood of international recognition for Slovenia and Croatia increased, the Bosniak and Croat parties in Sarajevo used their combined majority to ensure that Bosnia would not be left behind. In mid-October 1991, as war escalated in Croatia, the Bosnian Parliament declared the sovereignty of the republic within its existing borders. This prompted a walk-out by SDS deputies, who claimed that this vote violated the Bosnian Constitution, under which the concurrence of all three ethnic groups was required. Following the December 1991 meeting of the EC foreign ministers, Bosnia and Herzegovina applied for recognition as an independent state. The SDS responded by calling for a 'Serb Republic of Bosnia and Herzegovina' to be established if the Muslim and Croat peoples should "change their attitude toward Yugoslavia."

Responding to the EC ministers' deadline for republics seeking recognition of their independence, the Bosniak and Croat authorities submitted Bosnia-Herzegovina's application on December 20, 1991. In January, the EC Arbitration Commission noted that the Bosnian Serb leadership's hostility to independence meant "the will of the peoples of Bosnia and Herzegovina to constitute . . . a sovereign and independent state cannot be held to have been fully established." The Arbitration Commission suggested a referendum as the solution. Held at the end of February 1992, the referendum was in effect a census along ethnic lines: Serbs mostly refused to vote, while Muslims

39

and Croats (in sum, 63 percent of the electorate) mostly voted for independence, which was declared in Sarajevo on March 3, 1992.

By late March 1992, Serb irregular forces supported by the Yugoslav Army were attacking Bosniak and Croat settlements in northern Bosnia. EC and U.S. recognition of Bosnia and Herzegovina on April 6, 1992 had no deterrent effect. Serb–Yugoslav Army forces laid siege to Sarajevo and swept through eastern and northern Bosnia, waging campaigns of 'ethnic cleansing' against the non-Serb population. Local Muslim and Croat leaders were rounded up and often killed. Women and girls were raped, and men were herded into concentration camps at Manjaca, Keraterm, Omarska, Trnopolje, and elsewhere; many of the inmates were tortured and killed. The elderly, women, and children were forced to flee with no more possessions than they could carry. Householders were forced to sign over their property to the Serb authorities. Resistance was minimal; Bosnia at that time had no army. In the early stages of the conflict, the Bosnian leadership had demonstrated its trust in the Yugoslav Army by refusing (unlike Slovenia or Croatia) to build up one itself. The U.N. High Commissioner for Refugees estimated that, over the spring and summer of 1992, homes were destroyed at an average of 200 each day. In mid-August, the U.S. Senate Foreign Relations Committee put the death toll at 35,000. One Bosnian in three was by then a refugee, and Serb forces controlled some 70 percent of the country—leaving only central Bosnia and western Herzegovina under forces loyal to the Sarajevo government.

But the situation in the areas controlled by the Sarajevo government was complex. The Croat forces based in Herzegovina were only nominally loyal to Sarajevo; their chain of command led directly to Zagreb. Tensions between the Bosniak and Croat allies, evident since autumn 1992, escalated in 1993 into open conflict. In May, Croat forces tried to drive the Bosniaks out of Mostar. Multi-ethnic communities in central Bosnia were ripped apart; Croat forces inflicted a number of atrocities against Bosniak civilians and opened concentration camps in Herzegovina. The Bosniak SDA party tightened its grip upon power in areas controlled by the newly created Bosnian Army—to the detriment of the Serbs and Croats who had remained loyal to the Sarajevo government. But by the end of 1993, the Bosnian Army was gaining ground against the Croats. In February 1994, American diplomats brokered a Bosniak-Croat cease-fire that led to a "Federation" of these peoples.

The battle-lines in Bosnia-Herzegovina did not change significantly in 1993 and 1994, and the siege of Sarajevo continued, while successive peace plans were tabled by international mediators and rejected by the warring parties. The first major changes on the ground came in spring 1995. In April, just before the expiration of a four-month cease-fire, the Bosnian Army carried out its first successful offensives against Serb forces, taking high ground in central Bosnia-Herzegovina. Then Croatia recaptured the Serb-held region of Western Slavonia, and also made advances in western Bosnia-Herzegovina. In July, the Serbs carried out their long-predicted attack on the eastern Bosnian designated "safe area" of Srebrenica, where some 40,000 people had relied for their safety upon the battalion of U.N. peacekeepers. The town was soon overrun, and in front of Dutch peacekeepers and the world's television cameras, the troops commanded by General Ratko Mladic selected out the men and older boys. The evidence indicates that they were taken away to be slaughtered. Between 3,000 and 8,000 are missing. The rest of the population—desperate women, children, and old people—were expelled. The massacre at Srebrenica was the worst single war crime in Europe since 1945.

In July 1995, as Mladic's men closed in upon Zepa, another designated "safe area" in eastern Bosnia-Herzegovina, the Contact Group states and other interested parties convened in London. The European states agreed to an American proposal for a "substantial and decisive response" in the event of further attacks on "safe areas," with special emphasis on Gorazde. At the beginning of August 1995, NATO formally extended the new cover to Bihac, Sarajevo, and Tuzla, stating "any attacks will be met with the firm and rapid response of NATO airpower." The British battalion of U.N. peacekeepers in Gorazde, the third "safe area" in eastern Bosnia, was not replaced when its tour ended in August. Toughened rules of engagement excluded U.N. civilian authorities from the chain of command.

Throughout this period, Croat forces in Bosnia-Herzegovina and the Croatian Army were gaining ground from the Serb forces in western Bosnia—approaching the heavily Serb-populated Krajina region of Croatia. The Croatian attack on the Krajina came on August 4, 1995—three days after the U.S. Congress had voted to lift for Bosnia the arms embargo (imposed on the warring republics in 1992). There was scant resistance, and no support from Belgrade. Zagreb's military offensive was followed by a Croat campaign of 'ethnic cleansing' against the Krajina Serb population. Almost 200,000 people fled—possibly the largest movement of Serbs in history.

On August 28, mortar shells assessed by the United Nations to have been fired from Serb positions killed 37 people in Sarajevo. Early on August 30, action was initiated by NATO aircraft and the Rapid Reaction Force (RRF), composed mainly of newly arrived British and French ground forces with heavy artillery and attached to the U.N. mission in Bosnia. Serb military targets were attacked throughout Bosnia-Herzegovina, including the command and control infrastructure and lines of communication. Under Operation 'Deliberate Force,' NATO conducted over 3,500 missions, including 850 bombing sorties, while the RRF shelled Serb targets around Sarajevo. The international forces suffered no fatalities, and it is believed that Serb casualties were few.

Croat and Bosniak forces now attacked across a wide front in western Bosnia-Herzegovina, routing the Bosnian Serb forces. By the last week of September 1995, the territory held by the Serb side had been cut from some 70 percent to less than 50 percent. Under constant American pressure, and with Milosevic's assistance, the Serb leadership in Bosnia was persuaded to comply—principally by withdrawing heavy weapons from around Sarajevo—with the West's conditions for ending its military operation. A cease-fire was soon achieved, and the prospect of further serious military defeats pushed the Bosnian Serbs to the conference table. The peace conference was held at American initiative in Dayton, Ohio, with President Milosevic of Serbia representing the Bosnian Serbs.

THE LOGIC OF PEACE PLANS

The European, American, and U.N. diplomatic response to the war was embodied in a series of peace plans. Each represented a concentrated effort to devise a formula that would preserve as much multi-ethnic coexistence as could be rescued from the savagery of the war. Yet each succeeding plan preserved something less of this elusive quality—and, in the case of Bosnia and Herzegovina, also less sovereignty for its internationally recognized government. The succession of peace plans thus reflected a progressive deterioration that stemmed, at least in part, from American and European reluctance to use military force to uphold their professed principles, interests, and goals.

Last Chances

The first two plans represented two last chances: a chance to prevent war before it really got started, and a final opportunity for a comprehensive solution. The first of these was the *Common Declaration on the Peaceful Resolution of the Yugoslav Crisis*, known as the **Brioni Declaration**, signed in July 1991 by the Federal Presidency, Slovenia, and the European Community. The document confirmed the cease-fire in Slovenia and paved the way for the Yugoslav Army to withdraw from that republic. It deferred implementation of Slovenia's and Croatia's declarations of independence for a period of three months; committed all sides to refrain from unilateral acts, especially of violence; set guidelines for an international observer mission to Slovenia by the Conference on Security and Cooperation in Europe (CSCE); and set up negotiations "on all aspects of the future of Yugoslavia without preconditions . . ." These negotiations commenced in September.

But the EC mediators suffered from a basic misunderstanding of what was happening. In July 1991, Slovenia and Serbia appeared to be at odds, but in reality their goals were compatible. Serbia's leadership was not as concerned about keeping Slovenia in a united Yugoslavia as about gaining control over Serb-populated areas of Croatia and Bosnia-Herzegovina. (At the end of June, military commanders in Belgrade had been astonished by political advice from the Serbian leadership that Slovenia should be allowed independence and that the Yugoslav Army should pull out.) The Brioni Declaration favored both Slovenia, because a three-month moratorium on independence was not a rejection of independence, and Serbia, because it left the Yugoslav Army free to regroup in Croatia and Bosnia-Herzegovina, where Serbia was preparing local Serb communities to wage war. Hence the Declaration's keenest opponent was the Federal Prime Minister, Ante Markovic, who was making a genuine effort to keep Yugoslavia intact. The EC ministerial troika's rapid success encouraged belief that they had addressed the underlying issues successfully. This delusion was consequential: Three crucial months—when the EC could have devised a strategy to prevent the spread of the conflict to Croatia and Bosnia—were virtually lost.

As the bloodshed in Croatia continued and intensified, European diplomats grasped at the last possibility for a comprehensive settlement of the Yugoslav crisis. In late August

1991, EC foreign ministers established a Conference on Yugoslavia, chaired by Lord Carrington, the EC Chief Mediator on Former Yugoslavia, with the broad objective "to bring peace to all in Yugoslavia and to find lasting solutions which do justice to their legitimate concerns and aspirations." The principles of this legitimacy were to be defined with the assistance of an Arbitration Commission chaired by Robert Badinter of France and composed of constitutional judges from several countries.[4]

In early October 1991, Carrington reached verbal agreement with Presidents Tudjman and Milosevic, and the Federal Minister of Defense, General Kadijevic, that negotiations should seek to reorganize Yugoslavia as "a loose association or alliance of sovereign or independent republics," with guarantees for human and minority rights, and no unilateral border changes. This encouraging development was formalized as an *Outline of the Arrangements for a General Settlement*, known as the **Carrington Plan**. In addition to framing "new relations between the republics," the plan envisioned a "special status" for areas where minority "national or ethnic groups" formed a majority of the population. Milosevic soon rejected Article 1 of the Outline, which proposed, *inter alia*, "sovereign and independent Republics with an international personality for those that wish it"; and, in the framework of a general settlement, "recognition of the independence, within the existing borders, unless otherwise agreed, of those Republics wishing it." (All other republics accepted the Outline, although President Momir Bulatovic of Montenegro soon reneged under Serbian pressure.) In rejecting the Carrington Plan, Serbia dismissed the first and last comprehensive settlement for the republics and peoples of Yugoslavia.

---

[4]At the end of November 1991, the Arbitration Commission attached to the EC Conference on Yugoslavia delivered its first opinion on constitutional issues under dispute. It advised that the Socialist Federal Republic of Yugoslavia was "in the process of dissolution," and the republics should settle their problems of succession while upholding the "principles and rules of international law," with special regard for human and minority rights. On December 8, the Serbian authorities rejected these findings. Meeting on December 16, the EC foreign ministers set a deadline by which republics could apply for recognition as independent. Applications would be assessed by the Arbitration Commission against a list of conditions (regarding democracy, human and minority rights, respect for international law, the inviolability of borders, and peaceful resolution of regional disputes). Successful applicants would receive recognition in mid-January. This was a turning point in European diplomacy and a watershed in international mediation of the conflict.

Croatia

The diplomatic effort now turned to stopping the fighting in Croatia. International diplomacy gave up on comprehensive efforts and concentrated on firefighting, now under U.N. auspices. The **Vance Plan** (a partial plan for peace between Croatia and Serbia) is the name given to the *Concept for a United Nations Peace-Keeping Operation in Yugoslavia*, brokered by former U.S. Secretary of State Cyrus Vance, the Special Envoy of the U.N. Secretary-General. Prepared at the end of 1991, the Vance Plan was eventually accepted by Serbian authorities, the Yugoslav Army, the Croatian leadership, and the rebel Serb leaders in Croatia. Peacekeepers began to deploy in late February 1992.

Charged with the "prevention of new conflict by interposition," the peacekeeping force was deployed "in certain areas in Croatia, designated as United Nations Protected Areas (UNPAs)." In practice, these were in the Serb-controlled parts of the republic, except in Western Slavonia, where control was divided. The population in these areas were to be protected "from fear of armed attack"—hence the mission's name: United Nations Protection Force, or UNPROFOR.

The Vance Plan was especially vulnerable to Serb non-compliance. The peacekeepers were mandated to "ensure" and "verify" that the four UNPAs remained demilitarized after the withdrawal of the Yugoslav Army, but they had no means of enforcing demilitarization when the Serb forces refused to disarm. Before withdrawing, the Yugoslav Army units distributed weapons to the Serb militias, which, instead of disbanding, donned 'police' uniforms. The U.N. police monitors were supposed to "ensure" that police in the UNPAs (i.e., Serb police) worked without discrimination; but the police monitors had "no executive responsibility for the maintenance of public order," and no recourse when the local police declined to cooperate. The peacekeepers would "facilitate" the return of persons displaced from their homes in the UNPAs (numbering a quarter of a million), in collaboration with the UNHCR; but they had no mandate to create conditions for the return of these people, who thus remained refugees. There was no progress toward an overall settlement. Although U.N. officials drew attention to these setbacks, the Security Council failed to draw the consequences.

Another flaw inherent in the Vance Plan was its assumption that the civilian population *inside* the UNPAs was more vulnerable than the civilian population *outside* the UNPAs. This was doubly mistaken. First, the overall balance of forces between the warring sides would have favored the Croatian government if demilitarization had been achieved, but it was not achieved. Second, civilians on both sides of the confrontation line were vulnerable to bombardment and attack; on several occasions in 1992 and 1993, the Croatian Army attacked civilian settlements in Serb-held areas, beyond reach of U.N. peacekeepers, who were too thinly spread to provide protection. In general, the civilians who most needed protection were the several thousand non-Serbs remaining inside the UNPAs, as well as those Serbs, numbering somewhat less than 200,000, living in Croatia outside the UNPAs. These civilians wanted no part in the fighting and were potentially a factor for reconciliation. Their concerns were not addressed by the Vance Plan. So-called 'soft ethnic cleansing' continued throughout Croatia without respite. Non-Serbs in the UNPAs were persecuted within view of the U.N. peacekeepers. Serbs outside the UNPAs continued to 'pay' for the defiance of the Serb insurgents. By early 1993, the Croatian Helsinki Committee for Human Rights, an independent monitoring group, estimated that up to 7,000 homes of Serbs outside the UNPAs had been attacked or blown up since January 1992.

The Vance Plan did not succeed in turning an unfinished war into a political negotiation. On the contrary, the two sides moved farther apart. By omitting mention of the restoration of Croatian authority, and insisting that "the special arrangements in these areas would be of an interim nature and would not pre-judge the outcome of political negotiations for a comprehensive settlement of the Yugoslav crisis," the Plan inadvertently nourished Serb hopes and Croat fears of eventual secession by the rebellious areas.

In early 1994, the Security Council powers appeared to accept that the Vance Plan was in effect obsolete. A way out of the impasse was sought by a new group, convened in Zagreb and comprised of two ambassadors from the International Conference on the Former Yugoslavia (ICFY) and the American and Russian ambassadors to Croatia. This group, which became known as the Z-4 (Zagreb Four), planned a three-step process for a settlement in Croatia: an overall cease-fire, agreement on economic cooperation, and then negotiations on a political settlement.

A new cease-fire was achieved in March 1994. UNPROFOR was charged with patrolling a demilitarized zone of separation between the sides. Serb hesitations delayed an economic agreement until December. By then, the Zagreb Four had drafted the **Z-4 Plan**, granting very extensive autonomy to the largest Serb-held area (the Krajina), while phasing out Serb control over the other two areas (Western Slavonia and Eastern Slavonia). The Z-4 Plan—officially the *Draft Agreement on the Krajina, Southern Baranja, and Western Sirmiu*—was a model for the virtual confederalization of Croatia; the Krajina area would have its own government, currency, and insignia, dual citizenship with Serbia—in other words, it would be a virtual state within a state. Yet the Serbs were not satisfied. Political negotiations were still a remote prospect in January 1995, when President Tudjman announced that Croatia would not allow the United Nations mission to renew its mandate at the end of March. When the *Draft Agreement* was presented at the end of January, Tudjman accepted it as a basis for further negotiation. But despite the negotiators' far-reaching concessions to Serb sensitivities, the Serb leadership refused even to receive the plan unless Croatia reversed its decision on UNPROFOR. Milosevic declined to exert pressure upon the Serb side, and the Z-4 Plan dropped from view—until the very eve of Croatia's full-scale military recapture of Krajina, when one of the Serb leaders announced on television from Belgrade his qualified acceptance of the plan. It was too late.

Bosnia-Herzegovina

All of the peace plans for Bosnia and Herzegovina had to grapple with a dilemma: how to reconcile the conflicting aims of the three national communities and at the same time preserve overall Bosnian sovereignty. In fact, *from the first plan to the last, ethnicity was accepted as an organizing principle*—so that the succession of plans for Bosnia reflected stages of ethnic partition.

The result of the Bosnia-Herzegovina referendum in February 1992 was accepted by the EU foreign ministers, despite the Serb boycott, as confirming that the majority of Bosnia's citizens supported independence. The next step was to convene talks in Lisbon for the purpose of agreeing upon, in Lord Carrington's words, "future constitutional arrangements in an independent Bosnia and Herzegovina." Chaired by Portuguese Ambassador Jose Cutilheiro, these negotiations included the leaders of the Serb and Croat nationalist parties: Karadzic and Mate Boban made their debuts as interlocutors of the European Community—thus setting the precedent of recognizing only "ethnic" politics and leaders in Bosnia and Herzegovina.

On March 18, these talks produced agreement on a *Statement of Principles for New Constitutional Arrangements for Bosnia and Herzegovina,* the so-called **Cutilheiro Plan**, by which the three sides agreed to reinvent Bosnia as a state of "three constituent units, based on national principles." A few days later, before the three units had been delineated, Izetbegovic, the head of the Bosnian collective presidency, repudiated the agreement. The Bosnian Croat leader Boban followed suit. The Lisbon initiative had collapsed. Meanwhile, American pressure on EC states to recognize Bosnia and Herzegovina achieved its goal at a meeting in Brussels on April 6.

The second phase of international mediation in Bosnia-Herzegovina opened in August 1992, when the European Community presidency (then held by the United Kingdom) and the United Nations jointly sponsored a conference in London, bringing together the regional leaders and international foreign ministers. The London Conference asserted strong principles, including non-recognition of territorial gains achieved by force, unconditional release of civilian detainees, protection of minority rights, closing of detention camps, an end to Serbian military flights over Bosnia, international monitoring of the Serbia-Bosnia border, full cooperation by all sides with the relief effort, recognition of Bosnia and Herzegovina by all other former Yugoslav republics, and acceptance of existing borders, as well as respect for all international treaties and agreements. The Bosnian Serbs pledged to withdraw from a substantial (though undefined) portion of territory and to place heavy weapons around key towns (Sarajevo, Gorazde, Bihac, Jajce) under U.N. monitoring within one week. The Serb forces soon violated these principles and undertakings.

The London Conference established a successor to the EC Conference on Yugoslavia. This *International Conference on the Former Yugoslavia* (ICFY) had two Co-Chairmen, Cyrus Vance, appointed by the United Nations and Lord Owen, appointed by the EC. Their task was to pursue a negotiated settlement in keeping with the conclusions and principles agreed in London. The result was the **Vance-Owen Peace Plan**.

This Plan would have recast Bosnia and Herzegovina as a decentralized state of three "constituent peoples," ten provinces, a special status for Sarajevo, and a loose central government. Regarding the all-important nexus of nationality and territory, power would have been shared in each province by a multi-national government, nominated by the three national leaderships, and approximately reflecting the prewar population balance. Muslims (Bosniaks) would have predominated in four provinces, Serbs in three, and Croats in two; the tenth province would have been "predominantly Croat/Muslim."

Despite the intentions of Vance and Owen to challenge nationalist strategies and restore a foundation for civic government, the three sides appeared to conclude from the Plan that each province would be controlled by one or another nation. The Croat side wasted no time in acting upon such a conclusion. At the end of December 1992, even before the Plan had been tabled, the Croat side withdrew from the Bosnian government in Sarajevo. In mid-January, they ordered all Bosnian Army forces in provinces earmarked for Croat predominance to recognize Croat authority. The countdown to war between Bosniaks and Croats in central Bosnia-Herzegovina may be said to have begun with this order. This interpretation was encouraged by the weakness or virtual absence of provisions to ensure implementation of controversial items in the Plan, such as "progressive demilitarization under United Nations/European Community supervision," the "return of forces to the designated provinces," freedom of movement, and the return of refugees. The result was a conundrum. The warring sides—especially the Serb and Croat sides, with their projects of territorial control within Bosnia-Herzegovina—could not be expected to take the Vance-Owen Plan seriously if it lacked a dimension of enforcement. But no enforcement was available.

Vance and Owen had wagered that the principle of "ethnic territory" could be adapted, not quite explicitly, as the basis of a voluntary settlement to preserve "multi-ethnic" Bosnia-Herzegovina. They lost the wager: in May 1993, despite pressure from every quarter (including Belgrade), the Serb leaders in Bosnia-Herzegovina rejected the Plan, with impunity. The principles and conclusions of the London Conference, which had been acknowledged by the Vance-Owen Plan, were buried along with that Plan at the May 1993 conference of five members of the U.N. Security Council at a special meeting in Washington.

The two subsequent peace plans (the Owen-Stoltenberg Plan and the Contact Group Plan) accepted *de facto* partition of Bosnia and Herzegovina into national territories. Negotiations consisted mostly of haggling over minuscule portions of strategically significant territory, trying to find a formula which would be freely acceptable to all sides. In practice, this was seen as bullying the Bosnian government into reducing its minimal

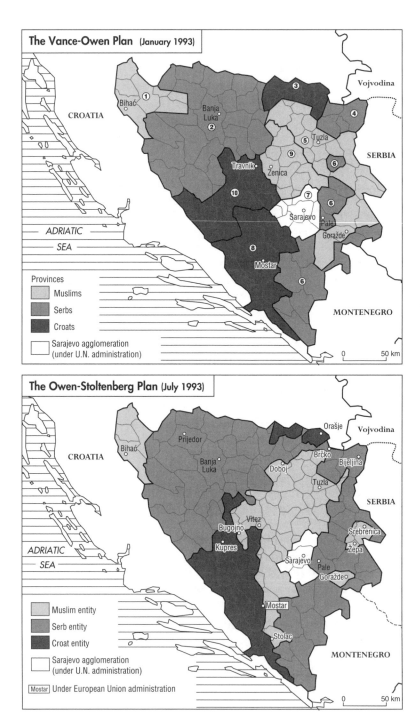

The Vance-Owen Plan (January 1993)

Vojvodina

CROATIA

Bihać ①

Banja Luka ②

③

④

Tuzla ⑤

⑨

⑥

SERBIA

Travnik• Zenica

⑩

⑦ ⑥

Sarajevo Pale

Goražde

ADRIATIC
SEA

⑧

•Mostar

⑥

MONTENEGRO

Provinces

Muslims

Serbs

Croats

Sarajevo agglomeration
(under U.N. administration)

0   50 km

The Owen-Stoltenberg Plan (July 1993)

Orašje   Vojvodina

Prijedor

CROATIA

Bihać

Banja Luka

Brčko

Bijeljina

Doboj

Tuzla

SERBIA

Vitez

Bugojno

Srebrenica

Kupres

Žepa

Sarajevo

Pale

Goražde

ADRIATIC
SEA

Mostar

Muslim entity

Serb entity

Croat entity

Sarajevo agglomeration
(under U.N. administration)

Mostar Under European Union administration

Stolac

MONTENEGRO

0   50 km

Maps on this and facing page are reproduced with the gratefully acknowledged permission of the publisher.
© Xavier Bougarel, *Bosnie, anatomie d'un conflit* (Paris: Editions La Decouverte, 1996).

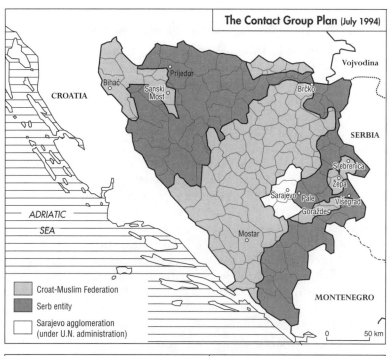

The Contact Group Plan (July 1994)

■ Croat-Muslim Federation
■ Serb entity
□ Sarajevo agglomeration
(under U.N. administration)

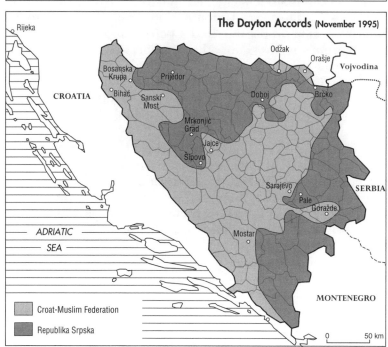

The Dayton Accords (November 1995)

■ Croat-Muslim Federation
■ Republika Srpska

demands. Not surprisingly, with all sides deploying the resources at their disposal, these negotiations failed.

Within weeks of the rejection of the Vance-Owen Plan, the ICFY Co-Chairmen (Thorvald Stoltenberg having replaced Vance) had endorsed a proposal by Bosnian Serbs and Croats to reduce Bosnia and Herzegovina to a 'Union of Three Republics.' Unlike the Vance-Owen Plan, this arrangement—known as the **Owen-Stoltenberg Plan**—would have given contiguous territory to the Bosnian Serbs. The Plan was a thinly veiled tripartite par- tition, indicating a return to the scheme endorsed by Carrington and Cutilheiro in March 1992. The central government would have retained residual competences and would have operated by consensus. Sarajevo would have been placed under U.N. admin- istration for two years. All sides agreed "in principle" to this pro- posal at the end of July 1993. Further refined, the Owen- Stoltenberg Plan would have given the Serb side 53 percent of the republic; the Croat side, 17 percent; and the Bosnian gov- ernment, the remaining 30 percent. The Plan collapsed when the Bosnian government demanded territorial adjustments unacceptable to the other sides.

The Owen-Stoltenberg Plan was modified at the end of 1993 into the **European Union Action Plan**. This grew from a Franco-German proposal to find 3 percent more of Bosnia and Herzegovina's territory for 'the Muslims' while linking sanc- tions-relief for Serbia and Montenegro to the implementation of a settlement. The Action Plan went the way of its predecessors— but not before the three sides had agreed upon a territorial apportionment of 33.5 percent for the Bosniaks, 17.5 percent for the Croat side, and 49 percent for the Serb side.

In early 1994, the negotiating terrain in Bosnia- Herzegovina was transformed. American envoys succeeded in brokering a cease-fire between Bosnian government forces and Croat forces in Bosnia. These two parties then agreed to form a "Federation" within Bosnia; this entity would confederate with Croatia at a later, unspecified date. In this new situation, an innovation occurred in multilateral diplomacy, reflecting a sense that European and U.S. mediation efforts could now be harmo- nized on a new footing. The Contact Group, comprising Britain, France, Germany, the United States, and Russia, was established in April 1994.

From the perspective of finding a settlement in Bosnia and Herzegovina, the creation of the Bosniak-Croat "Federation" had cleared the way for a simple territorial division. The **Contact Group Plan** was based upon the 51 percent: 49 percent territorial formula agreed during negotiations over the Action Plan. It also sought to involve President Milosevic more closely by linking sanctions relief for Serbia with a settlement in Bosnia.

Unlike its precursors, the Contact Group Plan was delivered as an ultimatum in the form of a map; constitutional arrangements would be refined *after* acceptance of the territorial deal. Like its precursors, however, the Plan omitted enforcement provisions. Again unconvinced that the international powers were serious about a settlement that would involve the loss of much Serb-held territory to the "Federation," the Serb leadership rejected the Plan. The resulting stand-off between the Contact Group powers and the Bosnian Serb leaders lasted until December 1994, when an American envoy offered to revise the Plan in one particular. Namely, the Plan had assumed confederal links between Croatia and the Bosniak-Croat "Federation," without a parallel allowance for the Serb entity. The Bosnian Serbs were now offered the right to confederate with Serbia, but the Serb leaders were not tempted. A four-month cease-fire was brokered at the end of December, with the assistance of former U.S. President Carter, but no headway was made in negotiations. American envoys spent two months urging the Bosnian Serbs to accept. In February 1995, one of the American envoys, Assistant Secretary of State Richard Holbrooke, declared failure.

The Contact Group Plan existed in limbo through the spring and early summer of 1995, as the Contact Group states tried to advance by bypassing the Bosnian Serb leaders altogether, offering Milosevic sanctions relief in exchange for recognizing Bosnia and Herzegovina. The situation on the ground was marked by all three sides undertaking offensives in Bosnia-Herzegovina or Croatia. From the perspective of the Contact Group, the most fateful of these operations came in early July, when Serb forces attacked the U.N. "safe area" of Srebrenica.

It was the Serbian seizure of U.N. soldiers as hostages in July 1995 following NATO air action that triggered a Western reappraisal of the use of force. The eventual outcome of this review was Operation 'Deliberate Force' in August and September 1995. This NATO-led operation to enforce U.N. Security Council Resolution 836 inflicted great damage on the Serb military infrastructure, creating an opportunity for the Croat and Bosnian government sides to capture territory. In this way—by using force massively but without granting any side victory—Operation

'Deliberate Force' helped create conditions in which the foreign ministers of Serbia, Croatia, and Bosnia and Herzegovina reached agreement on basic constitutional principles for Bosnia, signed in Geneva on September 8 and in New York on September 26. This agreement in turn led to the *General Framework Agreement for Peace in Bosnia and Herzegovina*, known as the **Dayton Peace Accords**, initialed by the presidents of Bosnia and Herzegovina, Serbia, and Croatia in Ohio on November 21, 1995 and signed by them in Paris on December 14, 1995.

The Dayton Accords proposed to recast Bosnia and Herzegovina as a state of two "entities": the Bosniak-Croat Federation and the Republika Srpska. These entities would have far-reaching autonomy, including "the right to establish special parallel relationships with neighboring states." The "common institutions" (the Parliamentary Assembly, the Presidency, and the Constitutional Court) would have power over foreign policy, foreign trade policy, customs policy, monetary policy, economic obligations of the state, immigration, refugee and asylum policy and regulation, international and inter-entity criminal law enforcement, inter-entity transport and communications, and air traffic control.

These constitutional provisions, including those for elections, represented a logical development of preceding proposals since the Vance-Owen Plan. The components of the settlement had been developed during the previous two years. The idea of using NATO air power to impose a settlement was proposed in May 1993 and again in June 1994. The idea of "compensatory air action" by the West (compensating, that is, for the weakness of Bosnian forces) dated from May 1993. The idea that a peace agreement should be implemented by a NATO operation had been raised in summer 1993. The linkage between sanctions relief for Serbia and Serbian compliance with a settlement had been around since autumn 1993. The 51:49 territorial formula dated back to December 1993. The Croat-Bosniak alliance had been developed since March 1994. The Clinton Administration had accepted in December 1994 that the Serb entity in Bosnia-Herzegovina could be permitted special links with Serbia. In short, the success at Dayton was not a result of new ingredients or new thinking but of new Western, above all American, resolve. Dayton was essentially a European plan with additional American input, imposed with American means.

Where Dayton was innovative was above all in the *regional approach* to a Bosnian settlement, and in the comprehensive *military provisions*, including deployment of "a multinational military Implementation Force" (known as IFOR) for the period of one year, in order "to help ensure compliance" by the local sides. The regional approach meant that Croatia and Serbia were consulted during the preparation of the agreement, which in its final form respected their strategic requirements in Bosnia-Herzegovina. As a result, the Croatian and Serbian regimes ultimately went along with the American-led diplomatic and military initiative, which came to a successful conclusion in Ohio; and they did this despite certain misgivings on the parts of the Croat and especially the Serb leaderships within Bosnia-Herzegovina.

The Dayton agreement stopped four and a half years of terrible conflict, but it did not foreclose either of the ultimate options for Bosnia and Herzegovina: reintegration or partition. The eventual outcome still might be the creation of a unified Bosnia-Herzegovina, or the opposite—a final splitting-up of Bosnia into two or three parts; or it might be an uneasy, indefinite survival of a nominally unified Bosnia.

TRANSATLANTIC STRAINS

The war against Bosnia and Herzegovina provoked the most severe crisis in transatlantic relations since the Suez Crisis. Nor is the rift necessarily over—making it doubly urgent to learn the appropriate lessons from its evolution. Where did the Atlantic Alliance fail, and what made it eventually get back on track?

Only the Western Alliance, embodied in NATO, had the capacity to stop the slaughter. The Alliance deserves credit for that achievement, but its governments must also accept responsibility for their earlier reluctance to use force. The people of Bosnia-Herzegovina paid dearly for transatlantic divisions.

Our purpose here is not to try to assign culpability to individual Western governments or leaders. There is enough blame to go around. There were also mitigating circumstances. An alliance of wealthy democracies had an inherent problem in dealing with such a crisis: the reluctance of any single power to lead, and the fact that each member state had to reach an internal consensus on what to do, as well as to strike a consensus among the various states. This often resulted in lowest-common-denominator policies that proved inadequate. Moreover, the leading powers were preoccupied in the early 1990s with managing the end of the Cold War. Although Western intelligence services were warning of the imminent threat to peace and stability in the region, no serious preventive measures were attempted. No attention was paid to the constructive ideas for turning Yugoslavia, a communist federation, into a democratic confederation—ideas that came first from Slovenia and Croatia in 1990, and then from Bosnia and Macedonia in 1991. The attention of Western foreign ministries was absorbed elsewhere.

The European Response

"This is the hour of Europe. It is not the hour of the Americans," said Jacques Poos, the Luxembourg Foreign Minister and thus the President-in-office of the European Community, upon arriving in Yugoslavia on June 29, 1991. For the then European Community, the beginning of the crisis in Yugoslavia seemed to represent an opportunity to demonstrate its enhanced role.

Looking back five years later, it can be argued that few things have done more to dampen public enthusiasm for the cause of European intergration than the inadequacy of European attempts at peace-making in former Yugoslavia. Extensive efforts were made by the European institutions and by individual member countries, but the judgment, in the Balkans as well as in Western Europe, is one of failure to act effectively.

Before examining the reasons for this failure, the extent of the EC/EU involvement should be considered. Although not a security institution, the EC took the lead in attempting mediation. The Arbitration Commission, established in September 1991 and chaired by Robert Badinter, was an innovative attempt to apply legal wisdom to the problems of a dissolving state. And the EC organized two major peace conferences on Yugoslavia— the first at the Hague from September 1991 to August 1992, and the second jointly with the United Nations in Geneva from September 1992 to December 1995. (Its EC/EU–appointed Chairmen—Carrington, Owen, Bildt—attempted to negotiate political settlements.) The EU decided in September 1993 to take responsibility for the administration of the divided city of Mostar and appointed successive administrators—Koschnik, Peres Casado, and Garrod—who attempted to resolve its problems. The European Community Humanitarian Office (ECHO) has been the principal contributor to the humanitarian aid and refugee programs of the UNHCR and, more recently, the European Union has assumed a major role both in financing the civilian side of the implementation of the Dayton Accords and in the reconstruction of Bosnia and Herzegovina. Perhaps the main achievement of the EU, however, was that it managed to contain its member states' different national perceptions on the Balkan crisis.

The crisis in Yugoslavia demanded from Europe a unified, focused, and resolute response, including the option of a direct military intervention. But although Europeans assumed the largest burden in resources, troops, and lives, without the direct involvement of the United States they were unwilling or unable to undertake such an intervention (and indeed explicitly excluded it by one of their earliest decisions at the EC Foreign Ministers Council of September 19, 1991).

Europe faced three different kinds of obstacles to an effective policy: (1) the lack of understanding of the nature of what was a very intractable conflict; (2) the social and cultural inhibitions concerning military force of rich Western democracies that had themselves enjoyed nearly half a century of peace; and (3) the institutional complications of a European Community trying to transform itself into a European Union with a Common Foreign and Security Policy. All of these constraints on effective policy-making merit thorough examination because this Commission, in offering certain critical judgments of Western policy, does not wish to imply that the way to a more effective policy was either obvious or easy.

The EC foreign ministers who tried to negotiate cease-fires in the summer of 1991 found it nearly impossible to understand that there were political leaders in Europe who would not hesitate to use military force, or that, for the Serbian and Croatian leaders, given their respective ambitions, war might be a deliberate, 'rational' choice. The EC took up the task of mediator in Yugoslavia assuming that it would be possible to negotiate a compromise agreement—as it normally has been possible to do in Western Europe. Postwar European experience also has been that, once negotiated, a compromise will stick because it is in the common interest.

The second group of constraints, social and cultural inhibitions on the use of force, were something that the members of the European Community shared with other Western countries, including the United States. These constraints derived, as Pierre Hassner has noted, from "the encounter between a world based on the search for peace, prosperity, and individual fulfillment and one which has not abdicated the search for glory, community, or territory." In the early months of the crisis, when a credible show of force from the West could have had effect, it probably would have been difficult to convince Western publics that their governments had to resort to military action, including aerial bombardment, in Europe. It would have been especially difficult if the action had lead to civilian deaths or high casualty figures. On the other hand, the public response to television pictures of death and atrocity, together with pressure from prominent intellectuals demanding an urgent European response, pushed reluctant leaders into taking a series of limited actions, even when the strategy underlying those actions lacked coherence. This helps explain the reluctance of Western European military commanders (like their American counterparts) to involve their forces in the conflict without a clearly defined political objective. Senior officers feared that governments might overreact to media-driven public opinion and commit inadequate forces to overambitious tasks without a satisfactory exit strategy. Western Europe's political leaders were in any case extremely hesitant about military involvement; for many of them, the name "Sarajevo" conjured up memories of Europe's earlier twentieth-century catastrophe.

The Yugoslav crisis inevitably came to be seen as a test case for European institutions and for the development of a Common Foreign and Security Policy. And whatever one's eventual expectations for that development, the experience indicated that the organic process of developing the common analysis, instincts, and reactions that are the prerequisites for such common policy is likely to be a more complex and protracted task than some had assumed in the heady days of 1991.

The first six months of the Yugoslav crisis coincided with the final stages of the negotiations of the Maastricht Treaty on European Union, involving complicated trade-offs on other sovereignty issues and an ambivalent spirit of rivalry and common interest. There were those who felt that precedents might be created by the way that Europe acted in Yugoslavia that could affect the future institutional pattern. The problem of foreign policy-making by consensus was illustrated by Greece's exercise of its veto on the question of recognition of Macedonia.

It is not clear, however, how far one can lay the blame for Europe's shortcomings on institutional weaknesses. Europe was not short of decisions on Yugoslavia. The failure of policy to be more effective should more justly be laid at the lack of priority that governments gave to the issue, the lack of understanding of the nature and implications of the conflict not only for those directly involved but more widely for Europe, and the lack of a positive consensus for resolute action.

In these circumstances, it was perhaps no small feat that the European Union achieved as much unity as it did. What seems remarkable, looking back over the half-decade, is that European governments were not more absorbed in calculating their separate interests.

The most important European powers—those which mainly shaped European policy—were Germany, Britain, and France. Of these three, it is **Germany** that has received the most criticism for allegedly going it alone in the early stages of the war. In mid-1991, Bonn, like most of its partners, still favored preserving the unity of Yugoslavia. But the German government changed its position as the war widened. This happened not least under the pressure of public (and published) opinion, which was immensely agitated by the unfolding horrors of the conflict and by the wave of hundreds of thousands of refugees beginning to arrive in the Federal Republic. The more military force Serbia employed against Croatia, the louder grew the voices advocating recognition of the dissident republics.

Serbian accusations that Germany pursued a grand design in the region, or was motivated by "revanchism," were patently absurd. But German diplomacy was at that time criticized in other Western capitals on three counts: (1) that it pushed its European partners too hard in the direction of recognition; (2) that it acted in a way that could be seen as against the advice of the Arbitration Commission; and (3) that it handicapped Lord Carrington's continuing efforts to reach a comprehensive settlement.

The record tells a more complicated story. It is true that, at the EC foreign ministers' meeting on December 16, 1991, the German Foreign Minister, Hans-Dietrich Genscher successfully advocated a timetable for the recognition of individual republics. But this had been preceded by a meeting at Haarzuilen on October 6, when the ministers had initiated a negotiating process aimed at recognizing those republics desiring independence. On October 10, Dutch Foreign Minister Hans van der Broek had declared that this process should be terminated within two months, after which the EC could no longer deny "the right to independence." Then Belgrade turned down the Carrington Plan, and on December 7 the Arbitration Commission reached the conclusion that Yugoslavia was in full disintegration. The Commission's advice was not actually followed by the EU. The Commission expressed reservations about the recognition of Croatia, but supported the recognition for Macedonia. Instead, the EU recognized Croatia and declined to recognize Macedonia. As for the Carrington Plan, while Carrington himself felt that recognition undermined his continuing efforts, the Plan had been rejected by Belgrade in November, and therefore the main responsibility cannot be placed on the decision to recognize Croatia. Vance and Carrington had already obtained a cease-fire agreement between Milosevic and Tudjman in Geneva on November 23, and this was confirmed on January 2 in Sarajevo by their military representatives. Thus recognition did not prevent the military cease-fire, but it did remove an important incentive that might have been used as leverage to restrain Croatia in its treatment of the Serbs in Krajina.

Some observers have faulted Germany for failing to consider the likely impact on Bosnia-Herzegovina, and it is true that Bosnian President Itzetbegovic had publicly warned of the dangers of recognition. Responsibility for the decisions of 16 December is, however, shared by all member states. Although Germany was widely criticized after the fact, no other state upheld an alternative approach. Moreover, it should be acknowledged that Germany's policy recognized, as Britain's and France's did not, that—after Belgrade's rejection of the Carrington Plan, the razing of Vukovar, and the bombardment of Dubrovnik—a strategy for peace needed to isolate and confront the Serbian regime. The vigorous German stance exposed the dearth of alternative strategies toward the conflict. But in retrospect it must also be said that neither the arguments of Germany's critics nor those of its defenders have been vindicated. Recognition may have "internationalized" the conflict and thereby delegitimized the Serb aggression, but it did nothing to stop it. (On the other hand, earlier international support for Yugoslav unity was interpreted by the Serb and the Yugoslav People's Army (JNA) leadership as allowing them a free hand.)

If Germany was the main force behind Europe's policy of recognizing the sovereignty of former Yugoslav republics in 1991, **Great Britain** was the power most consistent in discouraging the international use of military force. London insisted from the outset that nothing at stake in the region would justify military intervention, and that, without full participation by the United States, there was in any case no question of such intervention. There should be no attempt to "impose" a settlement; the sides should be urged to reach a "negotiated" solution. In the summer and autumn of 1991, Britain rejected tentative proposals to send armed European interposition forces to Croatia. On September 19, 1991, Foreign Secretary Douglas Hurd insisted that the Foreign Affairs Council of the EC expressly exclude the possibility of military intervention. After war started in Bosnia-Herzegovina, Britain doggedly opposed the use of force until 1995—although Hurd told the London Conference in August 1992 that "suffering in the former Yugoslavia" was "a direct result of blatant aggression."

France's view of the Yugoslav conflict was shaped by a tradition of pro-Serb/pro-Yugoslav diplomacy, World War I alliance, and a marked preference for the prerogatives of centralized statehood. A more immediately influential concern, as in Britain, was to preserve France's status as a front-rank international power, primarily by playing an active and distinct role within the EC, the Security Council, and NATO. This is one reason why France proposed a WEU intervention in Croatia in August 1991 and supported a similar proposal in September; the other reason was France's perennial ambition to strengthen the European "defense pillar" inside and outside NATO.

There also was concern among French decision-makers about Germany's new role in Central Europe after the disappearance of states (Yugoslavia, Czechoslovakia) that had been created after World War I with French sponsorship. Hence the tendency to give the benefit of the doubt and keep communication lines open to Belgrade, whether seen as capital of Yugoslavia or Serbia. President Francois Mitterrand was particularly representative of this view of French "historic ties" with Serbia going back to World War I. However, in June 1992, he paid a flying visit to besieged Sarajevo—a courageous act that led to the opening of the city's airport—and helped to channel the international response to the Bosnian conflict into humanitarian relief. France was the first EU state to commit large ground forces to the U.N. operation in Bosnia-Herzegovina. But, like Britain, France used its senior command appointments in UNPROFOR to discourage either military action by NATO or the lifting of the arms embargo against the Bosnian government. President Jacques Chirac's reaction to the taking hostage of French U.N. peacekeepers in 1995 broke the pattern of his predecessor's policy, however, and France's role in the American-led peace initiative received recognition when the Dayton Accords were formally signed in Paris.

The United States

Until late 1994, United States policy toward the war in former Yugoslavia veered between distance and engagement without fully embracing either option. Although rhetorically and ideologically inclined to see the conflict as a war of aggression against the Bosnian state and its people, and to advocate a robust military intervention, Washington was even more reluctant to deploy its own ground troops. Indeed, the American military establishment was, as noted above, particularly unwilling to be dragged into "another Vietnam." In contrast, many of the American intellectuals, journalists, and political figures who had opposed the war in Vietnam were vigorous advocates of a military intervention in Bosnia-Herzegovina.

Real isolation was never feasible, given that Bosnia-Herzegovina dominated the agenda of defense and security issues in Europe. The world's only superpower could not remain aloof; on the other hand, truly constructive engagement would have required military commitment and a coherent strategy, of which there was no sign until 1995. The Bush Administration's hands-off policy had been criticized by Governor Clinton in the 1992 presidential campaign. But the Clinton Administration needed two years to find a way to exert its prowess unilaterally and within multilateral initiatives to drive a settlement to the point of acceptance, and to commit itself to leading the implementation.

This delay has several explanations. Most career national security professionals saw no clear national or strategic interests at stake (in stark contrast with the recently concluded Gulf War). No less than European powers, the United States in the early 1990s was re-evaluating its defense and security priorities after the Cold War. Europe's new assertiveness was regarded equivocally by Washington, where many were tempted to respond that if "the hour of Europe" had truly dawned, Europe should go ahead and prove itself—if it could. In 1993, the incoming administration pondered Bosnia with the uncertainty of a party that had been out of office through the 1980s and of a leadership intent upon domestic reforms. Moreover, the American public was strongly against the deployment of U.S. ground forces in areas where U.S. vital interests were not considered to be at stake.

During the 1991 war in Croatia, the Bush Administration had tried to dissuade Germany and the EC from recognizing Slovenia and Croatia outside an overall agreement. Yet early in 1992, the Bush Administration pressed for recognition of Bosnia-Herzegovina—considered by many to be less viable than Croatia or Slovenia. When Bosnia recognition was followed by further Serb aggression, the Administration was no more enthusiastic to intervene than were its European allies. By the time the Vance-Owen Plan was presented to the sides, President Clinton had taken office. Inhibited by campaign promises of multilateral action in Bosnia, and in the light of media criticism of the Vance-Owen Plan, the Clinton Administration withheld approval, damning the Plan with faint praise. The Administration's only alternative to the Vance-Owen Plan was the policy of "lift and strike" (i.e., lift the U.N. arms embargo against Bosnia and use NATO air power to strike Serb targets while the newly strengthened Bosnian Army counter-attacked). If the internationally recognized Bosnian state could not be defended by outside powers, argued some Americans, it should at least be allowed the means to defend itself. But the White House itself remained hesitant about "lift and strike," which was championed most strongly by important segments of the U.S. Congress. The idea found no support in Europe. In effect, the United States undermined Vance-Owen without being willing to mount and enforce an alternative. What was ultimately made available at Dayton was, at least on paper, more damaging to Bosnia-Herzegovina's integrity than the terms of the Vance-Owen Plan.

In 1993 and 1994, as successive peace proposals were pressed by the International Conference on the Former Yugoslavia—led by the EU and the United Nations— Washington remained only semi-involved. To President Bush's disapproval of negotiating with the Bosnian Serb leadership or with Milosevic, President Clinton added a refusal to "impose" a settlement on the Bosnian government. Throughout this period, European leaders complained that the United States was encouraging false hopes in Bosnia of Western military intervention.

A shift began in early 1994, when the Clinton Administration saw an opportunity for unilateral mediation: American diplomats sought a settlement between Bosnian Croat forces and the Bosnian government. The new Bosniak-Croat

Federation created in March 1994 represented the first direct American achievement and investment in a peace effort. At about the same time, the United States was developing a regional Balkans strategy. It forged a military relationship with Albania and boosted its commitment of troops to the U.N. preventive mission in Macedonia. Both the Bush and the Clinton administrations had already warned Serbia to restrain itself in Kosovo (a warning that is taken very seriously in the South Balkans, as the Commission learned when it visited the region). Turkey and Greece were linked to U.S. strategy by membership in NATO. American diplomacy consolidated the periphery before moving toward the center. It was a truism among international mediators that the unresolved conflict in Croatia and the open conflict in Bosnia were interconnected; the evolving American strategy was the first to link a military resolution in Croatia effectively with a settlement in Bosnia. The Administration built a strategy for peace upon the Bosniak-Croat Federation—by fostering a Bosniak-Croat military alliance backed by Croatia proper that could become strong enough to roll back the Serb forces in Croatia and in Bosnia-Herzegovina to the point where the latter would compromise their maximal war aims.

These two developments—the growing U.S. military and diplomatic presence in the South Balkans, together with the new American engagement that led to Dayton and the IFOR deployment—have created high expectations in the region for a continuing U.S. role. This was a message that the Commission heard in countless meetings in the region. But when commissioners inquired in Washington about the depth and durability of that commitment, the answer was mixed. Congress was obviously most skeptical, particularly about the American troop deployment in IFOR. White House and State Department officials, on the other hand, maintained that the new engagement is a serious one. One official argued that "the whole question of what America will be in Europe is reflected in the Bosnia question. Bosnia is a microcosm of all the issues we think are important"—including the threat of European war, human-rights abuses, and ethnic conflict. He granted that it was more difficult to speak of Bosnia-Herzegovina as a "vital" American interest, but saw success in the Balkans as crucial to maintaining a "structure of democratic stability" and "constructive relationships with major partners."

What is clear is that America became more deeply engaged in Bosnia for essentially humanitarian and moral reasons: outrage at the atrocities being committed against defenseless civilians. Strategic analyses were generally formulated after the fact—to justify the decision to intervene. But the strategic analysis for deeper engagement is sound: If America is to play an important role in Europe, it cannot remain detached from such a critical European problem area as the Balkans. Moreover, wars of self-determination, joined by neighbor states related to the warring ethnic groups, are likely to be repeated in other regions (e.g., the former Soviet Union) if they are not resolved by the great powers and by the multilateral institutions they have formed. Unfortunately, it remains an open question whether this analysis will be compelling enough to keep both America and Western Europe engaged.

Russia

Russia's role in the Balkans has been profoundly reshaped by the simultaneous breakup of the Soviet Union and of Yugoslavia. It is worth recalling that in 1948 the defection of Yugoslavia was the Soviet Union's worst defeat by far. National communism (i.e., a communism independent of Moscow) made its debut in the Balkans. In the early 1960s, national communism inflicted two more defeats on the Soviet Union in the Balkans. First, Albania exchanged Soviet domination for Chinese patronage, and then Romania, also exploiting the then recently emerged Sino–Soviet schism, maneuvered to assure for itself a degree of international and intra–Soviet bloc latitude. Bulgaria remained the only Soviet dependency in the Balkans. By the end of the 1960s, just as Moscow appeared to have strengthened its position in East Central Europe by the invasion of Czechoslovakia, its position in the Balkans was in tatters. Moscow learned to live with its losses. It wrote off Albania, watched contentedly as Greece and Turkey became each other's worst enemies, developed an uneasy but workable relationship with Yugoslavia, and sat back as Nicolae Ceausescu gave national communism an increasingly bad name.

With the collapse of communism beginning in 1989, and the disintegration of both Yugoslavia and the Soviet Union itself, the parameters that had defined Russian international relations for most of the twentieth century were swept away. And for a time, the new ruling elite in Moscow was preoccupied primarily with domestic problems and the redefining of Russia's international role. The war in Yugoslavia was an immediate challenge to Russia's new, developing views of its national interest. Russian nationalists immediately put the government under pressure by invoking Slav-Orthodox unity and Russia's historic support for Serbia. There was also the strong temptation for any Russian leadership to back what seemed, for stretches of the war, to be the winning side—and thus to regain for Russia a degree of influence in the Balkans that it had not had since 1948.

But Moscow also supported Serbia for two other reasons: (a) concern over American influence spreading—especially through NATO—into Southeastern Europe at a time when NATO was threatening to expand into East Central Europe; (b) and recognition that communism's collapse left Russia and Serbia in similar situations. Both had large groups of kith and kin in newly independent, neighboring, and mostly unfriendly countries, and leaving Serbia in the lurch might have been taken as a sign that Russia was foreclosing its options of a more active policy in the future regarding the Russian minorities in its "near abroad." While many of those with whom the Commission met in Russia strongly denied that this second factor played any role in Russian policy, the very vehemence of their denials some-times lent it credence.

Although Mikhail Gorbachev brought Tudjman and Milosevic together for a meeting in 1991, Moscow gave no sign of craving a distinct role as a mediator. But, in Moscow's volatile political climate—as Russia smarted at its new ranking as a "post-imperial post-superpower," with its military resentful at "losing" the Cold War—Bosnia became an emblematic world stage on which no Russian government could afford to be pushed to the wings. At the same time, the Orthodox national-ist symbolism mobilized by the Serbs found some echo in Russia; a nascent "Balkan lobby" developed, even though pub-lic interest in the matter remained minimal.

By the time war was launched in Bosnia-Herzegovina, the inefficacy of the EC's efforts, combined with Washington's dis-tance, had created an opportunity for Moscow's involvement. Foreign Minister Andrei Kozyrev played a prominent role on several occasions, outpacing his partners among the U.N. Security Council states without confronting them. President Boris Yeltsin's special envoy to the former Yugoslavia, Vitaly Churkin, used more public diplomacy than Kozyrev and ensured Russia's prominence in the Contact Group. But Russia's internal disarray left little scope for developing a distinct strat-egy. Thus fear of a strong Russian reaction if NATO confronted the Bosnian Serbs was perhaps more a convenient alibi than a reality. When NATO did confront the Bosnian Serbs, Russia's response was relatively mild. Russia's policy in the Balkans before and since the peace settlement at Dayton, however prickly at times, has been remarkably restrained.

At the same time, developments in the Balkans convinced many Russians of their lack of clout on the international scene and of the increasingly powerful position of the Americans. This decisive loss of ground to the Americans was a constant theme in the conversations that Commission members held in Moscow. What Russians had once considered parity between two states had now become a paramountcy of one. The result was humiliation and sometimes anger—directed not so much against the Americans *per se* as at a situation that had developed so unfavorably, so quickly.

For the Russians, Dayton only dramatized American preeminence. Many of the Commission's Moscow interlocutors felt that Dayton demonstrated the alleged American-German bias in favor of the Muslims and the Croats and alleged American-German vindictiveness against the Serbs. They seemed convinced that the civil aspects of the Dayton Accords were unrealistic as well as unfair and could not last. On the Russian participation in IFOR, however, the Russians seemed satisfied at the "partnership" they saw as being involved in the special arrangements that were made for the Russian force to report to an American commander rather than a NATO commander. This could indeed become a precedent for closer American and NATO cooperation with Russia now that Boris Yeltsin has been reelected president. Such cooperation could not only improve the international atmosphere but also help lessen the sense of grievance that Russians feel over what they see as their Balkan debacle. Much will depend on how sensitively the West handles its side of any partnership and how realistically the Russians handle theirs.

The United Nations

No international actor suffered more loss of credibility through the Bosnia debacle than the United Nations. U.N. officials consider this unfair, given that the U.N. Secretariat had to implement policies handed down by a fitful and fractured Security Council. As suggested earlier, the lowest-common-denominator policies tended to be diluted further in a Security Council whose permanent members operate by consensus. Moreover, the prominent role accorded the United Nations from the beginning reflected the unwillingness of leading NATO powers to intervene forcefully in a war where such an intervention *could have helped*, as later events showed.

To be sure, the U.N. Secretariat did have a philosophy and an influence that tended to aggravate the failures of Western policy. One element of that philosophy was the Secretary-General's firm conviction, expressed on many occasions, that the war and suffering in Bosnia had received a disproportionate share of the world's attention and moral indignation. He drew a contrast with the relatively meager international attention given to crimes committed against non-European victims—the genocide in Rwanda being the most horrific example.

The United Nations certainly did not neglect Bosnia-Herzegovina; the mission there was the most expensive and complex peacekeeping operation in U.N. history. Its peak strength was over 19,000 personnel. Nonetheless, we note with regret that failure in Bosnia-Herzegovina is likely to have a negative impact on U.N. credibility for future missions to places of suffering throughout the world.

The United Nations became closely associated with three major errors of international policy: (1) a false definition of the crisis, leading to a *humanitarian* rather than a *political* response; (2) an extreme reluctance to use military force; and (3) the setting-up of so-called "safe areas" without the necessary resolve to make them safe. In fairness to the Secretariat, however, a major part of the blame for all of these errors belongs to the major Western powers, which have the dominant say on the Security Council.

Three Errors of Western Policy

Definition of the crisis as a humanitarian disaster rather than as brutal aggression. The United Nations became directly involved in Bosnia-Herzegovina to facilitate the delivery of humanitarian aid. In June 1992, UNPROFOR undertook to establish a security corridor for aid convoys between Sarajevo's airport and the city (and to monitor heavy weapons within range of the airport). In August, Security Council Resolution 770 enjoined "member states, acting nationally or through regional agencies," to use "all measures necessary" to deliver humanitarian aid.

The focus upon humanitarian aid reflected a genuine desire to ease the Bosnian misery. This Commission is well aware of the enormous contribution that humanitarian organizations made to relieving suffering and saving lives throughout the war in former Yugoslavia. And the Commission does not wish to imply that humanitarian aid should only be considered an adjunct of military action.

In the case of Bosnia, however, the prevailing definition among Western governments was that the war was primarily a humanitarian issue—indeed, a "humanitarian nightmare" (Secretary of State James Baker, April 1992). This minimal definition—as if the conflict were a natural disaster unrelated to political strategies—had the effect of dampening public pressure for robust action in response to news of atrocities by Serb forces, and later by Croat forces as well.

Despite valiant efforts by UNPROFOR personnel and the humanitarian agencies, most notably by the Office of the U.N. High Commissioner for Refugees (UNHCR), Sadako Ogata, the humanitarian mission failed to achieve its own targets. It was blocked by Bosnian Serbs and, to a somewhat lesser extent, by Bosnian Croats. In August 1992, at the urging of the United States, the Security Council called upon member states to take "nationally, or though regional agencies or arrangements, all measures necessary to facilitate in coordination with the U.N. the delivery by relevant U.N. humanitarian organizations and others of humanitarian assistance to Sarajevo and wherever needed in other parts of Bosnia-Herzegovina" (Security Council Resolution 770). However, U.N. officials in Bosnia and in New York insisted that force was of very limited use, if not counterproductive, in delivering aid. Force, ran the argument, was not compatible with the consensual environment upon which an effective humanitarian mission depended—or with the wider purposes and philosophy of peacekeeping.

Use of force. U.N. reluctance to authorize force in Bosnia-Herzegovina unquestionably reflected a concern for the safety of peacekeepers and for the humanitarian mission, as well as an institutional aversion to war-making. For much of the time, this aversion coincided with the political preferences of Britain and France—permanent members of the Security Council with troops in Bosnia—whose commanders in Bosnia usually opposed resorting to the threat or use of force in defense of the U.N. mandate.

In contrast, the United States was more inclined to interpret the conflict in Bosnia as a war of aggression, and to advocate forceful action in defense of the victim. As discussed above, however, this advocacy of force was for much of the time mainly rhetorical; Washington's European allies deemed it empty, even irresponsible, as long as they had troops in harm's way and the Americans did not. The evidence strongly suggests that this open transatlantic disagreement was followed closely by the Bosnian Serb leaders and contributed to their conviction that, notwithstanding all of the United Nations' and the West's solemn warnings and promises, the Serbs could literally get away with murder. Repeatedly, the Security Council let its resolutions be mocked:

—The initial humanitarian role around Sarajevo, established in June 1992, provided that all heavy weapons within range of the airport would be concentrated and subject to monitoring by UNPROFOR. This provision was not implemented until February 1994, under the terms of the NATO ultimatum, although Security Council Resolution 770 had authorized "all measures necessary" to facilitate delivery of humanitarian aid as early as August 1992.

—In the same way, air strikes by NATO forces in support of the U.N. operation, under discussion from July 1992, were only authorized in June 1993 by Security Council Resolution 836, in relation to the "safe areas" mandate.

—In July 1992, the Security Council president announced that UNPROFOR would supervise the collection of heavy weapons, as agreed by the parties; yet no effective regime of collection or supervision was established until February 1994.

—The Security Council imposed a ban on military flights over Bosnia-Herzegovina in October 1992, after months of discussion. This prohibition was explicitly linked to the prior provision for enforcement action in the service of the humanitarian mission. At first, NATO was mandated only to monitor compliance, which was non-existent; there were hundreds of violations. "No-fly zone" enforcement came only in April 1993—although NATO had offered to enforce the ban as early as mid-December 1992, if given U.N. authorization.

—The most egregious example of U.N. resolutions being flouted was the fate of the "safe areas" (see discussion below).

A significant element in the West's reluctance to employ military force was the complicated institutional "two-key" relationship between the United Nations and NATO. In theory, at least, the partnership would appear to offer unique advantages for addressing regional conflicts: the legitimacy of the world body plus the coercive resources of the most powerful military alliance. In reality, the two organizations have different, even contrasting philosophies, institutional 'cultures,' and procedures. Highly publicized strains developed between the two over Bosnia-Herzegovina. Centered on issues of command and control, these strains reflected political differences over strategy (or absence of strategy) among the Western powers in the Security Council and in NATO. The strength of British and French contingents in Bosnia had entitled those countries to effective military command within UNPROFOR. The British and French commanders often strove to prevent NATO action, in pursuit of both the United Nations' view of the conflict and its own role and their own governments' policies.

The strains did not prove that the two organizations cannot in future combine efforts successfully. They did, however, confirm that a successful combined operation requires a clear and achievable objective, and a chain of command that avoids confusion between the criteria of peacekeeping and those of military action. These conditions were lacking in Bosnia—essentially because, until summer 1995, the countries concerned had no united position on a strategy to end the war. UNPROFOR was deployed to *mitigate* and *contain* the conflict pending a settlement—functions that NATO was ill-suited to assist.

The use of force in the framework of a peacekeeping mission is necessarily controversial.[5] However, the subject cannot be considered only in terms of principle or institutional philosophy, divorced from assessments of the political context. In Bosnia-Herzegovina, the question of the use of force was seen by the warring sides as a question of the seriousness of the international community's commitment to the principles and values that it had proclaimed regarding borders, 'ethnic cleansing,'

---

[5]The argument against the use of force in the context of a peacekeeping mission was set out by the Secretary-General in May 1995: "The logic of peacekeeping flows from political and military premises that are quite distinct from those of enforcement; and the dynamics of the latter are incompatible with the political process that peacekeeping is intended to facilitate. To blur the distinction between the two can undermine the viability of the peacekeeping operation and endanger its personnel . . . Peacekeeping and the use of force (other than in self-defense) should be seen as alternative techniques and not as adjacent points on a continuum, permitting easy transition from one to the other."

and "safe areas." We note that the president of the Assembly of the Western European Union reported in November 1993 that "each time a NATO plane flew over the city [Sarajevo] at low altitude [as part of Operation 'Deny Flight'], Serb bombardments stopped, which meant a day of respite for the population." What also appears beyond doubt is the real deterrent effect when force was plausibly threatened around Sarajevo in February 1994, and even around Gorazde in April 1994—not to mention the use of force pursuant to Operation 'Deliberate Force' in 1995.

"Safe areas." The West's single greatest moral failure was to declare six "safe areas" and then fail to protect them— indeed, to allow thousands of inhabitants in one of them to be massacred. Moreover, the "safe areas" were the most notorious case of the Security Council's extending UNPROFOR's mandate without providing the military resources and the will to use them that would allow the mission to fulfill its new duties. The Secretary General asked for 34,000 troops, which may have been exaggerated, but he was given less than 7,000, which was certainly inadequate.

Like the "no-fly" regime, the "safe areas" regime evolved over a period of months in 1992 and 1993. In its final form, given by Security Council Resolution 836 in June 1993, the mandate established that six places across Bosnia-Herzegovina, all routinely bombarded by Serb forces (Sarajevo, Tuzla, Bihac, Srebrenica, Gorazde, and Zepa) were to be "safe areas . . . free from armed attacks and from any other hostile act." The general thrust of Resolution 836 was to ensure "the protection of the civilian population in safe areas." The Resolution offered wide scope for the use of force. (Operation 'Deliberate Force,' the NATO action in August and September 1995, was conducted under Resolution 836.)

U.N. officials did not conceal their unhappiness with this mandate. They deemed it "anti-Serb," because it neither ensured the demilitarization of the "safe areas" nor deterred military action *outward* from the areas; hence the mandate prejudiced the impartiality of the mission. The Secretary-General and UNPROFOR's leaders in the field interpreted the Resolution in the narrow sense intended by certain members of the Security Council (notably Britain and France): to wit, that UNPROFOR's task regarding the safe areas was to deter attacks, but should deterrence fail, UNPROFOR troops would use force only in self-defense, not to protect the civilian population. In the event, when "safe areas" were attacked in 1993 and 1994, force was generally eschewed by the United Nations *even* in self-defense. (The case of Gorazde in 1994 was an exception.)

In the spring and summer of 1995, the policies of the United Nations and of the Western powers reached their threshold of absurdity and ineffectiveness. Three outside factors forced changes. The most important was the *hubris* of the Bosnian Serbs in their offensive against the enclaves, the mass slaughter at Srebrenica, the bombing of Tuzla, and the taking hostage of several hundred U.N. Blue Helmets. The second was the pressure of the U.S. Congress to lift the arms embargo. The third was the successful Bosnian-Croatian offensive in Western Slavonia. Clearly a minimalist policy aimed at preventing escalation without running too many risks for the U.N. forces was no longer tenable. Authority moved from the United Nations to NATO when NATO decided to take responsibility as the only entity able to do something. A divided Alliance suddenly converged: Presidents Jacques Chirac and Bill Clinton were sending the same message. The creation of the Rapid Reaction Force, the "regrouping" of UNPROFOR (i.e., the abandonment of the eastern enclaves), the decision at the London Conference for massive air strikes, the Croatian-Bosnian offensive of August 1995, and, finally, the NATO bombings of Bosnian Serb installations led to the Geneva and Dayton agreements.

The military and diplomatic campaigns of late 1995 were distinguished from their predecessors by several factors:

—Washington's full engagement;

—The consensus among other international powers that a new, forceful strategy was needed in Bosnia-Herzegovina;

—The determination of these powers to succeed (there was no fallback strategy in 1995; had the initiative failed, UNPROFOR could not have resumed its former role);

—The linkage of the settlements in Bosnia and Croatia;

—The linkage of diplomacy and enforcement;

—The interaction between NATO and local ground forces. In 1995, the United States broke new ground by letting local forces fight other local forces. It gave its implicit blessing to the Croatian retaking of the Krajina and to the Bosnian-Croatian offensive against the Serbs in Bosnia-

Herzegovina. This and the subsequent NATO air action proved to be a major turning point in the war.

—The *hubris* of the Serb leaders in Bosnia-Herzegovina, on at least two occasions: first, in seizing several hundred U.N. personnel as hostages at the end of May 1995; and second, in capturing the "safe area" of Srebrenica in July and slaughtering thousands of its inhabitants—the worst single atrocity in Europe since 1945.

CONCLUSIONS

The achievement of Dayton cannot erase the shame and horror of allowing Srebrenica to happen. Responsibility for this failure is spread among many parties.

•**The primary cause of the failure of negotiations over Bosnia-Herzegovina, until summer 1995, was the refusal of the leading international powers to exert a credible threat of force much earlier in order to impose a settlement.** The West had the means to carry out its threat. An intervention would have had to have been militarily significant, but it need not have been overwhelming. Air power alone—posing no problems of an exit strategy—might well have been sufficient.

•**The gap between the rhetoric and the actual willingness of the leading international powers to back their words with actions had devastating and shameful consequences.** In the history of the Bosnia crisis, the disproportion between the U.N. Security Council's proclaimed decisions and the willingness of its members and the Secretariat to implement them was indefensible. This applies to the surveillance of the Serbia-Bosnia border (with some two dozen monitors), the "no-fly" zone, and, above all, the proclamation of "safe areas" that the Security Council was not prepared to defend. Each symbolic gesture, each U.N. resolution that was not followed by the evident will to act, became an object of derision. Each empty resolution was far worse than having made no declaration at all.

•**Given the forces deployed by the warring parties on the ground, the U.N. forces were seriously under-equipped to provide the level of deterrence required for successful peace-keeping.**

•**Bosnia showed that humanitarian intervention, although necessary in its own right, cannot substitute for a political strategy involving, if necessary, the use of force; it does limit options for more robust political and military**

intervention. Humanitarian intervention is a noble and often necessary response, but, as in Bosnia, it can prove to be insufficient and somewhat self-defeating.

● **The U.N. policy of impartial humanitarian intervention should be measured against the warring parties' respect for mandates handed down by the Security Council.** Instead, many U.N. officials in the former Yugoslavia maintained a conception of impartiality as neutrality toward the warring parties—even when one or more of them were violating the Security Council's mandates.

● **The U.N. Secretariat has its own institutional identity and interests. In Croatia and Bosnia and Herzegovina, the Security Council delivered impracticable, unenforceable, crucially ambiguous mandates. The U.N. Secretariat reacted by quietly 'redefining' the mandates in order to minimize the risks of implementation.** The Security Council powers who shaped these mandates knew this was happening (the "safe areas" mandate was the classic case).

● **The final conclusion is perhaps the most tragic. While the Dayton settlement was the best obtainable in autumn 1995, there is a strong argument that, with better coordination among the outside nations and institutions, a settlement at least as satisfactory could have been reached earlier.**

In making these sad judgments, the Commission recognizes that it enjoys the luxury of hindsight, and that a consensus on a credible threat and ultimate use of force might not have been within reach until lesser measures had been tried and had failed. But we believe that in the perspective of time, historians will confirm our view.

III. COUNTRY CONDITIONS, TRENDS, AND PROPOSALS

There are two major epicenters of conflict in the Balkans today. The first, the "northern tier," centers on Bosnia and Herzegovina but more broadly involves the Serb-Croat relationship. The Dayton agreement has put an end to the war, but not to the sources of conflict in the region. The second, the "southern tier," centers on Kosovo and directly concerns Serbia, Albania, and Macedonia—and potentially also Bulgaria, Greece, and Turkey. There is little direct interaction between the two, but it should be noted that solutions provided by Dayton for Bosnia are often seen in the region as a precedent for Kosovo.

The Commission's analysis of current developments and country-by-country proposals, based on extensive travel and discussions in the region, is therefore primarily concerned with these two areas of tension. Broader regional recommendations are taken up in part IV.

BOSNIA AND HERZEGOVINA

By the second half of 1995, when NATO finally used decisive force in support of the U.N. mandate, the Serb (and to some extent Croat) program to destroy Bosnia so as to make its reconstruction nearly impossible had advanced very far. It in no way detracts from the achievement of Dayton to observe that the agreement reflects Bosnia's advanced state of disintegration.

The Dayton agreement did not quite foreclose *either* of Bosnia's options: reintegration or partition. It left all sides with much still to play for. The agreement did in theory create a window of opportunity for new political forces to enter the political scene in Bosnia-Herzegovina in support of reintegration. But it has been clear from the outset that this opportunity depends upon rigorous implementation—by IFOR and the Organization for Security and Cooperation in Europe (OSCE)—of the integrative provisions of Dayton. At this writing, it remains to been seen whether this rigor will be supplied.

There is an inherent tension, a latent contradiction, in the Dayton settlement. With some exceptions, the settlement basically accepts the status quo of ethnic territorial lines within Bosnia-Herzegovina achieved by military force. But it also tries to protect and restore Bosnia's prewar multi-ethnic characteristics. This intention is explicitly stated and backed by specific measures in the agreement aimed at undoing some of the ethnic partitioning that war and 'ethnic cleansing' had produced. To that end, the Dayton Accords propose to erect an elaborate constitutional and institutional framework that will not, however, obstruct the already far advanced process of separate nation-state building by the three ethnic leaderships. And yet, what the war produced was also institutionalized at Dayton.

The central question thus remains: Can Bosnia become a viable state? In theory, under Dayton, a new, re-formed state of Bosnia and Herzegovina will bind together the Bosniak-Croat Federation and Republika Srpska (literally, the Serb Republic). But this new 'roof' has very limited authority. The central government of Bosnia and Herzegovina will have a presidency, a parliament, a constitutional court, and a central bank. It includes some Tito-esque features, such as a rotating presidency and the posting of assignments by nationality. This government is to be responsible for foreign policy, commercial and monetary policy, immigration, and international communications. All other powers, including defense, devolve to the two newly recognized "entities," the Bosniak-Croat Federation and the Republika Srpska, which occupy 51 percent and 49 percent of Bosnia-Herzegovina, respectively.

With so many prerogatives and so much power assigned to the entities, it is difficult to see the new Bosnia and Herzegovina operating as a state. The whole is not even the sum of its parts. If the entities had been on cordial terms, or at least ready to cooperate, a viable state could have been constructed. But they are not. No less important, they are bordered by Serbia and Croatia, which see themselves as the 'mother countries' of two of the three ethnic communities in Bosnia. Thus, with gravitation by Bosnian Serbs toward Serbia and Bosnian Croats toward Croatia, the Bosniaks will be left as the only one of the three constituent nations with an obvious, indeed vital, interest in preserving the new state.

The Dayton Accords grant the Bosnian Serbs and Croats the option of gravitating toward their 'mother' countries. The entities have the right to establish "special parallel relations with neighboring states consistent with the sovereignty and territorial integrity of Bosnia and Herzegovina." This formulation could be the most fateful in the entire Dayton agreement. It implies informal confederative relations. A "confederation" between the Bosniak-Croat Federation and Croatia was adumbrated when that Federation was established in March 1994, and suggestions were subsequently made about a similar relationship between Republika Srpska and Serbia. The word "confederation" was dropped at Dayton. As Croatian Foreign Minister Mate Granic told the Commission, this was to avoid creating a precedent for the Bosnian Serbs' association with Serbia. But future confederations have been universally inferred from the Dayton formulation about "parallel" relations. This tends to undermine the new Bosnia-Herzegovina from the start, by accelerating the process by which Republika Srpska gravitates toward Serbia and the Federation becomes a satellite of Croatia.[6] It could also set a precedent for other parts of the Balkans: for example, for the triad Kosovo-Albania-Western Macedonia; or for Turkey and those regions of Bulgaria heavily populated by the Bulgarian Turks.

Republika Srpska

Karadzic's Serbs did not quite triumph militarily, but their ideological or conceptual victory is nearly complete. They were beaten back from the 70 percent of Bosnia-Herzegovina that they controlled at their apogee of military success to less than the 49 percent accorded them at Dayton. Sarajevo remains undivided and in Bosniak hands. And yet the territory that the Bosnian Serbs hold is—subject to the agreement yet to be reached on Brcko—continuous, contiguous with Serbia, and 'cleansed' of Muslims and Croats. Everyone in Bosnia and Herzegovina must live according to Karadzic's conception of that country, where cultural distinctions are elevated to differences in species, and "cats and dogs" (Karadzic's phrase) are no longer expected to cohabit. At a meeting in Pale, 'capital' of Republika Srpska, the Commission was treated to a lengthy discourse by Nikola Koljevic, deputy president of Republika

---

[6] But confederation is not the only possible outcome in Bosnia-Herzegovina. As noted below, the Bosnian Serbs may be so angry with Belgrade that they may prefer either an equal role in Bosnia-Herzegovina over confederation with Serbia, or full independence.

Srpska, on the subject of the West's "hypocrisy" for perpetuating "this whole story of multi-ethnic Bosnia." Koljevic offered his vision of Bosnia: "In my home town of Banja Luka, [before the war] people lived in different parts of town, and mixed only when they wanted to. You have this in Paris, in [New York's] Chinatown, and in Harlem. . . . And yet you want Bosnia-Herzegovina to be different from everywhere else in the world."

Pale's sense of betrayal over Milosevic's concessions at Dayton may put a temporary brake on Republika Srpska's gravitation toward Belgrade. "We wanted to unite with Serbia," the Commission heard from Momcilo Krajisnik, president of Republika Srpska's self-appointed assembly. But "after they imposed a blockade on us (in 1994), our new wish is independence."

It was this estrangement between Milosevic and the Bosnian Serb leadership that the United States and Western Europe exploited to achieve the Dayton settlement. A similar opportunity may be offered by the rivalry between the Bosnian Serb stronghold of Pale, a ski resort in the mountains outside Sarajevo, and Banja Luka, the largest city in Republika Srpska. The visit of this Commission's members to Pale provoked a certain astonishment that this scattering of ski chalets had defied the civilized world for nearly four years. The future of Bosnia and Herzegovina may depend very much on a shift in power to Banja Luka, where political forces appear to be more pragmatic and on better terms with Belgrade.[7] Thus, while a leading role for politicians in Banja Luka might accelerate the political demise of Karadzic or Mladic,

---

[7] There is one issue, though, that unites these two cities, as it unites opinion in both eastern and western parts of Republika Srpska. The two parts are joined by the Posavina Corridor, a short and very narrow stretch of territory dominated by the town of Brcko. Historically, Brcko was a largely Muslim town, but it was 'ethnically cleansed' by the Serbs early in the war. It is now regarded by them as the crucial link between the two parts of Republika Srpska—essential to its unity and very survival. The Muslims demand that it be restored to them, and there was no agreement on the subject at Dayton.

Instead, the following compromise was reached, as stated in the agreement:

—No later than six months after the entry into force of this Agreement, the Federation shall appoint one arbitrator, and the Republika Srpska shall appoint one arbitrator. A third arbitrator shall be selected by agreement of the Parties' appointees within thirty days thereafter. If they do not agree, the third arbitrator shall be appointed by the President of the International Court of Justice. The third arbitrator shall serve as presiding officer of the arbitral tribunal.

—The arbitrators shall issue their decision no later than one year from the entry into force of this Agreement. The decision shall be final and binding, and the Parties shall implement it without delay.

in the long run it might also speed up the informal annexation of Republika Srpska to Serbia.[8]

The contest between Pale and Banja Luka reached a crescendo by mid-May 1996, and its outcome remains uncertain. It is clear, however, that the mere possibility of democratic politics and of any rapprochement between the two entities depends on the removal of Karadzic and Mladic. This was an often repeated message to members of this Commission in Sarajevo. "The removal of indicted war criminals from office is crucial, and that means first of all Mladic and Karadzic," said Mirko Pejanovic, a Serb who is a long-standing member of Bosnia's collective presidency. "As long as they are there, there can be no independent media and no free elections."

The Bosniak-Croat Federation

The Dayton agreement places more weight upon the Federation than that fragile structure may be able to bear. The United States treats the Federation as a building block. For the Bosnian Croat leaders of 'Herceg-Bosna,' and their sponsors in Zagreb, the Federation is a makeshift halfway house to secession by the self-proclaimed 'Croat Community of Herceg-Bosna.' For the Bosnian leadership in Sarajevo, the Federation may be a halfway house on a different route: the path to the reintegration of all of Bosnia and Herzegovina.

As long as Zagreb continues to back the 'Herceg-Bosna' nationalists, it is hardly surprising that the Bosniak leadership is wary. "Tudjman wants a piece of Bosnia," said Federation deputy president Ejup Ganic. "He thinks we are weak. He thinks the West doesn't care about Muslims. And he thinks he has a deal with Milosevic." A similar warning came from moderate

---

This stipulation for Brcko makes it the last place in either Croatia or Bosnia-Herzegovina where the question of sovereignty is still unresolved. It could become one of the most contested issues arising from the Dayton agreement. The Bosnian Serbs have no intention of leaving; they have settled many thousands of Sarajevo Serbs there. The Muslims still insist on having it back: in April, 15,000 Muslims, with Federation vice-president Ejup Ganic present, demonstrated for its return. Dayton is specific on the subject. Its credibility could depend on it.

[8] Mirko Pejanovic put the dilemma to us this way: "Two socialist parties in north Bosnia-Herzegovina are close to Milosevic and are now in conflict with Karadzic [partly over their greater willingness to recognize Bosnia's sovereignty]. But if they obtained power one does not know if they would push for separation." Pejanovic's conclusion is that the international community must keep relentless pressure on Belgrade (and Zagreb) to prevent that separation.

Bosnian Croat leader Ivo Komsic, a member of the collective presidency, who does not expect the Zagreb regime to adopt a constructive policy toward the Federation. It is up to moderate Bosnian Croats to make clear that they do not accept orders from Tudjman, he added. "We want cultural bonds with the Croatian state. But Zagreb politicians have to understand that Bosnia-Herzegovina is a sovereign state, and we live here with other people."

The problem with Komsic's proposal is that politically moderate Croats from Sarajevo and central Bosnia-Herzegovina, who support multi-ethnic society, have been dispersed and demoralized by the war. They lack political resources to influence the leaders in 'Herceg-Bosna,' where the majority of Croats in Bosnia-Herzegovina are now concentrated, and in Zagreb. When the Federation was established in 1994, many of these moderate Croats hoped it would be a means to maintain or restore the *status quo*, at least for themselves and the Bosniaks at a local level. But this has not happened. So far, the Federation has little substance. Bosnian Croat leaders complain about 'Muslim' dominance in the organs of government, while their Bosniak counterparts level charges of obstructionism. "It is difficult to reach decisions on even insignificant issues," said Kresimir Zubak, the Federation president. Zubak explained that the Bosnian Croats expect full equality within the Federation, including, for example, Sarajevo's radio-television center. But no Bosniak leadership is likely to fulfill that expectation as long as Bosnia-Herzegovina is threatened by partition and 'Herceg-Bosna' is a Bosnian Croat stronghold—effectively lawless, dominated by a mafia of smugglers and paramilitary bosses. And there is no prospect of change in 'Herceg-Bosna,' or in its role as the main institutional obstacle to the functioning of the Federation. It should have merged into the Federation in 1994, but it did not. Its dismantling by January 1996 was stipulated at Dayton, but this has not been done. In truth, the existence of 'Herceg-Bosna' is useful to Croatia as leverage against the Sarajevo government.

The Commission visited Mostar, the historic capital of Herzegovina, in December 1995. The local Croat leaders, as well as the Croatian government in Zagreb, have since 1993 treated the western half of Mostar as the capital of 'Herceg-Bosna.' In July 1994, Mostar was placed under a European Union administration headed by Hans Koschnick. The EU's mandate was to build a united, self-governing, multi-ethnic administration for

Mostar, within the Federation. Commissioners were impressed by the EU effort, which had considerably improved conditions in the city and its infrastructure. But there has been no real progress in uniting the city. The main obstacle to administrative unification was the impossibility of merging the two police forces. Resistance came mainly from the Croat side; the Croat mayor expressed the view that, as the Muslims "have" Sarajevo and the Serbs "have" Banja Luka, so the Croats should "have" Mostar. The Dayton agreement demands the total unification of Mostar's administration. By spring 1996, the prospects for this had receded, despite continuing pressure from international mediators. In despair about the lack of progress, and the lack of support from the European Union, Koschnick threw in the towel. The fact that he has had two successors within a few months (Ricardo Perez Casado from Spain and Sir Martin Garrod from Britain) suggests that the EU political efforts have not been more successful since Koschnick resigned. The municipal election held at the end of June 1996 only confirmed that ethnicity remains the primary divide in local politics. It also further diminished the hope that the September elections at the national and Federation levels might show greater tolerance for a multi-ethnic future.

New measures to shore up the Federation have included a customs union, a single state budget, a unitary banking system, and a single state flag (combining Croatian red and white with Muslim green). In May, there was a further agreement to combine military forces. If implemented, these measures would make the Federation more tangible. But Bosnian and international officials in Sarajevo stressed to the Commission that the Bosnian Croat leadership was unlikely to take them seriously unless pressured from Zagreb.

It is also clear that close and vigorous international monitoring will be needed of the new customs arrangements, especially to ensure that revenues are transmitted to Federation accounts rather than pocketed by the Croats, who control almost all of the Federation's international border. The agreements provide for financial penalties against local authorities that fail to comply with the new regulations.

The future viability of the Federation, and therefore of Bosnia and Herzegovina, will depend on the capacity of the two sides to reach a compromise on three strategically important issues: Mostar, Bihac (the fief of Fikret Abdic—the dissident Muslim leader with ties to Zagreb), and access to the Adriatic Sea.

Trends in Bosniak Politics and Society

Now, with peace, the divisions between Bosniak (Muslim) nationalists and proponents of democratic pluralism have come into the open. Prime Minister Haris Silajdzic resigned from the Bosnian government in January 1996, protesting against the ruling SDA's communal reflexes and, more generally, its tendency to run Bosnia like a party state. *Oslobodjenje* journalist Zlatko Dizdarevic has described the rift in stark terms: "Izetbegovic and Silajdzic represent two very different futures for an independent Bosnia: a return to the absolute power of a single-party state under the control of a party that is outdated, increasingly repressive, and taking over the country in the name of a fractious patriotism; or the Western-looking, democratic country its troops have been fighting for."

That the government of Bosnia and Herzegovina was far from a model democracy during the war did not by the remotest stretch of the imagination justify the aggression committed against it and its people. But now that the war is over, the international community should demand higher standards. The fate of Bosnia obviously depends on curbing the excesses of Serb and Croat nationalism. But it also depends on the Bosniak leadership's willingness to resist the communal reflex. Their commitment to an open society will be a necessary condition not only to win the loyalty of Croats and Serbs, but also to enjoy the long-term support of the West. This is the Bosniaks' only hope for maintaining Bosnia and Herzegovina as a sovereign state.

Conclusions and Recommendations

Excluding the worst case—that war will resume in 1997—three possible future scenarios can be discerned for Bosnia and Herzegovina:

Scenario 1: Restoration of a multi-ethnic Bosnia. The term "multi-ethnic" has been overused and simplistically praised by Western commentators on Bosnia; several of the Commission's interlocutors in Sarajevo spoke with irony about the "myth" of "multi-multi-multi" Bosnia. It will perhaps be important to avoid a new pitfall: judging multi-ethnicity in postwar Bosnia-Herzegovina by prewar norms.[9] There will be no restoration of

---

[9] Before the war, 12 percent of the marriages in Bosnia-Herzegovina were mixed, and 5.5 percent of the population declared themselves as "Yugoslavs" in the 1991 census (compared to 7.9 percent in 1981.) Multi-ethnicity was stronger in urban areas (over

the 1991 distribution of the population. What might be established, and must be encouraged, are public norms and institutions that are not dominated by ethnicity. Federation vice-president Ganic told the Commission: "We have to get people busy with something that is not nationalism." This would require a long-term international commitment and a carefully constructed framework. Thus the important question is: How can the domination of ethnicity in public life be diminished over time? Upon the answer to that question may depend the answer to another: Will those refugees and displaced persons who wish to return home across the inter-entity boundary between the Bosniak-Croat Federation and Republika Srpska ever be able to do so in safety and dignity?

Scenario 2: Peaceful coexistence of three communities within two "entities," under a common "roof." The "roof" would consist of the recognized sovereignty of Bosnia and Herzegovina, with a government of limited but accepted authority—i.e., the literal implementation of Dayton. In most respects, the two entities would govern themselves while respecting each other's prerogatives. If achieved, this state of affairs would be the closest possible approach to a restoration of multi-ethnic Bosnia. In the longer term, however, it would probably prove unsustainable—with a drift toward either full segregation or *detente* among the three nations. The former would mean partition. The latter would mean improved functioning of the Federation, economic interaction between the entities, and a progressive blurring of borders and distinctions.

Scenario 3: Partition—first into two, and then into three parts (since full separation of the entities would disintegrate the Federation). This could lead to *de facto* annexation by or confederation with Croatia and Serbia, leaving some 30 percent of Bosnia-Herzegovina as a tiny rump-state for Bosniaks. Formal annexation is unlikely, since Zagreb and Belgrade would probably avoid such a direct provocation to the international community. Besides, while Zagreb's desire for ever-closer ties with 'Herceg-Bosna' can be assumed, the same may not apply, or not to the same extent, to Belgrade and Republika Srpska.

---

a quarter of the population) than in rural areas. (Towns of more than 10,000 inhabitants are used as a criterion for urban.)

That demographic situation has been profoundly altered by the war: The plight of the urban elites and the massive displacement of the population account for the fact that refugees now comprise a half or more of population in Tuzla, Bihac, Zepa, and Gorazde.

This third scenario may be the most likely. There is also an argument—and it deserves a hearing—that the greatest hope for stability lies in full three-way partition. According to this view, the most sensible course would be to recognize the inevitability of partition and to take advantage of the temporary international presence to ensure a 'velvet divorce.'

But a three-way partition—leaving an Islamic state sandwiched between a Greater Serbia and a Greater Croatia—would be no recipe for stability. First, the segregation of Croats and Muslims is not yet finished; its completion would probably involve further violence. Second, the continued hostility of an undemocratic Serbia and an undemocratic Croatia would have a baleful influence on the character of the Sarajevo regime. A land-locked country, economically unviable, and wary of the depredations of its neighbors would likely succumb to the authoritarian tendencies that are already apparent. Third, although Bosnia's society is largely secular, the traumas of the war have made each community more closed than before. The fundamentalism of which Muslim Bosnia's enemies falsely accused it in the past cannot be ruled out for the future. Left to its own devices, a Muslim Bosnia *could* become a staging ground for "exporting trouble" (a phrase used with the Commission by Ejup Ganic).

Such an outcome in Bosnia would have a broader significance for Islam in Europe. It would be seen as a significant milestone, not least for Muslims in Western Europe, but more generally for Islamic societies torn between the Turkish and Iranian models. It could have the same implications for Turkey itself, where Islamists are already pointing to the fate of Bosnia as proof of the futility of tying Turkey's fate to the West. Finally, there could be grave implications for Kosovo and Macedonia, where Albanians, most of whom are at least nominally Muslim, can hardly be expected to be infinitely patient in the face of discrimination and even harsh repression.

The Contact Group countries must respond now if they wish to deflect this trajectory. While they should do everything possible to encourage the three ethnic groups to follow the first scenario over time, they should not—indeed cannot— impose it by some sort of Western *diktat*. Trying to do so could drive the parties to complete separation into three sovereign states—the worst of the three scenarios. The internal borders ratified at Dayton cannot be wished away, but a framework can be established to diminish their importance and to see that they become more permeable with every passing day.

A principled policy should demand strict adherence to the provisions of Dayton that are now flouted with impunity. Full implementation is one of the two general prerequisites of a strategy to prevent full partition and, over time, promote the reintegration of a truly multi-ethnic Bosnia and Herzegovina. The second general prerequisite is for the United States and Western Europe to make unity of purpose their number-one priority. The belligerents in Bosnia-Herzegovina have proven highly skilled at exploiting transatlantic divisions. If they succeed at this in the future, Bosnia's peace is probably doomed.

The Commission concludes that a united Bosnia strategy should be built upon the following principles:

1 **A reasonable guarantee of long-term security is the precondition for peaceful reintegration or even peaceful coexistence, and this guarantee can only be provided by an international military presence that continues for several years after December 1996.** Such a follow-on force could quickly be reduced to no more than one-third of IFOR's present strength. It should be even more heavily European. But it would require a small but visible American troop presence: perhaps 2,000 troops, or roughly 10 percent of the total. It would also require considerable U.S. military power in the background, including logistics, intelligence resources, and the credible threat of punitive air strikes as well as an over-the-horizon naval presence.

No one in Sarajevo believes the civilian "roof" will be ready by the end of 1996. The way that various parties are keeping their options open makes it very clear what kinds of risks are involved in a premature departure of IFOR. NATO countries have to make a strategic analysis of whether peace in the Balkans is an important interest: What is the price of staying in—but also what might be the price of leaving?

A counter-argument frequently used by Western governments is that the former warring parties have to make their own peace, and that one year of outside military presence is long enough to test whether they are willing to carry out the commitments they have already made. Indeed, some argue that the one-year deadline is a positive way to focus Bosnian minds on their own responsibility for their future. Yet there are clearly some powerful factions and individuals—Karadzic, Mladic, and their associates—for whom long-term peace would constitute an unmitigated disaster. Other individuals and civic forces that

87

want peace need the shelter of continued security in order to pursue it. For the near term, that shelter can only come from outside. Moreover, a meaningful assurance of internationally guaranteed security is needed to encourage significant numbers of refugees to return home—even to the area where their nationality is in the majority. Few refugees are willing to risk returning their children to an environment where war could resume within a matter of months. (The critical importance of refugee return is discussed under recommendation 9 below.)

"To deter the armies from coming back out of their barracks, you need air power, reconnaissance, intelligence—so you know what they are doing," the Commission heard from a military source in Sarajevo. "That might mean a brigade in each area, the equivalent of a large division." More important than size is credibility. The credibility of IFOR was well established by the robust bombing campaign of September 1995. ("Our people trust Admiral Smith," Assembly President Krajisnik told Commissioners in Pale. "When he said he would bomb us, he did. Now he says he will bring peace . . . ") To maintain its credibility, a scaled-down IFOR follow-on operation will need to insist on full compliance with Dayton.

The structure and command of this force will be critical to avoiding the kinds of transatlantic dissension and recriminations that have stymied coherent Western policies in the past. We are concerned about a resumption of those recriminations. Both sides' arguments have some merit. The Americans argue, reasonably, that Bosnia and Herzegovina is part of Europe, and American domestic politics will not support a risky, long-term mission to do what the Europeans could just as well do themselves. The Europeans argue that a major source of disunity since 1992 has been that the United States tried to determine policy without risking ground troops. London and Paris, in particular, are adamant that this pattern must not be repeated.

We believe that Western agreement on the force structure suggested above is the best possible compromise: Europe provides the bulk of the force; America shares the responsibility and some of the casualty risk. For Europeans, this would mean acknowledging unavoidable U.S. political constraints, which are likely to relax somewhat after the November 1996 election but are not likely to vanish completely. For Americans, it would mean acknowledging that the recent success of U.S. leadership can only be preserved through long-term commitment and continued sharing of some of the burdens and risks.

The other reason for insisting on a small but significant American ground presence is that the credibility of American power is now very high in the Balkans. Thus, the deterrent value of American troops is disproportionately effective. The same holds true for NATO as an institution. Both are needed in Bosnia-Herzegovina at least through 1997. If, as we expect, a *much reduced* military presence remains needed even after 1997, it might then be turned into a European operation, using NATO's command structures, intelligence, logistics, and communications resources—a move in line with current planning to reform NATO for post-Cold War missions.

Finally, we note that an IFOR follow-on mission may be the only way to avoid what looms as a major continuing source of transatlantic contention: the debate about arming and training the Bosnian Army. Again, both sides of the Atlantic have a point. Many Americans make a powerful moral argument that it would be unconscionable to once again leave the internationally recognized government of Bosnia and Herzegovina defenseless against attack. But Europeans also make sense when they argue that there would be no shortage of weapons from Russia and other sources to counter what might be provided to Sarajevo's forces. The result, they argue, would be a dangerous arms race and *less* security for the Sarajevo government. An international security presence seems the only way to resolve this dilemma.

2 **The institutions intended to provide a common roof for this divided country must be secured and strengthened in every possible way.** This concerns all the main institutions of Bosnia and Herzegovina binding together the Bosniak-Croat Federation and Republika Srpska—including the government, the presidency, the parliamentary assembly, the constitutional court, and the central bank. Pressure must be maintained on Republika Srpska (and if need be on Belgrade) to respect the new Constitution of Bosnia and Herzegovina. The other pressing challenge is to ensure the integrity of Dayton's other common roof, the Bosniak-Croat Federation. The Croatian government must not be allowed to continue treating 'Herceg-Bosna' as its proxy within Bosnia, encouraging Croats there to believe they have a political future outside the framework of Bosnia and Herzegovina.

The lack of support from the United States and the European Union for EU Mostar Administrator Hans Koschnick in the face of the violent intransigence of the local Croat leadership sent a negative signal. Koschnick resigned his position in March 1996, after the international sponsors of Dayton yielded to Croat pressure and modified Koschnick's plan for the administrative unification of the city. The Contact Group countries must be united in exerting pressure on Zagreb to permit and promote the functioning of the Federation as Dayton prescribes. (A general strategy for applying that pressure is discussed in the section on Croatia below, pp. 106–07.)

3 **The solemn commitment made at Dayton by all the signatories to cooperate with the International Criminal Tribunal on the former Yugoslavia should be enforced.** When arrest warrants are issued, all signatories (including Serbia and Croatia) are obligated to deliver the indicted individuals to the Tribunal. Failure to do so is a breach of the agreement. To suggest that it is possible to opt out of these obligations would be to imply that other aspects of the agreement are also optional. Therefore, compliance should be enforced.

The central controversy over the punishment of war crimes is whether peace and justice are contradictory or complementary. It is sometimes suggested that peace must take precedence over justice. Moreover, at the time that the Hague Tribunal was established, there was concern that some countries were using it as an alibi for their unwillingness to actually intervene to prevent continuing war crimes. There was also concern that the United Nations was again raising unwarranted expectations—promising a justice that it was unlikely to deliver. Finally, continuing practical objections to the pursuit of war criminals come from IFOR commanders, who warn that enlisting IFOR in such a manhunt could fatally undermine relations with the leadership of Republika Srpska and military stability in that entity. (It should be added that this argument was put to us not so much as a case against war-crime prosecutions, but simply against using IFOR as a police force.)

However, the Dayton agreement specifies that indicted war criminals—whether Serb, Croat, or Muslim—must be barred immediately from continuing to hold public office in Bosnia and Herzegovina or its constituent entities, and failure to implement this undermines the whole agreement. Thus, besides the legal aspects, this part of the agreement also has important political implications. This applies in particular to Karadzic and Mladic, whose continuing hold on power, whether official or unofficial, in Republika Srpska is a major factor blocking the implementation

90

of Dayton. They should go on practical as well as moral grounds. The Tribunal offers a way, through due process of law, to push aside some of the greatest threats to Bosnia's democratic development.

There are other reasons for thinking that international justice cannot be dispensed with. First, local institutions cannot yet provide justice, because none have credibility with the opposing camps; justice is the last area in which they can trust one another. Second, if there is no institutional justice, there is a risk of vigilante 'justice,' which could be a continuing poison for many years. Third, there is the problem of collective guilt. If the worst criminals are not prosecuted, then the logic of collective guilt will prevail ("all Serbs are guilty"), rendering reconciliation impossible.

Bosnia in 1996 is not Germany in 1945; the victors are not judging the vanquished. Instead, compromises are being made, some of them distasteful. Some of the guilty may never be brought to justice. However, the Tribunal can serve purposes other than strictly legal ones: Experience from other parts of the world suggests that, for the survivors and the families of victims, the possibility to say in public what happened has its own importance in coming to terms with the wounds of the past.

4 If the signatories of the Dayton Accords do not perform their commitment to deliver indicted persons for trial before the Tribunal, the Commission recommends that the Tribunal exercise its legal power to try them "in absentia."

Under the Civil Code systems of France, the Yugoslav Federation, and other European countries, indicted persons who are outside the physical jurisdiction of the state and do not appear for trial can be tried *in absentia*. In such a trial, the prosecutor presents all the evidence, counsel for the accused is entitled to cross-examine and present defense witnesses, and the Tribunal makes a reasoned decision of guilty or not guilty. If the accused returns to the jurisdiction, he may reopen the case and present further evidence, and the Tribunal reconsiders its judgment.

The Tribunal has the power to conduct trials *in absentia* when the accused does not exercise his right to be present. The Tribunal has so far determined not to invoke this power but is understood to be reconsidering the question. Such trials, while less satisfactory than trials with the accused present, are far better than no trials at all.

5 **The existence of free and independent media must be guaranteed.** The Commission's interlocutors in Sarajevo all agreed that news media had played an immensely influential role in preparing the war in Bosnia by sowing hatred and fear. There was general agreement, too, that the media would be indispensable to building a lasting peace. "If you had asked me how to stop this war," said Cardinal Pulic in Sarajevo, "I would have said three things: media, media, media." This may be an overstatement, but it highlights the crucial importance of media for the future of democratic development.

The Dayton Accords contain provisions for the freedom and international monitoring of the media in Bosnia. The signatories pledged "full support" for "freedom of speech and of the press" as one of the *Further Basic Principles* signed by the Foreign Ministers of Bosnia and Herzegovina, Croatia, and Serbia on September 26, 1995. In relation to the elections, the Dayton agreement envisaged high standards of media conduct ("they will respect the freedom of the press"), standards which have been reiterated in the *Rules and Regulations of the Provisional Election Commission* (April 22, 1996). Furthermore, the Provisional Election Commission has appointed a Media Expert Committee to assist with the achievement of acceptable standards for the elections.

However, the signatory states have ignored their promises regarding the media. At the time of writing, the most influential media in Bosnia-Herzegovina, Serbia, and Croatia still continue to serve the various party-regimes; the incitement of fear and hatred continues unabated. The Bosnian air waves are effectively monopolized by four nationalist broadcasting systems—controlled by the Bosnian government, by the Bosnian Serbs, and by the Serbian and Croatian state networks, whose transmissions are relayed inside Bosnia and Herzegovina.

There is virtually no freedom of movement or access for journalists across the inter-entity boundary line, just as there is none for refugees. It remained almost unthinkable for journalists from the Federation to work freely in Republika Srpska; Bosniak journalists are also at risk in Croat-controlled parts of the Federation.

The three regimes in Bosnia and Herzegovina continue their well-worn techniques of exploiting the dominant media and intimidating the independent media. IFOR has been obliged to passively witness continuing propaganda and incitement to hatred. Following the Dayton agreement, Serb media in Bosnia-Herzegovina deliberately inflamed fears in the Serb-controlled districts around Sarajevo that were scheduled for transfer to the Federation. These media campaigns seem to have played a very considerable part in persuading Serb residents to flee before the transfer dates. In early January 1996, President Izetbegovic sent an open letter to Bosnian state television (RTVBH) criticizing the coverage of Christmas and New Year celebrations; in May 1996, he reportedly convened high-level discussions on a plan to convert RTVBH into an explicitly Bosniak station.

Although the state- or party-controlled television and radio news stations retain their overwhelming influence, there have been some positive developments in Bosnia-Herzegovina. Peace has brought a veritable bloom of new media, especially in territory controlled by the Bosnian Army. A first meeting of independent journalists from both entities occurred on April 10, 1996, in Banja Luka—an exception that proved the rule. Also worthy of mention is an international project to transmit live television broadcasts on Bosnian state television from the International Criminal Tribunal for the Former Yugoslavia in the Hague. The project was conceived by *Internews*, a media consultancy based in California, explicitly as an instrument for social catharsis and reconciliation.

Most notable of all, and most encouraging, is the establishment in May 1996 of the Open Broadcast Network by five independent television stations from around Bosnia-Herzegovina— including one station from Republika Srpska. The Open Broadcast Network will use the existing network of transmitters to broadcast six hours daily of combined output, concentrated on current affairs. Organized by the Office of the High Representative at the request of the stations concerned, often in the face of obstruction by the regimes, this project cost some US$17.5 million. The Network was due to become operative only one month before the elections, and its signal only covered some 70 percent of Bosnia and Herzegovina; thus the programming is unlikely to have made much dent in the effective monopoly of regime-controlled media. The project's real significance lies elsewhere. First, it has longer-term potential for attracting a wider public audience and growing interest in independent television across the country—a development that could compel improvements in the regime-controlled media (provided that it does not trigger simple repression as soon as the subsidies and the international publicity have dwindled). Second, the project has set a precedent for international intervention on behalf of democratic media. Unless the project is assessed as an outright failure, the precedent should expand the repertory of techniques for addressing the deeper causes of conflict in post-authoritarian and multi-national societies.

Clearly, this ingenious arrangement alone cannot compensate for the continuing deficit of impartially gathered and impartially presented information. In the media case as in other respects, the situation in Bosnia and Herzegovina cannot be much improved without equivalent or prior improvements in Serbia and Croatia. Several Western non-governmental organizations and trade unions have given much help to independent media in former Yugoslavia; but these media cannot have a wide impact on public opinion. What has been absent is high-level support from Western governments to pressure the local political leaders to stop their manipulation of the media.

More extensive recommendations concerning the role of media throughout the region are presented in the section below entitled Democracy: Civil Society and Media, pp.152–57 below.

6 A critical task for Western governments, foundations, and non-governmental organizations is to help rebuild "civil society"—the nationally mixed institutions and social infrastructure destroyed in the war. This recommendation is discussed in a Balkan-wide framework on pp. 148–152, below.

7 International efforts should now focus on ensuring that a further round of elections can be held within two years under truly free and fair conditions. The first Bosnian elections under the new constitution are scheduled to be held in mid-September 1996—just before the release of this Report. Hence there is little sense in our entering into the controversy over whether it was wise or not for the OSCE to certify them. We do want to comment, however, on where the elections are likely to leave Bosnia and Herzegovina, and to suggest some next steps for the process of democratization.

As of July 1996, few of the conditions for free and fair elections were in place. Freedom of movement between the Federation and Republika Srpska was nonexistent. Opposition parties had no real access to the official broadcast media, which were, particularly in rural areas, virtually the only source of information on the elections. A "politically neutral environment" certainly did not exist in either entity—especially not in Republika Srpska. (One brighter note is that, although their strength is yet to be tested, new multi-ethnic parties are actually being formed.)

Under such conditions, there is an inherent danger that the elections might strengthen nationalist or separatist forces rather than promote state integration along multi-ethnic lines. In Bosnia-Herzegovina, voters have had little choice but to vote on the basis of ethnicity, which encourages the tendency toward territorial fragmentation. Such is the overwhelming influence of the three nationalist parties (SDA, HDZ, SDS), that the existing "civic" parties tend to be marginalized. There is a further danger that, as after the municipal elections in Mostar in June 1996, the losing parties may contest the final outcome of the elections on fraud or other grounds.

The challenge now is to mitigate the damage that is likely to be done by nationalist parties enjoying new electoral legitimacy—and to prepare better conditions for the *next* elections. The former calls for relentless pressure on the nationalist leaderships to contain their political programs within the framework of a single Bosnian state. They must be firmly discouraged from interpreting electoral victory as a democratic license for separation.

As for the next elections, we emphasize two general requirements. First, a continued international presence should assure that the various conditions—freedom of movement, media, etc.—*are met* in the next electoral contest. Second, the next electoral contest should be sooner rather than later. The mandate of the newly elected government should be limited to two years. The new Constitution already provides for a two-year term for the plural presidency, and the Bosnian Assembly can legislate the term of office for its own members.

8 **Reconstruction should give priority to projects that promote the economic reintegration of the country.** The war has ravaged Bosnia and Herzegovina, which already was one of the poorer republics of the former Yugoslavia. As of September 1995, about 145,000 war-related deaths had been registered. The real death toll is probably higher. About 174,000 people have been injured—some 75,000 of them seriously injured or disabled. Economic activity, especially in the industrial centers, came to a virtual standstill. As of August 1994, domestic production had declined to some 5-10 percent of the 1990 level.

95

Industrial output was at about 5 percent of the 1990 output, and electric consumption was below 10 percent of the 1990 level. In the four years of war, the per capita GDP of Bosnia-Herzegovina dropped from US$ 1,900 to US$ 500. About 80 percent of all power generation was put out of operation. Power distribution has been almost totally destroyed. Manufacturing industry has been almost totally destroyed or crippled. Coal output is reported as having dropped from 18 million tons in 1990 to about 1 million tons in 1994. Agricultural production has also dropped drastically.

The greatest damage has been inflicted on the infrastructure. Before the war, Bosnia-Herzegovina had about 1,000 km. of normal track railways. By 1995, only about 300 km. were still in use. About two-thirds of the main roads and of the regional road systems have been damaged. The energy system (electricity and gas) has suffered immense destruction, as has the telecommunications system. About 70,000 of the total housing stock has been either destroyed or damaged, and health care facilities and schools have suffered extensively.

It has been estimated that, as of 1995, about US$ 9 billion had been spent by the international community on operations in the former Yugoslavia, most of it through U.N. agencies. The contributions of the European Union have been estimated at about one-third of this. There have been various estimates for the cost of reconstruction in Bosnia-Herzegovina. Probably the most relevant is the one given by the World Bank: US$ 5.1 billion over the next three years. This appears to be well in excess of anything the international community has promised so far. As of the beginning of 1996, the U.S. government had declared its readiness to contribute US$ 600 million, and the commitment by the European Union stood at about US$ 2 billion. At the beginning of 1996, the World Bank provided a first installment of assistance in the amount of US$ 150 million. In April 1996, the international community pledged US$ 1.23 billion for reconstruction in Bosnia-Herzegovina.

What will be important ultimately—regardless of the actual amount of aid—is how that aid is provided. This raises several issues:

- *Neither the Bosniak-Croat Federation nor Republika Srpska is viable on its own; economic reconstruction can have positive 'spin-off' effects in terms of unifying the country, provided that economic and infrastructural reconstruction projects are crafted to unify rather than separate.* If enough can be done in this regard—and here the international commitment would have to be long-term—the attraction of Serbia and Croatia for the Bosnian Serbs and Croats might be less strong. Reconstruction aid should help rebuild the local economy and should, through employment, help to reintegrate personnel from the wartime armed forces.

- *Although there is agreement about the general approach to reconstruction and the principle of conditionality, there are some differences as to the interpretation of the latter.* The Americans have wanted to withhold aid from Republika Srpska until it complies with the Dayton Accords, while the Europeans have been concerned that certain forms of reconstruction aid to the Serbs would help integrate them. No less important is the lack of a concrete mechanism for the implementation of conditionality by the World Bank and other financial institutions in case of non-compliance with Dayton.

- *One of the most serious aspects of the entire war in former Yugoslavia is gangsterism and corruption on a huge scale.* Muslims have supplied weapons to Serbs for use against their nominal allies, the Croats. Croats have made similar deals with Serbs. And gangster bands from all three nationalities—continuing a long and much too romanticized tradition—have preyed incessantly on their own kith and kin as well as on the 'enemy.' Some members of UNPROFOR also have been involved. Gangsterism and corruption have disgusted and demoralized members of all ethnic groups and repulsed foreign observers and potential investors. Now that international aid is pouring into several regions of former Yugoslavia, the strictest local and international supervision is necessary. There is corruption at the highest level and at all levels. Now the opportunities for it will grow. So will the cynicism if nothing effective is done.

9 The civilian side of the Western presence must be rationalized and strengthened. Lines of authority need to be rationalized. The difficulties faced by the High Representative Carl Bildt and the first EU Administrator in Mostar, Hans Koschnick, prove the point. Never has there been a greater need for Europe to speak with one voice. Likewise, Western criticism of Bildt's performance has had the unintended consequence of undermining his authority among the local parties. The next year in Bosnia is the time to show that both a Common Foreign Security and Policy (CFSP) for the Europeans and transatlantic unity can have concrete meaning. The Commission considers a number of improvements imperative:

- *The role of the High Representative should be strengthened and given a long-term mandate.* In addition, the High Representative should consider establishing a permanent peace-building forum—consisting of members of the international donor community and local (government and entity) authorities—to foster the policy framework for future peace-building activities, identify key tasks, and promote reconciliation. The forum should also be mandated to help ensure that peace-building programs are not diverted or misused for the political domination of one group by another.

- *Coordination between the civilian and military aspects of the Western presence should be improved.* One shortcoming of the current peacekeeping mandate is the lack of inter-linkages between IFOR and the civilian components. Under a new mandate, the post-IFOR troops should be expected to fulfill, or at least actively support, civilian tasks. The dangers of 'mission creep' are real and cannot easily be dismissed. But the high degree of separation of roles between the military and the civilian parts of the operation has created a vacuum in which many urgent problems remain unsolved. Some degree of mission evolution is indispensable. Peacekeeping is a political activity *per se* that requires the capability to mediate and de-escalate *non-military* as well as military conflicts.

- *Better coordination of peace-building activities should have high priority in the implementation process.* (The current peace-building activities fall within the mandates of various institutions, agencies, and offices that are entrusted with numerous and varied political, socio-economic, humanitarian, and human-rights tasks.) As the peace-building activities succeed, increasing responsibility should be given to local institutions.

- *A fundamental reform of the public security sector is required.* Assistance should be given to develop good budgeting practices and to civilianize the police forces. While IFOR will be scaled down, there is a case for building up the International Police Force (IPTF). The IPTF's mandate should be specified, and it should be given the means (including weapons) to implement that mandate. Civilian-military dialogue and civilian control of all security forces should be encouraged.

- *Western funding must be assured, but conditioned on the parties' fulfillment of their own commitments under Dayton.* Promises made regarding money and manpower (e.g., police contingents) must be kept.

10 Persistent efforts to implement the right of refugees to return home should be accompanied by generous conditions for those who choose to remain abroad. This may be the most difficult issue of all. According to the Dayton agreement, all refugees are entitled to return home. Yet refugees are unable to return across the inter-entity boundary line; inside the Federation, too, there has been no breakthrough on this issue. In fact, the war aims of the parties have been consolidated since Dayton; the exodus from 'Serb Sarajevo' is the best-known case, but the burning of the towns of Sipovo and Mrkonjic Grad by Croat forces before their evacuation is another. The main sizable returns to date have been those of Croats to Croat-held areas and of Serbs to Serb-held areas—though not always to their homes of origin. So far, some 100,000 people have returned, mostly to 'majority areas.' Croats are re-populating Kninska Krajina and western Bosnia with refugees from central and northern Bosnia; Sarajevo Serbs are being encouraged to re-populate Brcko and Srebrenica. These movements are expedited by the Serb and Croat authorities precisely to forestall the 'other' refugees, whose return would represent a direct blow to those authorities' war aims—aims that were curbed but not abandoned at Dayton. Meanwhile, relations between Bosniaks and Croats within the Federation continue to be so poor that even the "symbolic return" of several hundred Muslim and Croat families to towns where they had lived before the war—as agreed at Dayton—has been obstructed by both sides.

Bosniak refugees have not been able to return to Republika Srpska; those who have tried have been attacked by enraged Serbs. The Bosnia-Herzegovina government has taken the position, reasonably if improperly, that it cannot be expected to accept Croat and Serb refugees as long as a vastly greater number of Bosniaks cannot return elsewhere. It is highly unlikely that the authorities anywhere in Bosnia-Herzegovina will be more flexible on this theme after the OSCE-endorsed September 1996 elections than they were before. Yet the refugees are the prime living victims of this war. If they cannot go home, can we really speak of a peace settlement at all, rather than a deal fixed between the warring sides? In this confusing scene, several things are clear:

—First, the *right to return* must be secured.

—Second, since wartime Bosnia-Herzegovina was afflicted by the brain-drain on a massive scale, persuading significant numbers of the skilled, the educated, and non-nationalistic (or at least less nationalistic) urban elite to return is critically important for reconstruction and reconciliation.

—Third, although not all refugees will want to return home, a good many—scores of thousands—would probably be willing to return with only minimal assurances of future security. As in so many respects, *security is the fundamental precondition.*[10]

Many refugees would rather face risks at home than a life of exile. However, according to the UNHCR formulation, there can be no international assistance for return except "in safety and dignity"—and even if IFOR commanders were willing to escort refugees home to 'enemy territory' and to guard them until IFOR's mandate expired, this would not create enduring safety or dignity. Moreover, the material conditions for return— such as housing, employment, and basic physical security—are virtually nonexistent in many or most areas.

Thus, unlike the displaced persons (DPs) on the territory of Bosnia and Herzegovina, the refugees in neighboring countries or in the West are unlikely to return in large numbers. They are likely to go back only on a modest scale, and only to where they will be in an ethnic majority and where economic conditions permit.

This raises the broader issue of the relationship between refugees, diaspora, and minorities. In the Bosnian case this means, for instance, that the 320,000 Bosniak refugees in Germany, like the 80,000 from Croatia and Serbia, are likely to stay—adding to the 700,000–800,000 ex-Yugoslav guest workers

---

[10] Clearly the general insecurity is worsened by the estimated 4-6 million mines planted across the country.

already in that country. Refugees and diaspora have an impact on Balkan politics, and this, too, is a warning for Bosnia—particularly in relation to the political exploitation of the refugee problem for irredentist agendas (which tend to encourage radical nationalist solutions, such as incorporating co-ethnics from the other side of the border; or reducing or marginalizing minorities inside the boundaries.) More generally, there is a tendency in the Balkans for diaspora to play a political role in the post-communist transition. In varying degrees, they have supplied money and political advice. On the whole, they tend to radicalize political discourse rather than to foster the introduction of democratic practices; a problem with exiles and diaspora can be that, as a former Croatian Prime Minister told the Commission, "they love the country so much that it can be counterproductive." They perpetuate a mythified image of the 'mother' nation and tend to forget that it has neighbors.

In conclusion, the Commission would emphasize that even under the most optimistic scenarios for refugee return, most refugees will remain in the West. The Western countries must therefore confront the question of accommodating them indefinitely. Here we would make two general suggestions. First, the financial burden should be shared among EU countries, and not left disproportionately to those countries, such as Germany, who have the most refugees. Second, the EU countries will need to be more forthcoming on offering permanent visas to refugees and their families.

The ultimate challenge, we would suggest, is to create a framework that gives each party a stake in the success of the Dayton agreement. The former warring parties, including the Bosniaks, are of two minds about what they want. The Bosniaks have resisted aggression, but they are not victors, and they now find themselves facing the Croats and the Serbs. In order to avoid a new nationalist eruption, it is not enough to propose technical solutions. Each side must feel it is gaining something in exchange for sacrificing something. The Western powers are not ready to maintain their forces in Bosnia-Herzegovina forever. Each side must be made to see that the cost of resuming war is higher than that of maintaining peace.

CROATIA

Croatia was the first victim of Serbian aggression in 1991. Its regime is arguably today the main 'victor' of the war. Nevertheless, while Western public opinion often identified with the Bosnian cause, the unattractive nationalism of Croatia's leadership has generally prevented the country from arousing sympathy abroad. But Croatia has had two powerful backers on the international scene: first Germany in 1991 and 1992, and then the United States, especially in 1994 and 1995. This sponsorship brought Croatia international recognition in 1992, saved it from international sanctions in 1993 and 1994, and then, in 1995, enabled it to roll back Serb forces in Croatia and Bosnia-Herzegovina.

Croatia achieved most of its war aims. Only Eastern Slavonia remains under Serb control, and it, too, is due to revert to Croatia by January 1997 at the latest. Moreover, the large Serb minority—which before the war comprised over 12 percent of Croatia's total population of some 4,800,000—was reduced to under 5 percent by the mass exodus that followed the Croatian Army's recapture of the Krajina region in August 1995. This successful military action was followed by looting and the burning of Serb property in the recaptured area. According to EU monitors, several hundred Serbs, mostly elderly civilians, were killed during this period of several months. The Croatian authorities made no serious effort to halt these crimes or to bring the criminals to justice, pointing to their complicity in what was in effect a campaign of 'ethnic cleansing.'

With sovereignty about to be established over the last Serb-held territory, two issues are of overriding importance for Croatia: (1) its relationship with Bosnia and Herzegovina, and (2) internal democracy. The most controversial and, for the future of regional stability the most important, is the nature of Croatia's relationship with Bosnia. President Tudjman's long-standing belief in the necessity of dividing Bosnia and Herzegovina into Croat-controlled and Serb-controlled portions is well known. From early on, he sought opportunities to discuss such 'solutions' with his Serbian counterpart, President Milosevic. Under American pressure, Croatia recognized Bosnia and Herzegovina in April 1992, but it had already established a para-state in Herzegovina, the 'Croat Community of Herceg-Bosna,' endowed with its own army, the Croat Defense Council (which many Muslims also joined because it was a more effective force than the then nascent Bosnian Army). As Serbian aggression tore apart Bosnia (and the Western powers decided not to intervene with force), Croatian policy changed. In early 1993, the Croat Defense Council ended its alliance with the Bosnian Army, purged Muslims from its own ranks, and made land-grabs in Herzegovina and central Bosnia.

This Croat-Muslim war ended in February-March 1994, when American diplomacy first achieved a cease-fire and then pressed for the establishment of the "Bosniak-Croat Federation" on territory controlled by their two armies. Within the "Federation," an uncompromising political struggle continued. The clearest symbol of this struggle is the divided city of Mostar, much of which was reduced to rubble by Croat artillery in 1993. Croatia and the mini-regime of 'Herceg-Bosna' seek a maximal degree of territorial autonomy for areas controlled by the Croat Defense Council, with Mostar as their capital. Indeed, the area has been quietly absorbed into the neighboring state: Croatian currency, telecommunications, and media are all in use. In 1995, the Bosnian Croats were granted a number of directly elected members in the Croatian Parliament.

The Croat side continually obstructed the European Union administration of Mostar during its two-year attempt to reunify the city before the municipal elections on June 30, 1996. Unfortunately, these obstructions—including two attempts upon the life of the EU Administrator, Hans Koschnick—were sufficient to dissuade the European powers from pursuing their project of reunification. Nevertheless, this Croat 'victory' cannot herald conditions of lasting peace, security, or prosperity—not even for Croats. Indeed, 'Herceg-Bosna' represents the negation of these values. Croat-controlled western Mostar is a lawless place, where a wartime mafia continues to rule by terror and corruption.

The second related issue concerns the Croatian regime's curtailment of democratic practice. In parliamentary elections called in October 1995, after the reconquest of the Krajina, Tudjman was widely expected to reap a 'victory dividend,' a vote of gratitude delivered in the glow of victory. The Croat Democratic Union (HDZ) got 45 percent of the vote—more than any other party, but still a relatively lukewarm endorsement. It was clearly less than the majority needed to change the Constitution to give the presidency still more powers. Tudjman has consolidated his hold on Croatian politics just as Milosevic did in Serbia. He shows little sign of greater flexibility toward political pluralism. Nowhere has this been more evident than in the recent struggle over the mayoralty of Zagreb. Tudjman repeatedly vetoed the mayoral candidate—put forward by the majority of members of the Zagreb city council, elected in October 1995—because the candidate was from the opposition. Tudjman eventually dissolved the council. Zagreb, the capital of the state, he argued, cannot be governed by an opposition mayor.

The Zagreb mayoralty issue is not the only case of democracy flouted. There have been manipulations of the senior judiciary. Severe pressure has been put on the media. State television is strictly controlled. Independent radio stations have been closed, and the opposition press has been subjected to blatant chicanery. All this has been done within the framework of two major amendments to the criminal code, which are aimed at inhibiting journalists in their coverage of the government.

Tudjman's line of attack against his opponents is simple and predictable: Anyone who is against him and the HDZ is against Croatia and its independence. They are, therefore, not democratic opponents but "enemies of the state." This goes for striking workers, human rights activists, independent journalists, or elected politicians. Government propaganda insists there is a plot, with conspirators outside the country and inside it, to force Croatia back into some kind of re-created Yugoslav, or even larger Balkan, confederation. At a party meeting in February 1996, Tudjman stated that 15-20 percent of the population had never wanted a Croatian state and still rejected it; hence independent Croatia was still in danger—indeed virtually under siege. This stance is hardly conducive to democratic dialogue.

The Opposition in Croatia

The evolution of the Croatian regime is of utmost importance to peace prospects in the region. Was Croatia's transition to democracy derailed by the pressures of nation-state building under external threat? War is not the most conducive environment for the development of democratic pluralism: *l'union sacrée* and outright nationalism were used to curtail the development of democratic institutions. The end of the war, the achievement of most Croatian goals, could open up greater space for pluralism. While the opposition parties' joint stand on the issue of Zagreb's mayoralty may indicate a new trend, these parties remain generally fragmented and ineffective, and they are not reluctant to use nationalist discourse. They have not collectively challenged the regime on the issue of the return of Serb refugees to Croatia.

There is also a strong regional component in the Croatian opposition. Two regional parties—the Istrian Democratic Forum and Dalmatian Action—have national profiles. Both question Tudjman's centralized concept of the state and his dual approach of wishing to make Bosnia as decentralized as possible while keeping Croatia as centralized as possible. Istrian regionalism is politically and economically liberal, favoring a parliamentary rather than a presidential system and a decentralized state on the lines of Spain or Italy. It also seeks the creation of a "Euro-region" allowing for cross-border cooperation with regions of Slovenia and Italy. The IDF regularly achieves over 60 percent support in elections in its own area. Dalmatian Action, which lost its representation in the Croatian Parliament in the October 1995 elections, could be described as a 'regionalist left,' reflecting the strong partisan tradition in Dalmatia since World War II. The party is critical of Western democracies for not supporting their real allies in former Yugoslavia, instead of helping Tudjman and Milosevic.

Against the broader background of Croatian politics, these two parties count for little. But their demands and Zagreb's reaction to them, their geopolitical location, and the history of their constituencies well illustrate the problems of regionalism—and the possible opportunities for it—in Central and Southeast Europe. For these two parties, democracy, decentralization, and minority rights are part and parcel of the same agenda.

The "Euro-region" concept of cross-border cooperation originated within the framework of the EU but has now been extended to include some of the new democracies of Central Europe (for instance, the Euro-region along the German-Polish border). In the Croatian case, it is particularly attractive to Istria, which is seeking closer ties with its Western neighbors and the EU. However, having secured independence, the Zagreb government and many Croats see any plans for "regionalism," especially "Euro-regionalism," as ill-concealed threats to dismember their young state. These sensitivities obviously need to be taken into account, although it must be said that the regime exploits them to consolidate undemocratic methods of government.

Conclusions and Recommendations

Croatia is a sovereign state, an internationally recognized member of the United Nations, that fought hard for its independence. Those countries which have contributed to Croatia's achievements so far should wish it to succeed as a democracy and help it contribute to peace in the region. But Croatia is no longer under siege, and now that peace has returned, the country should be held to much higher standards.

"It is a fact that Croatia, culturally and geographically, doesn't belong to the Balkans," President Tudjman assured this Commission when it met with him: "Croatia in geopolitical, cultural, civilizational terms belongs to Central Europe. All our endeavors are focused on reintegration with Europe." This insistence is part of the national self-perception, or mystique. The Croats' Roman Catholicism, their Central European history and culture, their inclinations and aspirations induce them to see "Europe" not just as their refuge but as their home, to which they have an undeniable right of return. But one can doubt to what extent the Zagreb government appreciates what Europe stands for, or what it at least aspires to: liberal democracy; flourishing civil society; a decent, pluralist political culture; a means to overcome chauvinism; and a set of values and legal norms that stand in contradiction to much of Croatian policy toward its Serb minority or toward Bosnia.

Another of our interlocutors in Zagreb said of Tudjman's government: "Europe is a threat to them; it means democracy, free markets, and monitoring." Europe should make good use of that "threat." The vote of the Parliamentary Assembly of the Council of Europe in favor of Croatia's membership on the Council, and then the decision of its Committee of Ministers to postpone Croatia's membership, are indications that Europe is of two minds on this issue and does not always make effective use of its leverage. The Commission recommends that the European institutions as well as the United States government—a close ally of Zagreb—should raise the price of their friendship and support. Both European governments and the U.S. government should make clear their expectations for change in the following areas.

11 **The treatment of minorities should be improved. Peace with its neighbors will largely depend on Croatia's action on this issue.**

12 There should be a serious attempt, internationally monitored, to promote the return of the refugee Serb population.

13 Real freedom of the press must be guaranteed, to end party or government control of the national broadcast media and make frequencies available to independent broadcasters.

14 The local dimension of democracy—decentralization and regional status—should be promoted.

15 The government in Zagreb should be expected to establish constructive relations with Bosnia and Herzegovina, help dissolve the 'Croat Republic of Herceg-Bosna,' promote the functioning of the Bosniak-Croat Federation, and take part in Bosnia-Herzegovina's economic recovery.

SERBIA

Serbia remains the pivotal state in Southeast Europe. It is the geopolitical link between the Northern Balkans (Croatia and Bosnia and Herzegovina), neighboring Romania, and the South Balkans (Macedonia, Albania, and Bulgaria). Serbian policy will also affect the future roles of both Greece and Turkey, while its large Hungarian minority in the province of Vojvodina gives it a connection with Central Europe. Perhaps most crucial, its future policy in Kosovo could decide whether the South Balkans will suffer or avoid the fate that overcame part of Croatia and the whole of Bosnia-Herzegovina.

Opinions differ over whether Serbia won or lost the war in the former Yugoslavia. Certainly the war ended with Serb military defeats: the rout from the Krajina, Bosniak-Croat advances in central and western Bosnia-Herzegovina, and the final NATO air bombardment. On the other hand, the Bosnian Serbs succeeded in carving out for themselves an 'ethnically cleansed' Republika Srpska, and they achieved their program of an ethnically divided Bosnia-Herzegovina. The argument is also bound up with the question of what the aims of Serbia's President Milosevic really were. Did he have a serious pan-Serb or Greater Serbia agenda, or was his conduct during the war built on more mundane opportunism?

Milosevic was undoubtedly perceived by many Serbs as a Messiah figure who would unite them in one state, righting the wrongs of history and saving them from the dangers of minority status in hostile successor states. Consequently, whatever Milosevic's original aims may have been, he is now seen by many Serbs from Croatia and Bosnia-Herzegovina as having raised hopes and then betrayed them. In Serbia itself, there is no evidence of physical war damage, but the embargo took its toll, refugees came by the hundreds of thousands, and the country is isolated and stigmatized. For *all* Serbs, there has always been the powerful myth of solidarity: "Only Solidarity Saves the Serb!" is the most famous nationalist slogan. A sense of common identity persisted despite all the differences.

What both Serbia and the Serb nation now need is a national reappraisal. Where do they stand after this war? What is the relevance today of the myths that have carried them through the centuries? Instead of seeing themselves as an "exceptional" nation in the Balkans, is it not time to see themselves as a partner in a regional community, as a nation that must cooperate or condemn itself to isolation and backwardness?

Who can make the needed reappraisal? The Serb Orthodox Church and a good part of the intelligentsia are too blinkered by traditional nationalism to be capable of fresh thinking. The liberally inclined intelligentsia has been decimated by emigration and demoralized by continual defeats. The political parties that belong to the so-called 'democratic opposition' have discredited themselves politically—by their ineffectuality, inconsistency, and disunity. The only important thing they can agree about is that they detest Milosevic. They have also discredited themselves morally, as many of their leaders first preached the nationalist crusade in Serbia in the 1980s and were aggressively nationalistic while Serb forces were winning the war.

Still, new directions might be taken by the younger generation that has so far kept out of politics. Some of its members have already shown an independence and breadth of spirit that gives hope for change—change in the way Serbs look at their neighbors and the way they are governed at home. In both Serbia and Croatia, there are rudiments or remnants of a civil society, and it is in helping to foster this civil society that the West might help.

Milosevic's political ability stems from an instinctive pragmatism that enables him to take up or shed options not *when*, but *before*, it becomes essential to do so. In Serbia itself, he had been doing this since the mid-1980s. Since 1994, he has applied the approach with extraordinary success in the international field. He saw defeats coming and accommodated them by refashioning himself as a peacemaker. In doing so, he gained an aura of indispensability. To be sure, Milosovic made an important contribution to Dayton—not least by isolating the intransigent leadership of the Bosnian Serbs. Yet he also used the Dayton talks to save himself, and in this he appears to have succeeded. The Commission came away from its January 1996 visit to Serbia with the impression that Milosevic's political supremacy currently seems unassailable. He controls the police and, apparently, the senior officer corps in the Yugoslav Army. He also controls the greater part of the media. His own Serbian Socialist Party is a convenient 'transmission belt.' In his meeting with the Commission, he exuded confidence—a confidence that is also reflected in last year's purge of some of his former supporters, who had regarded the Dayton agreement as a disaster.

But Milosevic's position may not be as safe in the future as it looks today. His Serbian Socialist Party is much less powerful than he is. It is short of a majority in Parliament and can only form a government with the support of a splinter group. Milosevic has had little to fear so far from the democratic opposition, and he can present himself as a 'lesser evil' compared to the nationalist right—spearheaded by Vojislav Seselj and the Radical Party—which has recently lost much electoral ground but might make up some of it among those Serbs not persuaded by Milosevic's propaganda campaign about Dayton. First among them are the half a million homeless Serbs from Croatia and Bosnia-Herzegovina who have entered Serbia over the last year. (If fighting were to break out in Eastern Slavonia, there could be 150,000 more. Even without fighting, a peaceful Croatian reoccupation could eventually lead to a Sarajevo-like exodus—although the Serb strategy at present is to remain and to demand the maximum territorial autonomy.) These Serbs are refugees—with no residential or automatic citizenship rights. They are therefore no immediate electoral threat to Milosevic. But they represent the kind of brewing discontent that Serb nationalists could exploit to their own advantage and against Milosevic.

Milosevic also faces a constitutional problem that will test his political skills. His second term as President of Serbia is due to expire in 1997, and the Serbian Constitution forbids more than two presidential terms. Since it is highly unlikely that he can get the necessary majority to amend the Constitution in the present Parliament, he needs to get around this legal difficulty in order to retain constitutional power. Two possible solutions to this dilemma have recently been discussed. The first would involve Milosevic's giving up the Serbian presidency and standing for election to the (rump) Yugoslav Federation presidency. This would seem to have the virtue of simplicity, although there is strong Montenegrin opposition to it on the grounds that it would demean their republic. The second is much more elaborate and complex. It would involve a complete territorial-administrative reorganization of the entire rump-Yugoslavia. The current administrative units—Serbia, Montenegro, Kosovo, and Vojvodina—would be formally replaced by a number of self-governing or federated regions (six or eight are the figures mentioned), the administration of which would be pyramid-shaped. Atop the pyramid would be a president: Slobodan Milosevic. But this solution, falling foul of a number of nationalisms, looks much less viable than the first. One thing is certain: Milosevic will show all his resourcefulness in trying to keep power.

Meanwhile, the Commission believes, Serbia's priorities should be: (1) a national reappraisal; (2) political democracy; (3) the rule of law; and (4) a market economy that can be constructed without a still deeper plunge into gangsterism and without being so severe as to destroy the society it is supposed to benefit. Milosevic is unlikely to bring about any of these. Indeed, the months since Dayton have seen a tightening of political control. The regime has further cracked down on the media by taking over the independent television station, Studio B—the only source of television news beyond control of the regime. As for the economy, instead of market-oriented reform there is continuing state control. The head of the Serbian State Bank, Dragoslav Avramovic, who impressed members of the Commission with his lucid devotion to market virtues, was dismissed in May 1996.

There are two explanations for these moves. First, they should be seen in the context of the rise to prominence of the Yugoslav United Left (JUL), a grouping of communist, neo-communist and left-socialist parties or splinters. No members of parliament but several members of the government belong to JUL. The group's chief ideologist is Mirjana Markovic, the wife of President Milosevic. Markovic is an unreconstructed international socialist and makes no bones about it.

The second explanation for the hardening of the domestic line since Dayton is that Milosevic perceives the role he played

at Dayton as a 'service' he rendered the international community, entitling him to a 'free hand' at home. And a free hand means
reversion to his true political nature. Indeed, according to Veran
Matic, editor-in-chief of the independent radio station B-92,
"the elevation of Milosevic in the West to the position of chief
guarantor of the Dayton Accords has been greeted with the
deepest despair" by democratic circles in Serbia. This situation
is not likely to improve unless the major powers disabuse
Milosevic of his notion of what their 'bargain' with him was.

Conclusions and Recommendations

There is no sense in denying that President Milosevic became a
key political 'partner' for the West. But it would be very dangerous to consider him the *only* interlocutor, or to encourage the
notion that the implementation of Dayton requires giving
Milosevic a free hand in Serbia and Kosovo. In the long run,
peace and democracy in Bosnia require democratic development in Serbia and Croatia, as this Report has already emphasized. As with Croatia, Europe and the United States should
make some fundamental demands of Serbia:

16 Serbia's reintegration into the community of nations
should be made contingent on its respect for the sovereignty of Bosnia and Herzegovina and its compliance with
the Dayton Accords. This includes the provisions relating to
indicted war criminals in Serbia itself as well as in Republika
Srpska. President Milosevic, as the tie-breaking head of the
Republika Srpska delegation at Dayton, should be called
upon to fulfill the commitments he made there in its name.

17 Belgrade should accept the draft treaty regarding the
succession of the former Yugoslavia, regulating the
distribution of its debts and assets. The lack of resolution of
this issue has serious implications for all the Yugoslav successor states, including their relations with international
financial institutions.

18 Freedom of the media must be guaranteed (see the
specific recommendations regarding media starting
on p. 152 below).

19 There should be a coordinated Western strategy for
recognizing the new Yugoslavia, and integrating it into
international institutions. Serbia's quest for legitimization

offers the West a leverage that should not be wasted. Serbia and Montenegro call themselves Yugoslavia; yet there is a U.N. resolution stating that Yugoslavia has ceased to exist. Belgrade should be expected to reapply for its admission to these organizations, and that context offers an opportunity for addressing the fundamental outstanding issues. Chief among these is Kosovo.

KOSOVO AND SERBIA'S TANGLED ETHNIC RELATIONS

Before the recent war, only about two-thirds of the population of Serbia (including the formerly autonomous provinces of Kosovo and Vojvodina) was Serb by nationality. While no reliable statistics are yet available, the war has certainly increased that percentage considerably through the influx of Serb refugees, mainly from Croatia. Although this will numerically strengthen the Serbs as the largest national grouping, it will do nothing to diminish the serious ethnic tensions. The most fundamental of these involves Kosovo. But before turning to the simmering Kosovo crisis, it is important to note that there are other points of actual or potential tension:

Serbia-Montenegro. The Serb-Montenegrin relationship has historically been marked by a closeness of identity and usually a closeness of purpose. But the Montenegrins have always been conscious of their distinctive history and are very sensitive to the Serb tendency, real or imagined, to take them for granted.

Sandjak. This region, with a population of 200,000–250,000 and a clear Muslim majority (67 percent in 1991), lies mostly in Serbia but partly in Montenegro. It has become a restive region, but so far not a rebellious one. Political formations are still quite poorly developed, but most Sandjak politicians favor specific designation as a province with a large degree of autonomy. Sandjak's ties with Bosnia and Herzegovina could become important. The Bosnian government grants citizenship to Sandjak Muslims, and the Party of Democratic Action (SDA) dominates political life among Muslims. The province could become another serious problem for Belgrade, forming a link between Kosovo and Bosnia.

Vojvodina. The 1991 census showed that 54 percent of the population of Vojvodina was Serb by nationality and 22 percent was Hungarian. In Tito's time, the treatment of the Hungarian community was better than that of any large minority anywhere else in Eastern Europe. In 1974, Vojvodina, along with Kosovo, gained an autonomous, quasi-federal status in the former Yugoslavia. After 1990, both provinces lost their 1974 autonomous status and were downgraded to a status which, though officially autonomous, has meant the loss to Belgrade of much of their previous local authority. Vojvodina also began to lose its distinctive historic identity.

Multi-ethnic society was once a reality here, as in Bosnia. Vojvodina had a high proportion of ethnically mixed marriages—a rate twice as high as in Bosnia—and a greater national diversity. But between 1991 and 1995, Vojvodina's population structure changed radically. It has been estimated that, while at least 50,000 Hungarians and between 30,000 and 40,000 Croats left the province, more than 300,000 Serbs from Croatia and Bosnia-Herzegovina moved into it. Compact Hungarian and Croat settlements have been broken up to make room for Serbs, and some Hungarians have been evicted from their homes. There has been no large-scale 'ethnic cleansing' as in Bosnia, but the tension could lead to a series of escalating incidents culminating in confrontation—followed by a further exodus to Hungary. The Hungarian government, at least, is aware of the dangers. As early as October 1992, Hungary's President Arpad Goncz, a man not given to nationalist drum-beating, described Vojvodina as a "powder-keg," with the very survival of the Hungarians there endangered. In August 1995, the Hungarian government formally demanded that Belgrade take adequate steps to protect the Hungarian minority. If it does not, then this could have implications for the situation of Hungarian minorities in Slovakia and Romania, and therefore Hungary's relations with several of its neighbors.

Kosovo

The Serbs consider Kosovo their historic heartland—the "cradle" of their nation. It was the historic place of origin of the Serbian Orthodox Church. The Serbian Patriarchate was at Pec until it was abolished in 1766. Several famous Orthodox monasteries survive. Kosovo Polje, just outside the capital town of Pristina, was the site of the famous Battle of Kosovo in 1389, which caused the downfall of the Serbian medieval kingdom and helped consolidate Ottoman power in the Western Balkans. The battle, celebrated and commemorated in folklore, remained a major trauma in national memory.

Kosovo has for many years represented a dual minority problem. Albanians—who make up the majority in Kosovo—are a minority in Serbia, while Serbs are a minority in Kosovo. The Serb minority in Kosovo has been dwindling, due to increasing out-migration and a much higher Albanian birth rate. In 1961, the Serb minority was 27 percent of the population; now it is less than 10 percent. Attempts to 're-colonize' the province, including last year's effort to resettle Krajina refugees, have failed to change the demographic reality.

The conviction that time is on their side has so far led most Albanians in Kosovo to support a policy of "time and patience" regarding the future sovereignty of the province and its independence from Serbia. This is advocated by Ibrahim Rugova, writer turned politician and president of the Albanian 'parallel state' in Kosovo, which began to be formed immediately after 1989. It was then that the Belgrade government abrogated the constitution of 1974, which had given the province a very large degree of autonomy; suppressed all provincial government bodies; dismissed thousands of Albanian officials, professional people, and workers; and declared martial law. Rugova's policy has been one of non-violent waiting while trying to win support abroad for Kosovo's independence and perfecting the parallel state at home. The existence of the parallel state reflects self-confidence among the Albanian population. It also would not have been possible without a cadre of officials, experts, and entrepreneurs, many of whom benefited from the province's early autonomy and were educated at the University of Pristina. This institution, founded in 1970, had soon become a center of Albanian nationalism. The University has been closed to Albanians for several years.

The parallel state includes a limited health system and an education system up to university level. There are also Albanian newspapers and magazines—tolerated by the Serbian authorities. Perhaps most striking of all is the way the Albanian-dominated second economy is flourishing. Obviously some of this Albanian activity could not exist without the acquiescence of the Serbian authorities. A mutually accepted stand-off has evolved between oppressors and oppressed—between the official Serbian state and the 'parallel' Albanian one—with each side apparently careful not to upset the tenuous balance of activity, responsibility, and authority.

The situation is not, however, one of coexistence based on tolerance, but more one of an apartheid based on growing hate and fear. On the Albanian side, the anger stems mainly from the absence of justice for Albanians in Kosovo. Without necessarily accepting all the reports coming from Albanian sources, it is quite clear that members of the Albanian community are continually maltreated or humiliated by the Serb police and judiciary. The fear on the Serb side is one of being eventually overwhelmed. The tension permeating the situation erupted into violence and further repression in April 1996, and there could be more violence soon. One thing is obvious: the coexistence of the official Serbian state and the 'shadow' Albanian one simply cannot last.

Is there room for compromise? The Commission found scant readiness for dialogue in either Belgrade or Pristina. Very few of the Commission's interlocutors were ready to offer any variation on the basic Albanian demand: complete independence for Kosovo. The only qualification on that demand was that they would accept a transitional international trusteeship—hardly the kind of creative compromise designed to interest Belgrade.

This is not to deny that the Albanians' arguments were in most instances compelling, as was their basic plight. Rugova told the Commission: "To stay with Serbia is no solution. Yugoslavia was destroyed, and with it, our ability to remain." Commissioners repeatedly heard the lament that if the various Slavic peoples of former Yugoslavia—the Macedonians, Croats, and Bosnians—could not find an acceptable arrangement with Serbia, how could the world expect an Albanian-populated Kosovo to be the exception? "Slavs, people with the same roots, could not bear the Serb regime," said the writer and human-rights activist Adem Demaci. "Yet we, as Albanians, who have nothing in common—we are expected to live under them." The Commission's Albanian interlocutors dismissed the notion of '1974-plus' (that is, an enhanced version of the autonomy that Kosovo enjoyed under the 1974 Yugoslav constitution)—by pointing out that the original 1974 formula was very much a product of the ethno-national balance of the larger Yugoslavia and would hardly be worth much now, given how easily it was abolished in 1989.

The colonial aspects of the Serbia-Kosovo relationship are certainly striking. To meet with the Commission, District Governor Aleksa Jokic had to fly in from Belgrade, where he is Serbia's Minister of Traffic and Communications. And although the mass firing of Albanian state workers in the early 1990s is

115

well documented, Governor Jokic's Vice-Governor, Milos Nesovic, explained to the Commission that, "as you probably know, in 1989 and 1990, all workers, under the direction of their separatist leadership, quit their jobs in the state services, with the aim to paralyze the work of the state . . . The Republic of Serbia succeeded in restoring services by bringing in Serbs from outside."

It is easy to see why the Albanian leadership is afraid to discuss compromise proposals that might concede in principle that Kosovo is part of Serbia. Paradoxically, the combination of pacifist strategy and maximalist demands could solidify a stalemate, which in turn might breed terrible violence. Almost all of our Kosovo Albanian interlocutors said that, for now, they support the Rugova strategy. As suggested above, however, pressures do seem to be slowly building for a more aggressive, *intifada*-like strategy which, even if it initially did not involve armed violence, could invite a Serb crackdown leading to an explosion. Rugova's supporters argue that the massive Serb military presence in Kosovo makes an *intifada* tactic dangerously irresponsible. But it seems doubtful that this argument can prevail much longer.

A few of the Commission's Kosovo Albanian interlocutors were willing to discuss the possibility of some solution short of complete independence—at least on an interim or transitional basis. Mahmut Bakalli, formerly a chairman of the Communist League of Kosovo, was one of them. Although he favors Rugova's policy for complete independence, Bakalli acknowledged the problems that Serbia would have in granting independence: "If Milosevic were to recognize the Republic of Kosovo, he would be toppled. If the opposition did it, they would never attain power. Albanians should understand the false unity of the Serbs regarding Kosovo and look for a compromise: a new confederation or federation." He stressed that he did not mean accepting anything like the current Yugoslav federation, but rather a new federal structure that might include Serbia, Montenegro, Kosovo, Vojvodina, and perhaps even Macedonia and Republika Srpska.

Blerim Shala, a political editor of the Kosovo weekly *Zeri*, also thought a possible solution might involve Kosovo as a republic inside a restructured federation—perhaps, as a concession to Serbia, a republic without the right to secede. "But it must have a large measure of real self-government." Shala admitted frankly that the "balance of power is on the Serb side. For this reason, independence cannot be realized." On the other hand, "the Serbs don't know what to do with Kosovo. They know that sooner or later some sort of self-government is inevitable"—not least because of the demographic imbalance.

Kosovo Albanians feel they are the forgotten of Dayton. If the Dayton agreement allows two separate entities within Bosnia and Herzegovina, and Republika Srpska ties to Serbia, they ask, what is the argument against Kosovo independence or even ties to Albania?

What is clear is that the prospects for democracy in Kosovo and Serbia are linked. Without freedom in Kosovo, real democracy in Serbia seems unlikely—and vice versa.

Conclusions and Recommendations

The Kosovo problem is very much here and now. Its solution could still be some way off. But the longer it is delayed, the greater the risk of a conflagration that might easily spread beyond Kosovo's borders. At the time of Yugoslavia's disintegration in the early 1990s, there were warnings of an impending South Balkans war spreading from Kosovo and Macedonia to Albania, Greece, and Turkey. That this nightmare did not come to pass then cannot justify complacency now; the fundamental problems remain unsolved. Ethnic entanglements and tensions in the south are connected to the postwar wounds of the north: a resumption of violence in Bosnia-Herzegovina might have violent repercussions in Kosovo. Even the moderate Rugova has stated that, if Republika Srpska achieves confederation with Serbia, Kosovo will demand the same with Albania. Beyond such geostrategic concerns, there is a compelling moral interest, for the plight of the Kosovo Albanians is the plight of a people who feel that they are treated "like foreigners in their own country."

The status quo cannot—nor should it—endure. Present dynamics point to the violent breakup of rump-Yugoslavia. Avoiding such violence would require an urgent international peace process; and even if such a process were to begin soon, Kosovo independence might be unavoidable.[11] But other solutions—such as a re-balanced federation consisting of Serbia, Kosovo, Montenegro, and Vojvodina—have been suggested.

---

[11] If so, several Serb enclaves, including the Kosovo Polje battlefield and the great monasteries, could be put under permanent Serb control guaranteed by the United Nations.

The overriding question is how to start a genuine dialogue between Belgrade and the Albanians of Kosovo. Such a dialogue seems unlikely without a stronger push and long-term honest brokerage from the West. For that to happen, the Western powers must come to a shared understanding of the very high stakes involved, and also some clearer idea of what such a dialogue should achieve. This is not to say that the final form of a solution need be described explicitly. But it is possible to articulate some starting principles:

20 Serbia should lift martial law entirely, restore Kosovo's status of autonomy, and effect a gradual withdrawal of troops and police, unilaterally, before the start of negotiations.

21 The Kosovo Albanian leadership should, in return, be ready to enter negotiations without further preconditions, thus backing off from their refusal to talk about anything other than independence.

22 Although the final outcome cannot be prejudged, it would be expected to take legitimate Serb concerns into account and, at the same time, to acknowledge the right of the Kosovo Albanians to self-government, including but not limited to:

—The right of the Albanians to control their own police and judiciary as well as health, cultural, and educational institutions.

—Reliable guarantees of the rights of the Serbian minority in Kosovo.

If no agreement can be reached within a reasonable time, say two years, the Commission feels that the future status of Kosovo should be submitted to legally binding arbitration and, if the arbitrators so recommend, a Kosovo-wide referendum on the various options.

A concerted international effort should buttress this process. A long-term presence of an OSCE monitoring mission would be indispensable.

23 Along with the lifting of martial law, a coordinated effort is needed by the Albanian leadership, Western foundations and NGOs, and the Serbs, to restore a normal civil and cultural life to Kosovo. This means, above all, a unified Pristina University, with financial aid, technical help, and academic exchange programs aimed at restoring the University as an open and pluralistic institution.

THE ALBANIANS

The collapse of Yugoslavia and the war of succession that followed at first seemed to pose serious dangers for Albania. In Tirana's eyes, Serbia was going on a rampage and its strength seemed to be increasing. But Serbia was eventually turned back. The net effect has been an increase in Albanian self-confidence. The Balkans had again become unstable, but with Serbia checked, this gave Albania space to maneuver, and more diplomatic opportunity than it had ever had. And the new international situation enabled it to gain two new powerful patrons—Turkey and, even more important, the United States. It still needed patrons, but these patrons were different: They were not threats to, but guarantors of, Albania's existence.

It is important that the international community—if it is not to misunderstand one of the most important trends in the entire Balkans—begin to think not only about Albania itself, but also about the Albanian peoples, spread over four states in the region. It is not just Albania that is growing in self-confidence, but the Albanian people as a whole, inside and outside Albania. There are about 3.4 million Albanians in Albania itself; nearly two million in Kosovo; between 500,000 and 600,000 in Macedonia; and about 60,000 in Montenegro. The fall of Yugoslavia and the containment of Serbia convinced all Albanians that the obstacles to their self-expression, perhaps to their self-determination, and possibly to their eventual reunion, are now less formidable than ever been before. The key to the future of the Albanian people may lie in Kosovo. But an increasing role is also being played by the Albanians in Macedonia.

Albanians in Macedonia

During the Serb repression of 1981 and after, many Kosovo Albanians fled to or through Macedonia. Many thousands have done so ever since, swelling the number of Albanians living in Macedonia. The 1994 national census in Macedonia, conducted under the auspices of the Council of Europe, put the officially registered Albanian population at 22.9 percent, or just under 500,000. But to these should be added the approximately 130,000 unregistered Albanians. The overwhelming majority of the latter originally came from Kosovo, and the Macedonian government refuses to officially recognize their existence.

The situation of Albanians in Macedonia is hardly comparable to that of Albanians in Kosovo. Although the Slavic Macedonian majority national group refuses to grant what many politically moderate Albanians have demanded—constituent-nation status—the government in Skopje is increasing its efforts to integrate Albanians into public life; it is, for example, recruiting them into the police force, the civil service, the army officer corps, and other public bodies. The Albanians have their own schools, and although their attempt in 1994 to set up Albanian-language university courses in Tetovo was forcibly suppressed, such classes are now unofficially held in private buildings—a situation that Skopje tolerates. There also are more television and radio programs in Albanian and a considerable Albanian press. Most striking of all is the fact that the Albanians now have their own political parties, the largest of which, the Party of Democratic Prosperity, is represented in parliament and has five ministers in the ruling coalition government. There is much more extensive dialogue between the Albanian and the Macedonian leaderships in Macedonia than there is between the Albanian and Serbian leaderships in Kosovo. There is also much more flexibility on both sides.

The obvious differences between Serb repression of the huge Albanian majority in Kosovo and Skopje's policy and methods toward its Albanian minority should not, however, divert attention from the shared interest of both states in addressing their "Albanian problem." Each knows that developments in one will have repercussions in the other. If Kosovo's Albanians were to gain increased status—say, full autonomy, not to mention independence—the Macedonian Albanians would certainly press for improved status for themselves. Thus, despite the tensions and the strained relations that have existed between them, Serbia and independent Macedonia are bound together by this shared predicament. When the Albanian-Slav tensions become more acute, Belgrade and Skopje may be drawn into an alliance of necessity.

A growing number of Albanians, especially the younger people, feel a deep estrangement from the Skopje government and most Slavic Macedonians. This is only partly caused by the conditions obtaining since Macedonia became a sovereign independent state in 1991. The feeling is embedded in the memory of repression during the first, post-Versailles Yugoslavia as well as during periods of the second, Titoist, Yugoslavia. Under Tito, some safeguards were established at the federal level in Belgrade, and there was at least lip-service to the ideological notion of the brotherhood of man. Indeed, one feature that was noted by Commission staff members in conversation with Macedonian Albanians was that, while their despisal of communism was evident, they looked back on certain aspects of Tito's rule with some nostalgia. Now there is no Belgrade to protect them. And many of them deeply mistrust Skopje.

In Yugoslavia's later years, the situation of Albanians in Macedonia deteriorated. Tito's response to the growing national crisis in the 1970s was to grant increasing powers to the federation's republics. The Albanians in Kosovo gained from this policy; their province, in whose governing bodies they were then strongly represented, was elevated almost to republic status. In Macedonia, however, the Albanians suffered. The authorities in Skopje became more powerful and more nationalistic.

Now, in the 1990s, while the Albanians in Kosovo have lost the constitutional rights they gained in 1974 and suffer severe repression, many have kept the self-confidence those rights gave them. And this confidence has in many cases been reinforced by the successful operation of their 'parallel state' and their inexorably growing numerical preponderance over the Serbs. In Macedonia, the Albanian minority, although growing relatively quickly, still officially amounts to less than a quarter of the total population. Nor does it have any real sense of public achievement. Hence the growing tendency among Macedonian Albanians to dismiss those who cooperate with Skopje's policy of integration as "opportunists" taking part in "tokenism"; in doing so, however, they also dismiss the main section of the Albanian Party of Democratic Prosperity for its participation in the political process in Skopje.

There have been four outlets for those Macedonian Albanians who reject cooperation. One is nationalist agitation—aided and abetted by some of their kinsmen from Kosovo. The suppressed effort to set up a university at Tetovo was a striking example of this. Another is emigration. A third is economic progress, especially in some of the towns of western Macedonia—most notably Gostivar, where an astonishing construction boom has taken place. In this regard, the Albanians have shown real entrepreneurial skill.

The fourth outlet is Islam. For Albanians anywhere to embrace militant Islam is something relatively new. In Kosovo, the Albanians are mostly Albanians first and Muslims second. Their leadership is decidedly, often emphatically, secular. It is much the same in Albania itself. Since the fall of communism, there has been a general return to religion—to Islam, mainly, but also to Orthodoxy. Prewar Albania was 70 percent Muslim, 20 percent Orthodox, and 10 percent Catholic.) But the Islam to which most Albanians have returned is the moderate type that they had historically practiced. They have remained relatively immune to rigorous proselytism. The religious militancy of some of the Albanian minority in Macedonia is thus an exception. But, if the general sense of alienation deepens, it is likely to grow.

Albanian Union?

Any comparison between Albanians in the three states in which they live logically leads to a subject that is increasingly being discussed: their attitudes toward eventual union. How much support there is for the concept of a 'Greater Albania' is difficult to judge. But most Albanians recognize that even if this were desirable, it is not at present a practical option.

There are significant differences among Albanians on this issue. In Kosovo, it is true, the view of Albania proper has often been one of disparagement. Although Kosovo was by some distance the poorest part of communist Yugoslavia, economically it was clearly well ahead of communist Albania. And as the Kosovo Albanians advanced, however bumpily, toward political autonomy, their lot was compared favorably with the suppression in Enver Hoxha's republic. At the personal level, the Kosovo Albanians, like many Macedonian Albanians—with their ability to travel and work in Western Europe—undoubtedly were much more aware and broader in outlook than most of those in Albania. Indeed, although these two parts of the Albanian nation were not totally cut off from each other, their situation and their apparent future course of development seemed so different that some observers spoke of the development of two distinct, even incompatible cultures. Union will always be an option, but it would be wrong to see it as an inevitable outcome.

If the movement for Albanian union begins, it will require zealous support within Albania itself. Statehood, strength, and historical primacy may encourage this. Because of its isolation during the period of communism, and also because of the cautious policies of the Tirana government in the 1990s, Albania's relations with the Albanians of Kosovo and of western Macedonia have been much less intimate than the relations of these two with each other. In fact, the bonds between Albanian Kosovo and Albanian Macedonia—although reduced due to the Serb repression in Kosovo—are still considerable. Just as an Albanian 'parallel state' exists in Kosovo, so an Albanian 'shadow union' could develop between Kosovo and western Macedonia.

Kosovo has always taken the lead in this association, which dates back to the 1970s—the hey-day of Albanian power in the former Yugoslavia. The role of the University of Pristina in forming a nationalist elite on both sides of the Macedonian border must again be stressed, but this sense of mutuality is not confined to elites. The issue of relations between Albanian communities will remain an important issue on the Balkan agenda.

Albania

Albanians in Albania always enjoyed one distinction over those in Kosovo and Macedonia. However much they were oppressed, they were at least oppressed by their own people. And Hoxha did at least strengthen the national consciousness of many of his countrymen. Albanians now feel that their national consciousness is rounded out with the pride of having achieved their own freedom. However impoverished their country, it is free, and so are its citizens. And, however shakily, some economic and political progress is being made. This, and the Albanians' growing contacts with the outside world, will in time alleviate the backwardness to which they were so long condemned. Some indices of economic life have improved over the past two years, especially in the countryside, where most people still live, and agriculture is again functioning. Improvement was to be expected, of course, from the dismal starting point of Hoxha-era Stalinism and its even more miserable aftermath, when the population vented its pent-up rage in a frenzy of destruction, smashing factories, greenhouses, schools, hospitals—any remotely plausible symbol of authority. The consequent collapse of even subsistence-level production helped provoke the mass exodus to Italy.

Albania's first free election since the early 1920s took place in February 1991. It was won by the Albanian Socialist Party—the renamed, but only partially reformed, Albanian (communist) Party of Labor. This leftist, or "post-communist," victory was part of a South Balkan post-communist electoral pattern that also included Bulgaria and Romania. But just a little more than a year later, in March 1992, the militantly anti-communist Albanian Democratic Party swept to a convincing electoral victory. The

123

Democratic Party leader Sali Berisha has dominated Albanian politics since. A young cardiologist, scion of a communist family, educated partly in France, Berisha soon showed himself to be a leader of ability and energy. The Albanian Constitution gives the presidency considerable powers which Berisha has used to the fullest. It was largely due to his determination that the rampant public disorder sweeping the country in 1991 and 1992 began to recede. Berisha and the Democratic Party government also embarked on a radical economic reform in agriculture and industry, and both he and his program initially made a favorable impression in Western Europe and the United States.

But Berisha's style of governing has seriously detracted from his achievements. He professes his basic devotion to democracy, but some of his methods—interference with the work of the Constitutional Court, removal of its president, repressiveness toward political opponents—are anything but democratic. He seems to equate democracy with anti-communism. The Albanian population has registered its unease in a way that tends to repudiate the notion that Ottoman rule, national authoritarianism, and then communist dictatorship, had made them unduly submissive. In a referendum in November 1994, they rejected by a clear majority Berisha-inspired proposals for a new constitution that would have further strengthened the powers of his presidency. The vote expressed the popular view not just on one specific issue, but on a whole range of issues concerning governmental performance and behavior. In the May 1996 parliamentary elections, Berisha's methods of manipulation and intimidation caused outrage in both Europe and the United States. They led to demands that the election be held again and to calls for the suspension of Albania's membership in the Council of Europe.

Perhaps the greatest long-term problem remains one of public confidence, especially among the young, in Albania's future and its ability to overcome its impoverishment. Since 1991, when freedom of travel was introduced, some 400,000 Albanians—about 12 percent of the population—have left the country. Many of them are working illegally in neighboring Greece and may return, willingly or unwillingly; some are also in Italy. Their regular remittances home are essential for the domestic economy. But many of these young men would leave Albania forever if they could. Italian television and the "good life" it projects, the comparisons they make with the condition of their own country, their reaction to the 50 years of almost total insulation—these are some of the factors that have prompted an exodus that could seriously undermine Albania's progress.

Albania's foreign policy has been much influenced by the United States. American-Albanian cooperation has developed remarkably in the 1990s with military, intelligence, and, to some extent, economic ties. Washington undoubtedly has had a moderating influence on Albania's policy in the Balkan region. Tirana has softened its original policies toward its three Balkan neighbors: with Serbia, over Kosovo; with Macedonia, over its Albanian minority; and with Greece, generally. With regard to Kosovo, Tirana has qualified its backing for the Rugova leadership's insistence on total independence. It still supports independence, but now less ebulliently, and it has disappointed Kosovo Albanians by not officially recognizing their 'parallel state,' although it permits them a quasi-diplomatic presence in Tirana.

Relations with Athens seem to have improved. In the past, unofficial Greek claims to part of southern Albania (Northern Epirus), and the treatment of the Greek minority in southern Albania (ranging from 40,000 to 300,000 depending on whether Tirana or Athens estimates the number) were the main specific causes of dispute. The appointment of a Greek national to head the newly re-activated Albanian Orthodox Church only served to remind Albanians of Greek hierarchical authority and was deeply resented by many. The recent huge, illegal influx into Greece of Albanians looking for work—and their subsequent expulsion, with threats to expel more—have caused tension. The poisoned atmosphere that developed was further aggravated by a number of exaggerated provocations by both sides. Indeed, between 1993 and 1995 it sometimes seemed only a matter of time before some serious incident would lead to hostilities. Then both sides, apparently realizing the calamity toward which they could be heading, took steps to relieve the tension. Greece, for example, finally recognized the border between the two countries, while Albania agreed to expand education facilities for Greek minority schoolchildren. There is little doubt that Washington contributed to this improvement in relations—the most important symbol of which so far has been Greek President Konstandinos (Kostis) Stephanopoulos's visit to Tirana in March 1996.

Albania's relations with Turkey have become closer in the 1990s. The end of communism and the breakup of Yugoslavia revealed convergent strategic interests. Military cooperation is

particularly close, and Albania certainly regards Turkey as its closest ally and strongest support among the countries of the region.

But Albania has also looked to other Muslim countries,
particularly for economic support. Ties to some of the wealthier
Arab countries were already growing by early 1993. What
Albania has seemed bent on doing is getting the best and the
most from both the Western and the Muslim worlds. It provided
striking evidence of this at the end of 1992, when, virtually
simultaneously, it joined the Conference of Islamic States and
formally applied to join NATO—the first former communist
state to do so. Tirana was obviously aware of its room for maneuver. More recently, however, responding to America's undemon-
strative push to shore up stability in the South Balkans, it has
tended to lean Westward. And certainly among the Albanian ruling and cultural elite, regardless of their religious background,
there is a strong Western orientation.

Conclusions and Recommendations

Albania is by far the poorest country in Europe, and what it
needs more than anything else is the benevolent interest of a
larger power. The U.S. role has been very positive in this regard,
exerting a pedagogical influence that has led to improved relations with Greece and Macedonia, and a more moderate stand
toward Serbia-Kosovo. The European Union's considerable
presence has also been constructive. In this context, the
Commission emphasizes the following priorities:

24 Albania's pro-Western orientation should be encouraged, but the Berisha government must not be allowed
to interpret it as a license for undemocratic behavior.

25 Concerted assistance should aim to bring Albania up
to the economic level of its neighbors; the key task is
the building of infrastructure. The European Union and the
proposed Balkan Infrastructure Association (see below,
p. 144) should play a significant role in this. Italy and Greece
have unique roles to play, both because of traditional ties and
because of their Albanian immigrant workers.

26 Turkish and other Balkan ties should be encouraged
over other Islamic ties. Joining the Islamic
Conference was a unilateral decision by President Berisha.
Many leading Albanians felt disquiet over it, for they do not

define their country in religious terms—a feature that distinguishes Albania from almost all other countries in the Balkans. Any move to define Albanian nationhood in terms of religion would be a mistake.

MACEDONIA

When the Commission visited Macedonia in November 1995, it gained the impression of a country that had emerged from its period of acute danger. However, for the Slavic majority and the Albanian minority, the long-term problem of coming to terms with one another inside a single state is still to come.

All four of its neighbors have now accepted, if only grudgingly, the existence of the new Macedonia. The Albanian attitude has already been discussed. Bulgaria, whose historic claims on Macedonia were a principal cause of the first two Balkan wars, quickly recognized the new state but retained its communist-era refusal to acknowledge the existence of a Macedonian nation. It continued to maintain that Macedonians are ethnically Bulgarians and their language a dialect of Bulgarian. Serbia, of which Macedonia (South Serbia) had been part in the prewar Yugoslav kingdom, initially adopted an unfriendly, at times threatening, attitude. In April 1996, however, as part of Milosevic's continuing peace offensive in the region, Belgrade agreed to establish full diplomatic relations with Skopje, acknowledging and recognizing the name Macedonia, much to the annoyance of the Greeks.

Greece's attitude has been the most hostile and damaging of all. It complained that the very use of the name "Macedonia" was not only a usurpation of an essential part of its identity, but also a potential threat to Greece's integrity; so were, Greece alleged, the new Macedonian flag, with its 16-point Star of Vergina, and some articles in the new state's Constitution referring to Macedonians abroad. Greece imposed a full economic blockade against the new state in February 1994. It was a drastic measure; had it been maintained indefinitely, it could have crippled Macedonia's prospects for survival. The blockade was lifted in September 1995, after negotiations in New York that led to important Macedonian concessions—especially regarding the design of the national flag. But the Macedonians remained determined to keep their country's name, and the Greeks remained just as determined not to accept it.

127

The Greek blockade may well have prompted the European Union nations as well as the United States to provide more financial and economic aid to Macedonia than they would have otherwise. This Western solicitude reflected the strong belief that Macedonia's survival is crucial to the stability of the South Balkan region. If Macedonia collapsed, another Balkan war might break out. This view was generally shared in the Balkan region itself. In Sofia, even Bulgarians who still smarted under the "historic injustice" of the loss of Macedonia were nonetheless adamant about the need for its survival.

Macedonia has survived with surprising tenacity. Its economic policy has been characterized by tough macro-economic stabilization measures, introduced at the beginning of 1994, that have earned the praise of international financial circles and considerable credits from the International Monetary Fund. Inflation, for example, has been drastically reduced, and so has the budget deficit. It is too early to describe Macedonia as an economic success because of persisting weakness at the micro-economic level. Privatization is proceeding slowly, as is the reform of banking. At first sight, the Macedonian economy seems characterized by a large number of small-scale entrepreneurs and socialist nostalgia. Both to some extent reflect the differing policy preferences or the vested interests of the ruling elite.

The political process in Macedonia since the overturn of communism has developed smoothly. The Macedonian League of Communists renamed itself the Social Democratic Union and has ruled effectively ever since. Whether it has ruled democratically is another question. But many Macedonians, although aware of the new state's democratic deficiencies, argue that the circumstances of their country's birth made stability essential, and stability has stemmed from the continuity that the new government both reflects and projects.

So far, though, stability has been dependent less on institutions and procedures than on the personality and ability of one man, President Kiro Gligorov. His narrow escape from death in the (still officially unexplained) assassination attempt in October 1995 and his eventual recovery were greeted with general relief. But Gligorov is nearly 80 years old and has certainly been weakened by his recent ordeal. Macedonia must therefore face the prospect of a future without him. Through his towering prestige he effectively transformed what is purportedly a parliamentary system of government into a presidential one. It was encouraging that, in the immediate aftermath of the attempt on his life, both the government and parliament functioned well. But the real test is still to come.

The Commission was impressed by the optimism in Skopje—among the political elite, academics, journalists, and Western officials—about Macedonia's future. Some expressed nervousness about the post-Gligorov situation, but a few argued that the "Gligorov system" was stifling democracy. Among the examples they gave were the situation in parliament, where the government was supported by over 80 percent of the members, and that in the media, where the government enjoyed a decisive monopoly, despite some small signs of relaxation recently. Nearly all the Commission's interlocutors pointed to the psychological value of UNPREDEP (the United Nations Preventive Deployment force). This force, stationed mainly on or near the Macedonia-Serbia frontier, consists of over 1,000 troops, partly Scandinavian and partly American. The Scandinavians (mainly Finns) are held in high repute, but it is the symbolism provided by the 500 Americans that is really important. Their presence seems to be construed locally as virtually an American security guarantee to Macedonia.

Yet along with all the hopeful signs, there remains the looming and potentially destructive problem of the Albanian minority. Probably nowhere else are the ethnic issue and opposing perceptions of how it should be approached focused as sharply as in Macedonia. The Skopje government offers Macedonian Albanians participation and justice; the Albanians demand constituent-nation status and a degree of autonomy commensurate with it. They want collective rights as a minority; but the Skopje authorities reject this ethnic approach as divisive, and insist on the unitary state concept and the civic concept of equal individual rights. Skopje fears secession will follow if the Albanian demands are met (and a growing number of Albanians want eventual secession). But there is a danger that the Skopje government's resistance will only hasten the pressure for secession.

Conclusions and Recommendations

Given the odds it faced at the beginning, Macedonia has proven to be one of the most stable successor states of former Yugoslavia. But its future viability will depend on its capacity to deal with the problem of its Albanian minority. As is the case between Kosovo and Serbia, the Albanians and the Slavs in Macedonia seem unlikely to resolve their differences without help from the outside. The Commission therefore recommends that:

27 The primary goal of outside influence should be to encourage an Albanian stake in Macedonian statehood. This implies looking for a Macedonian-Albanian relationship within the framework of the existing unitary state. To work, however, this approach will require a high degree of decentralization and continued political restraint on both sides.

28 The presence of UNPREDEP, which provides a high degree of reassurance at a relatively low cost and risk, should be maintained pending substantial progress in resolving the Kosovo problem.

29 Steps should be taken to defuse the tense Tetovo University dispute. Such steps should include the restoration of normal operations at Pristina University in neighboring Kosovo, together with the complete opening of the Kosovo-Macedonia border; and the establishment of a Southeast Europe University (an international graduate school) in Macedonia with a curriculum designed to attract both Albanians and Slavic Macedonians, as well as Balkan students from outside Macedonia.

BULGARIA, THE BULGARIAN TURKS, AND TURKEY

In the 1980s, the Todor Zhivkov regime's brutal policy of forced "assimilation" of Bulgarian Turks caused many casualties and induced over 300,000 Bulgarian Turks to migrate to Turkey. When Zhivkov's successors at least partially reversed the effects of his regime's 'ethnic cleansing'—in the only move by a Balkan country to reverse such a policy—this helped restore Bulgaria's international standing. Perhaps a half of those who 'moved' to Turkey have since returned. But relations between the Bulgarian "national state" and the Turkish minority, numbering over a million, are still sometimes tense, and it would not take much for a new crisis to develop.

Historically, Bulgaria has treated its minorities relatively well. On an individual basis, relations between Bulgarians and Turks are usually respectful and friendly. But there is undoubtedly apprehension, even among many liberal Bulgarians, about the presence of Turkey as a powerful and increasingly assertive neighbor as well as about Turkey's interaction with Bulgaria's Turkish minority, many of whom live adjacent to or near the

Turkish border. Turkey is sometimes depicted as a 'once and future menace' that might one day demand an *'Anschluss'* with the 'Turkish' regions of Bulgaria. In those districts of Bulgaria that have mixed Bulgarian and Turkish populations, there have been some cases of serious antagonism. The fear of Turkish citizens buying chunks of land in Bulgaria has caused legislation to be enacted barring any foreign ownership of land. Many Bulgarians are also ready to listen to the swelling Balkan Slavic-Orthodox chorus about the general 'Muslim threat'—seeing their own country as Europe's first line of defense against this threat.

The main political parties in Bulgaria have adopted a relatively flexible attitutude toward the Turkish minority; both the liberal Union of Democratic Forces (UDF) and the ex-communists have relied on the Turkish minority's representatives in Parliament for government support. But there is some anti-Turkish sentiment across the whole political spectrum, and the present Socialist government is often criticized for playing on it. A danger exists that, in view of its feeble showing in office so far, the Zhan Videnov government might play the nationalist card in the forthcoming elections.

The Turks in Bulgaria are now mainly farmers, small artisans, and traders wanting to keep to themselves and be left alone. But for some Bulgarians, they are a humiliating reminder of past servitude under the Turks and an insuperable obstacle to national homogeneity.

There is therefore some prejudice, worry, and even neurosis on the Bulgarian side. But there is also insensitivity, and occasionally provocation, on the part of Turkey. Sections of the Turkish media, the military, and sometimes members of successive Turkish governments, have referred to parts of Bulgaria as if they were parts of Turkey. Government officials have also occasionally visited (or tried to visit), heavily Turkish-populated parts of Bulgaria without advance clearance from Sofia. There have also been suggestions in Turkey that Turkish aid be provided directly to the Bulgarian Turks. It might be noted in this context that since the early 1960s Bulgaria has been the transit station for vast numbers of Turkish workers and families going to Western Europe and returning from it.

Yet it would be a mistake to conclude that Bulgarian public life is dominated by ethnic tension. For example, the Turkish political representation in the Bulgarian Parliament, the Movement for Rights and Freedoms, has played a key power-

131

balancing role on several occasions. But to many Bulgarians, it is galling that the political stability of the country might depend on a small group of Turks. And it should be noted that many Bulgarian Turks (like many Albanians in Macedonia) see their representatives in Parliament as caught up in the corrupt tokenism of the majority national grouping.

GREECE AND TURKEY IN THE BALKANS

Both Greece and Turkey have been drawn into recent Balkan developments, and their own strained relations with each other have been reflected throughout the region. The tension between the two countries has its origin in the nearly five centuries during which Greece was part of the Ottoman Empire, in the unique (and in some ways, privileged) position that Greeks enjoyed in the Empire, and then in the long and bitter process of encounter and disentanglement in which the two nations have been involved since Greece achieved independence in 1830. The process has by no means ended. Its most important and bitter aspect since the Greek-Turkish war of 1921-22 (and the population exchange that followed) has been the continuing dispute over Cyprus. Even in 1985—with the Cold War still on and Greece and Turkey in the same anti-Soviet NATO alliance—the Greek government announced a "New Defense Doctrine" that pointed to Turkey as the main enemy.

The Greek economic blockade of Macedonia between 1993 and 1995 has been the most direct form of intervention on the Balkan peninsula by either country so far. It did great harm to the Macedonian economy, but much greater harm to Greece's international stature. Greece's reputation has also suffered because it has been Serbia's most consistent diplomatic ally in the region throughout the recent war.

There is a tremendous sense of anxiety in Greek political and military circles over issues that are construed as relating directly or indirectly to Greek security. And pervading this is Greek fear of Turkey, Turkish power, and (real or imagined) Turkish machinations. The Greeks, much more than the Turks, see their mutual rivalry as a 'zero-sum' relationship. This is especially so when it comes to the Balkans—any Turkish gain is seen as Greece's loss; any increase of Turkish influence means a loss of Greek influence; any Turkish ally is potentially an enemy of Greece; any state unfriendly to Turkey is favored by Greece.

Nothing has been less rational than the hysteria whipped up in Greece over the new state of Macedonia. There was nothing in the name of Macedonia that implied a present or future threat to Greek Macedonia or to Greece as a whole—a nation five times as big as Macedonia, with armed forces several hundred times more powerful. Yet, although many Greeks admitted that Athens had handled the Macedonia controversy badly, the Commission met no one among the Greek establishment who was willing to concede that it was illegitimate for Greeks to react emotionally to Macedonia's simple act of calling itself Macedonia. The Commission's interlocutors tried to convey their strong convictions that Skopje, although clearly no strategic threat to Greece, does represent a "cultural threat" to Greece's sense of identity.

The Greek campaign—indeed, its virtual act of war against a tiny neighbor—was all the more disappointing because Greece *could* play a constructive and influential role in the Southern Balkans. "The blame is with the press and politicians," said one of the Commission's interlocutors in Athens, former Foreign Minister Michalis Papaconstantinou. "It is their fault that people don't realize the new situation we are in. In fact, Greece is the most powerful country in the Balkans. Instead of seeing this, we keep getting into quarrels with weaker neighbors. We could play a role, assisting them to join Europe. We could have been a big brother. Instead, we manage to convert foreign-policy issues into domestic issues. No one can surpass us at this."

The Commission did sense that Greek elites were starting to understand that they had squandered some opportunities. Movement toward a settlement with Macedonia was the most important evidence of the increased realism of Athens. Branko Crvenkovski, the Macedonian Prime Minister, told the Commission in November 1995 that, although Macedonia's foreign policy was based on the principle of "equidistance" from all its neighbors, Greece was the country—despite the hostility it has shown so far—with which Skopje would want to develop the closest relations. Greece, a member of the European Union and NATO, could be Macedonia's conduit to the wider world—politically, commercially, and intellectually.

Minorities in Greece

A country's treatment of its minorities is the single issue on which EU membership should have the most positive effect. Yet

Greece is far from exemplary in this regard. The Greek government recognizes no Macedonian minority. The issue of its recognition is tied up not only with the recent allegations of
Macedonian irredentism, but also with bitter memories of the
civil war, in which Macedonians sided mainly with the
Communists. Yugoslav Macedonia was the springboard for Tito's
attempts to subvert Greece. The Macedonian minority representatives with whom the Commission met insisted that they sought
only to preserve their culture against strong pressures of assimilation. "We want ethnic rights as European citizens," said one of
them. "We are not trying to change borders, and we are not ask-
ing for autonomy. There are no areas that are mostly
Macedonian, so autonomy is not a solution to our problem."

For the ethnic Turks living mainly in Western Thrace, the
problem is not one of assimilation. They are harassed through a
series of administrative measures. If that does not induce them
to leave permanently, they may find their citizenship revoked
and be barred from returning to Greece under Article 19 of the
legal code when they travel abroad temporarily.

Turkey's Role in the Balkans

In Turkey, the Commission observed two countervailing attitudes
toward the Balkans. In strategic terms, the Balkans do not seem
to be an overwhelming preoccupation. Turkey may very well be a
Balkan power, but it has equally pressing interests and concerns
in the Caucasus and Central Asia, and in the Middle East. For
Turkey, these regions have strategic priority over the Balkans.
But in emotional terms, the Balkans loom larger. They are a grim
emblem of secular Islam's fate within Europe. Balkan peoples are
sprinkled liberally among Turkish society. And there is an element of 'Ottoman nostalgia' that makes it impossible for Turkey
to ignore the fate of Turkish and Muslim communities in Europe.

Even so, the evident strategic detachment does contribute
to relatively dispassionate discussion of Balkan issues among
Turkish elites (compared to the passion that these issues evoke
among the Greeks). Conversations with government officials are
as likely to concern the Caucasus and pipeline diplomacy as the
Balkans. "A new world is coming up around here," President
Suleyman Demirel told the Commission with obvious excite-
ment. "We can feel it. A new continent has emerged—Central
Asia—as big as Europe, with enormous resources: gas and oil
reserves *at least* as great as the Persian Gulf."

Turkey's Ethnic Entanglements

There was perhaps a distortion in the Commission's discussions of minority problems and minority rights; because we were concerned about the treatment of minorities *in the Balkans*, the problems of minorities within Turkey (e.g., the Kurds) got rather short shrift. The serious grievances that we heard mainly concerned the treatment of Turks in Western Thrace by Athens (see above). Minority communities within Turkey were discussed as factors pushing Turkish foreign policy toward a more active role in the Balkans. The Commission repeatedly heard that there are more Bosnians in Turkey than in Bosnia, and more Albanians than in Albania. Many came in the nineteenth century and early in this century, and their descendants form a strong lobby today. "The founders of this Republic were from the Balkans," said one journalist. "When the Ottoman Empire collapsed there, it was over." A newspaper columnist told us that the intensity of Turkish interest in Bosnian affairs had taken him by surprise— it was comparable to the concern over Cyprus. While Cyprus involved ethnic Turks, Bosniaks, although not Turks, were somehow recognized as "people like us."

This degree of recognition of course has a religious dimension, which was put to the Commission passionately and plaintively. It came in two basic forms. The crudest version was that the West would not have allowed the Bosnian carnage to happen had those being massacred been Christians. Either the West did not care as much about Muslims or (in a more sinister version) it actually let Serbia do the "'dirty work." We heard this argument repeatedly—from a group of Islamist editors, for example, as well as from somewhat more moderate participants in a roundtable organized by the Research Center for Islamic History and Culture (funded by the Islamic Conference). There was an illogical connection here: Western Europe, however serious its failure to intervene earlier, was neither killing Muslims in Bosnia nor sympathetic to their mistreatment by the Serbs. Moreover, our Islamic interlocutors did not seem to take note that the West had been just as passive (in fact, far more passive) when Roman Catholic Croats were the victims.

On a more sophisticated level, however, the Turkish complaint demands more attention. Turkey, and especially secular Turkish elites, see themselves pursuing the same sort of national experiment as Bosnia. "Allowing Bosnia to survive as a pluralist Muslim community in Europe is critical to Turkey seeing itself the same way," said one Istanbul journalist. "If Bosnia fails, can Turkey survive?"

At bottom there is the grievance that Western Europe cannot identify itself with a Muslim society, however secular. This grievance is of course linked—sometimes implicitly and sometimes explicitly—to the question of Turkish entry into the European Union. It was put to us by the new Foreign Minister Deniz Baykal, on his first day in office: "For 70 years we internalized European culture. What other nation has opened itself up to such culture shock for so long? In European terms, we compare favorably with Romania, etc. But we have a different religion, it is true. This is a trial for Europe. It is a trial for us too."

Another recurrent theme in many of the Commission's meetings in Istanbul and Ankara was the idea of Turkish democracy, somewhat authoritarian, as a bulwark against Islamic fundamentalism (just as it was once seen as a bulwark against Soviet communism). Put in more positive terms, Turkish society is a constructive example of reconciling Islam with modernity. The Bosnia theme also plays a role here, since it is a potent weapon in the domestic political debate and, it was argued, could help the Islamists. "Tolerance for ethnic cleansing provoked the Turkish people very deeply," said Baykal. "The government is under pressure, subjected to the criticism that they have not been able to force the West to do anything, and the Islamic opposition tries to generate support based on that theme."

The Islamic Welfare Party's accession to government raises the specter of a fundamental strategic realignment. This concerns policy in the Middle East (Ankara's strategic relationship with Israel is threatened), and the threat of war in the Aegean (Turkey and Greece are competing in a dangerous arms race). Above all, it could have dangerous repercussions in the Balkans, for it could undermine the very notion of a Turkish model of secular Islam.

IV. THE REGION:
CONCLUSIONS AND PROPOSALS

Very few Balkan problems can be solved on a national basis. The Commission stresses the importance of a regional framework for dealing with the potentially dangerous issues and disputes that we have been considering.

Dayton was the response to over four years of war and atrocity in Bosnia and Croatia. But potential for new conflicts also lurks in other parts of the Balkans: Kosovo and western Macedonia are the most frequently discussed. At the eastern periphery of the Balkans, the eventual possibility, however remote at present, of union (or reunion) between Romania and Moldova could cause an international crisis involving not only those two countries but also Ukraine and Russia—and perhaps Hungary as well. In the meantime, the enmity between Greece and Turkey simmers on; although mainly centered on Cyprus, it is multi-dimensional, and every incident between the two countries reflects suspicion and threatens conflict.

A preemptive initiative—one designed to secure peace before war, not after it, and to anticipate and neutralize the danger of conflict instead of having to respond to it—certainly would be desirable. But did the war in former Yugoslavia provide a sufficient warning and impetus for a preventive international mediation or arbitration on a regional scale? The potential for further conflict has raised suggestions for some form of preemptive international conference on the Balkans. Two ideas in particular have been discussed.

The first suggestion is an ***International Conference on Security in the Balkans,*** under OSCE or Contact Group auspices, with the main purpose of guaranteeing the stability of borders and mutual confidence-building measures. A preliminary step for the preparation of such a conference could be carried out by extending the framework of the Stability Pact (initiated by the EU but now under OSCE auspices) to the Balkans through bilateral or trilateral negotiations on the stability and openness of borders as well as on guarantees for minority and human rights.

A second, more ambitious initiative would involve a *South Balkans Conference, under the auspices of the United States and the European Union, with the goal of creating a South Balkans Confederation.* The chief purpose of such a confederation would be to avert and defuse the impending confrontation between Albanians and Slavs, centered in Kosovo-Serbia and Macedonia, but potentially involving all of their neighbors, including Turkey.

However, the Commission in its travels has found grounds to question the feasibility of such preemptive conferences, organized by international institutions, for the benefit of the Balkan countries. There are two reasons for this in particular.

First, the major international settlements have been essentially postwar, made possible by the exhaustion, defeat, or the fading victory prospects of one or more of the combatants. Though limited in its geographical scope, Dayton was the latest in a long line of international conferences that attempted to secure peace after war. Its predecessor in the nineteenth century was the Congress of Vienna (1815), and in the twentieth century, the Paris treaties after World War I. The Congress of Berlin, although it came after a bloody Balkan war, was mainly a deal among the major European powers aimed at checking the expansion of one of their number—Russia—in the Balkans. In this it probably succeeded, but in general it was a depressing example of international greed and shortsightedness, a principal cause of the Balkan wars of 1912 and 1913, and one of the causes of World War I.

Second, compromise by all parties to Balkan disputes would be necessary. Compromise would involve the Balkan countries surrendering something they regard as an essential part of their national identity—territory, historical claims, kith and kin, some aspects of sovereignty, or parts of their patrimony. It is difficult to see any of the Balkan countries doing this. It is likewise difficult to see the major powers in effect forcing them into doing so. Neither military nor economic pressure would be possible in this case. And the threat of international ostracism of the whole region would simply leave the field clear for the stronger Balkan states to bully the weaker. The result could be the opposite of that intended.

A preemptive conference would exemplify a one-time, "top-down" approach that might well end in failure and cause damaging mutual recriminations on both sides. The best way to try to head off conflict is through Western-initiated preemptive diplomacy from below—"bottom-up" rather than "top-down."

30 **The Commission recommends the establishment of a network of regional commissions, corresponding to the issues and areas of potential conflict discussed in this Report.** These commissions, composed of both governmental and non-governmental representatives, would be set up to focus on specific issue areas—for example, ethnic and minority relations, religious reconciliation and cooperation, civil society, economic and infrastructural development, the environment, transnational crime, and relations with Western institutions. These issues would necessitate commissions composed of Western specialists and representatives of all or most of the Balkan states. Hence, their very establishment would begin the slow process toward Balkan cooperation. The potential areas of conflict for which commissions would be needed include Kosovo, western Macedonia, and their relations with each other and with Albania; Serbia and the South Balkans; Greek-Macedonian relations; the cluster of Turkish-Greek problems; Moldovan-Romanian-Ukrainian-Russian relations; and Bulgarian-Turkish relations.

The lead in this diplomatic initiative could be taken by the European Union and the United States. Russia and Ukraine could participate from the beginning, and their representatives could sit on many or most of the commissions. Some Balkan nations might be unwilling or strongly opposed to the very creation of some commissions and reluctant to take part in them. Here, though, Western pressure—economic, diplomatic, or related to aspects of acceptance by Europe—could justifiably be used. This could indeed be "the hour of Europe."

The commissions should be set up for a reasonable, specific duration—say, two or three years. Their work should be coordinated by a bureau to which the commissions report and make recommendations at regular intervals. The bureau should inform the relevant governments and multilateral institutions of progress and problems.

There would be no assurance that concrete, constructive suggestions would emerge. But Winston Churchill's statement that "jaw, jaw is better than war, war" needs to be kept in mind. And getting the Balkan nations into the habit of talking, or even arguing, would be a step forward. If and when enough progress had been made in the work of some of the commissions, that might be the time to think about one or more bigger conferences.

Clearly, the top-down and bottom-up approaches are not mutually exclusive. Above all, they both concern the same cross-border difficulties. The remainder of this section makes regional recommendations according to five categories: (1) Balkan regional cooperation; (2) reconstruction and economic development; (3) democracy, media, and civil society; (4) ethnic relations and the treatment of minorities; and (5) security.

BALKAN REGIONAL COOPERATION

Historically, most of the best-known schemes for cooperation devised have reflected tensions rather than good will among Balkan nations, and they have been aimed, at least in part, *against* other countries in the region. It has been conflict and suspicion, rather than the will to cooperate, that has resurfaced since the end of communism and the collapse of the Soviet Union.

Since 1989, several ideas have been put forward. Former President of Turkey Turgut Ozal's "Black Sea Economic Cooperation" scheme at first captured some attention as a new framework for trade and political dialogue. Although it has since lost some of its initial momentum, it remains a useful forum involving several Balkan countries: Bulgaria, Romania, Albania, and Greece. More recently, in July 1996, a meeting of foreign affairs ministers from the countries of Southeastern Europe—Bulgaria, Romania, Yugoslavia, Greece, Turkey, Albania, and Bosnia and Herzegovina—was convened in Sofia to discuss the possibilities for improving "good neighborly relations, stability, security and cooperation in the Balkans." Croatia and Slovenia, among others, sent observers.

But the idea of cooperation needs a new impetus from the West as well. Without external inducement, there is likely to be little progress toward meaningful cooperation in the Balkans. The difficulties and reasons for reluctance of the states in the region are numerous.

First, both Croatia and Serbia, for different reasons, appear to pose problems regarding their participation in regional cooperation. Croatia seems anxious to disqualify itself. President Tudjman insists that his country must be considered Central European and not Balkan, and Croatia is therefore reluctant to take part in any schemes of regional cooperation or to attend any "Balkan conferences." What made Croatia "Balkan," the argument goes, was its being part of Yugoslavia; now that it is free and independent, it wants to resume its rightful place in "Central Europe." Part of Croatia's determination to reject Balkan cooperation lies in its anxiety to avoid contact with Serbia as much as possible. But it may well find, and fairly soon, that some degree of regional cooperation is advantageous and presents no dangers to either its independence or its self-image.

As for Serbia, it has been ostracized, at least for the time being, by its recent record in relation to both the Balkans and other parts of the international community. But, looking to the future, Serbia remains the pivotal country in the entire Balkan region and now seems rather eager to participate in various aspects of regional cooperation.

A second reason given—in Zagreb, Sarajevo, Skopje, Ljubljana—for reluctance about Balkan cooperation is that it could be tantamount to the "re-creation of Yugoslavia." This in fact tends to be regarded as the unstated aim behind the West's advocacy of various cooperative schemes and the support they receive in Belgrade. Any plausible case for closer regional economic cooperation must take that reluctance into account by offering a broader framework.

Third, mutual distrust between most countries of the region can hardly be overestimated. The deepest distrust of course exists among the belligerents in the recent war—Serbs, Croats, and Bosniaks. But in the entire peninsula, the prevailing mood is more conducive to separation than to cooperation. Such cooperation as does exist—between Turkey and Albania, for example, or between Greece and Serbia—can hardly be seen as a possible foundation for or stepping-stone to wider regional cooperation.

Fourth, the recent war in Yugoslavia has only strengthened what might be called the 'opting-out of the region' inclination of some of the Balkan countries—their pronounced preference for bilateral ties with Western institutions or countries over ties of any kind with their neighbors. What attracts them is the idea of Europe as their 'home'—and a panacea for all their problems. Any commitment to regional cooperation is seen by many as only postponing the aim of joining Europe, not as preparing for it.

Finally, even among those Balkan public figures who might be receptive to notions of cooperation, there is a widespread feeling that the individual countries must put their own (mostly post-communist) houses in order first. Domestic preoccupations therefore have priority.

141

Because of this reluctance, reliance on regional initiatives alone will not be effective. There is a need for Western initiatives in devising Balkan schemes for cooperation as well as for Western inducements to get the initiatives accepted and started. The European Union, as a role model and sponsor, has an important part to play in this connection. Referring to trade and cooperation agreements with the Balkan countries, EU Commissioner Hans van den Broek told us in February 1996, "We are stressing that for fruitful cooperation with us you will need fruitful cooperation among yourselves."

Economic Cooperation

Senior officials of the European Union, as well as several economic spokesmen in individual Western European states, have strongly recommended that Balkan regional economic cooperation be set in motion. These Western suggestions are being resisted by the Balkan states for the reasons just discussed. They want bilateral relations with Brussels leading to associate membership and, eventually, full membership in the European Union.

But some of them may soon be persuaded, with some Western prompting, that a degree of economic cooperation within the region is to their advantage. Even if Croatia succeeds in re-establishing and further developing its tourist industry, it will soon find that tourism alone cannot be the sure foundation of economic prosperity. It will also soon realize that it is unlikely to equal the Slovenian success in redirecting its trade westward. Croatia might therefore rediscover, however unwillingly, the advantages of economic ties with some of its former Yugoslav associates.

The case for more intensive cooperation and closer economic integration between Bosnia-Herzegovina and Serbia on the one hand and Croatia on the other is particularly strong. (There is, however, a danger that Serbia and Croatia will seek to bypass the central government in Sarajevo and concentrate instead on tightening economic links with their corresponding "entities" within Bosnia—Republika Srpska and the Bosniak-Croat Federation—with a view to eventually absorbing them.) Macedonia's pragmatic approach suggests that political fear can be overcome. For other South Balkan countries, the fear of reincorporation is irrelevant. All would benefit from a greater stimulus to regional trade. Different forms of economic integration are possible and desirable.

31 The Commission advocates a free-trade area as the most politically realistic and economically expedient starting point. A Balkan free-trade area would afford its members maximum economic and political sovereignty—in contrast to a customs union (which implies a common external trade regime vis-a-vis non-members), a common market (which implies the liberalization of capital flows as well as labor migration), or an economic union (which implies a monetary union).

32 Such a free-trade area might eventually become part of the Central European Free Trade Area (CEFTA). Some CEFTA members (most notably the Czech Republic) might object to this, but support from Brussels, together with the prospects of eventual advantage, could facilitate acceptance. Bulgaria and Romania are likely to be admitted to CEFTA before the end of 1996, and Macedonia has also applied. Among the Balkan countries, the CEFTA connection would certainly weaken fear of attempts to re-create another Yugoslavia. And the Balkan governments—especially those of Yugoslavia's successor-states—should be reminded of the fact that, given the importance of intra-regional trade, a liberalization of extra-regional trade that is not matched by intra-regional liberalization could be a net loss for their economies.

Assuming that regional cooperation gets under way, the next step will be for the European Union to offer some form of bilateral connection with each of the cooperating states. Brussels already has a range of agreements and arrangements with several Balkan states. Greece is a member of the EU. Turkey has a customs union with the EU. Bulgaria, Romania, and Slovenia have associate member status. The best eventual Western opening for Croatia, Bosnia-Herzegovina, Serbia and Montenegro, Macedonia, and Albania would be through bilateral Trade and Cooperation Treaties—the first step on the ladder leading to eventual full membership (although full membership is not likely to be attained by any of them until well into the next century).

The second generation of association agreements between the EU and its East European partners—known as Europe Agreements—go beyond the 1972 Free Trade Agreements with European Free Trade Area (EFTA) countries. They might serve as a rough guide for relations between the EU and Balkan countries. The main articles are: (1) free trade with the European Community; (2) a long-term program of financial assistance;

(3) industrial, technical, and scientific cooperation; and (4) establishment of an institutional framework for political dialogue.

Some initiatives for highways (e.g., between Durres in Albania and Istanbul) and rail links have been mooted for several years now. There is a real need for some communication links to be in a West-East direction to avoid total dependence on the existing South-North communications.

33 **The Commission recommends the creation of a Transport and Infrastructure Association for the entire Balkan space.** This would not conflict with European Union regulations, and it could be of considerable value to provide a framework not merely for raising funds from the World Bank and European Bank for Regional Development (EBRD), but also for planning major rail, road, and telecommunication investments and ensuring a rational development of air transport.

34 **There should be a concerted, regional effort to combat organized crime, particularly drugs and arms trafficking, and terrorism.** This is a seriously growing transnational economic, social, moral, and political problem in the Balkans. In the former Yugoslavia, war profiteering has led to the criminalization of large parts of society. Its impact on Western Europe (and even on the United States) should not be underestimated. An EU initiative setting in motion larger- and smaller-scale cooperation in fighting all aspects of crime would seem to be both imperative and feasible.

35 **The European Union should provide support, technical and financial, for regional efforts to counter environmental degradation.** The devastation left from the communist era and the significant reliance of some of the countries (Bulgaria, Romania) on unsafe nuclear installations means that this is important not only for the region but for the EU countries as well.

RECONSTRUCTION AND DEVELOPMENT

Most of the current difficulties of the post-communist Balkan economies have two main causes: (1) the transition process from state socialism toward market economies, and (2) the impact of the war and sanctions in former Yugoslavia and the region as a whole. The first reveals the obstacles to the dismantling of state/political control over economic activity and the post-communist reorientation of foreign trade. The second, war and sanctions, have not only disrupted the established regional pattern of exchange but also encouraged the criminalization of large sections of economic life. Three elements are needed to help overcome these obstacles: (1) a proper banking system has to be put in place in order to avoid the all-too-frequent confusion of personal and state interests in economic decision-making; (2) a legal and fiscal institutional environment is needed that will clarify the rules of the game and create a more reliable framework for investors; and (3) existing trade barriers need to be dismantled in order to help regional cooperation.

Bosnia is a special case. There, the need is for reconstruction, and in the foreseeable future it will remain a virtual economic protectorate. But the regional economic environment might have positive effects there, too. The figures for economic losses in other parts of former Yugoslavia may be less devastating, but still serious. Between 1989 and 1994, economic output in rump-Yugoslavia dropped by 75 percent and in Croatia by 50 percent. In Macedonia, it dropped by over 30 percent, and subsequently by considerably more because of the Greek embargo. In 1994, the highest rates of unemployment were registered in rump-Yugoslavia and in Macedonia, where they reached about 35 percent.

Developing the Economies of the Region

Western investment in the Balkans, particularly in former Yugoslavia, is not likely to be significant in the near future. Except in the case of Slovenia, prospective Western investors are understandably reluctant to commit themselves and look likely to remain so.

One obstacle continues to be the fact that the claims of international banks, governments, and private citizens on the Yugoslav successor-states cannot be settled until these states agree on the allocation among them of the old Yugoslav debt. This stood at over $16 billion before the collapse of the Federation and the ensuing war. Early in 1996, Slovenia concluded an agreement with about 400 Western banks in which it agreed to assume 18 percent of that former Yugoslav debt. Negotiations are also proceeding apace with Croatia and Macedonia on the apportioning of debt. But in March 1996, the Central Bank of rump-Yugoslavia in Belgrade and several

Serbian commercial banks lodged a formal objection to the Slovene agreement. Before any composite agreement is finally reached, the negotiations are likely to be bitter and protracted.

Nor is this the only problem. There are also the potential claims of millions of refugees for restitution (or compensation) for lost property, and arguments among the Yugoslav successor-states over ownership of former federal property. Problems like these are simply unprecedented, and they easily dwarf the difficulties of settling the accounts of former COMECON countries and the Soviet successor states. Any resolution of these problems will have to include: (1) considerable debt forgiveness by Western and international creditors; (2) the creation of oversight mechanisms to supervise the balancing of inter-governmental claims.

Two other key obstacles to foreign investment in Yugoslavia's war-affected successor states are: (1) the absence of physical infrastructure, ranging from transport and telecommunications networks to well-functioning public health and safety institutions; and (2) political instability. The combination of economic nationalism and militarization has left almost all of these economies highly politicized and made subject to state control—and thus subject to economic and regulatory instability generated in the political sphere. The end of the fighting and the consolidation of democratic political mechanisms should reduce the scale of the second problem. Western and international development aid must inevitably play a large role here.

Thus foreign investment is likely to be sparse and slow for the foreseeable future. Here Greece, Italy, and Austria—as EU members and with the strongest economic regional potential—have a major role to play. There already is extensive small-scale Greek investment in Bulgaria, Romania, and Albania and, since the lifting of the Greek embargo, there is reported to be Greek interest in investing in Macedonia. There is considerable Turkish investment in Bulgaria, especially in the regions with large Bulgarian-Turkish populations. Albania is developing close economic relations with Turkey and Italy. In Bosnia-Herzegovina, there could be some outside investment for strictly non-economic reasons: Croatia might invest considerably more than it can afford to bind the Federation more closely to itself; Middle-Eastern countries might invest considerably more for reasons of Muslim solidarity. Slovenia, for obvious reasons, looks like the one bright spot in terms of foreign investment. Croatia might expect considerable Austrian and German interest in fully reviving its tourist industry, although in view of the huge financial costs of integrating the former East Germany, German financial and economic backing for Croatia is likely to be less than the Croats originally hoped for.

As a rule, it is the big investments that get the publicity. However, with the exception of infrastructure investment (especially in Bosnia-Herzegovina), future prosperity and cooperation in the Balkans will depend less on large-scale projects conceived for political reasons than on the development of small investments that help to create small firms and small-scale entrepreneurs—in industry, agriculture, commerce, and services. Small-scale capitalism can become the backbone of economic recovery and eventual economic prosperity in the Balkans.

36 The Commission considers that the following forms of international assistance should be made available:

—*Improved market access for Balkan exports, especially those of Yugoslavia's successor states.* This means accommodating the desire of the successor states for EU association, once they (like Slovenia and Croatia) have achieved the requisite macroeconomic stability. Generously asymmetrical association agreements (in which Western barriers to former Yugoslav exports are removed faster than former Yugoslav barriers to Western exports) would seem most appropriate.

—*Quick financial assistance for infrastructure reconstruction and refugee resettlement.* The private capital flows that the region desperately needs are unlikely to appear until basic infrastructure is put in place and refugee issues have been dealt with.

—*Traditional IMF balance-of-payments assistance and World Bank and EBRD development assistance for stabilization, market reform, and structural adjustment efforts in Bosnia and Herzegovina (and possibly other countries).*

—*Engagement in helping to settle the mutual claims of international banks, governments, and citizens of the Yugoslav successor states will be critical.* When the resident governments become willing to accept a broad-stroke, 'zero-option' type of solution to what are likely to be otherwise insolvable problems, the West should be ready to help with oversight mechanisms for netting out inter-governmental claims.

DEMOCRACY: CIVIL SOCIETY AND MEDIA

The case of Yugoslavia certainly highlights some of the more general problems facing the transition to democracy in the Balkans, although the region should not be seen solely through the prism of the Yugoslav crisis. It can be argued that in Bulgaria, and to some extent also in Macedonia, Albania, and even Romania, the choice of domestic economic priorities has prevailed over nationalistic foreign policy agendas. For them, the war in former Yugoslavia has served as a warning, and the hope of a rapprochement with the European Union is a positive stimulus. However, their progress in the creation of democratic institutions should not obscure the fact that the passage from communism to open societies has been beset with considerable difficulties and remains vulnerable to setbacks, as the Albanian elections in May 1996 have shown.

Obstacles to Democracy

In identifying obstacles to effective democracy in the Balkans, one should therefore distinguish how they relate to the legacy of war in former Yugoslavia, the legacy of communism, and the legacy of Balkan history. These legacies apply in varying degrees in different countries, and recognizing them is important in attempting to suggest lasting remedies.

•*The weakness of parliamentary democratic traditions.* There were positive developments in this respect in the latter part of the nineteenth century and in the immediate aftermath of World War I, but the Western-style constitutions that were adopted were rarely put into practice. By the end of the 1920s, most of the countries of the area—like several Central European countries—had succumbed to various forms of authoritarianism (Bulgaria in 1923, Albania in 1924, Yugoslavia in 1929, etc.). No less important, there was little or no tradition of the rule of law in the Ottoman period. Half a century of communist rule only reinforced many of these traits, so that there was **little democratic political culture** to sustain the transition after 1989.

•*The fragility of civil society* in the absence of institutions independent of the state and of social forces capable of sustaining such institutions. The very nature of the communist experience was to abolish or curtail the autonomy of social actors and to reinforce reliance on the state. It was the state that shaped society rather than the other way around.

•In Bulgaria, Albania, and Romania—in contrast to Poland, Hungary, or Czechoslovakia—there was **no organized democratic opposition** to communism from which a new political elite could emerge as the old regime disintegrated. (To the extent that it existed in Yugoslavia, it was at the level of the republic, rather than as a country-wide force. Even today, it remains weak, divided, and more reminiscent of "dissent" during the communist period than of parliamentary opposition in a mature democracy.)

•The legacy of the communist period in almost all the Balkan countries is best described as *'apparat nationalism,'* the origins of which were the successive (and in their own terms successful) attempts by Balkan communist leaders to achieve independence or a degree of autonomy from Moscow while retaining the totalitarian features inside in the name of national unity. While ex-communists in some countries of Central Europe have returned to power as social democrats, in the Balkans they have tended to retain power by converting to nationalism.

•In the post-communist transition, some Balkan countries have developed *a presidential rather than a parliamentary system*. This tends to reinforce the centralized authoritarian features of the overall political system. The subordination of the state administration to the whims of the ruling party is considered normal practice in Romania, Serbia, Bulgaria, and Croatia. The arbitrariness of their bureaucracies is mitigated only by inefficiency and corruption.

•Almost everywhere in the region, the *media* have become *a key instrument of political control*. Television and radio in particular are considered a prerogative of the ruling party, leaving the opposition without a voice.

•But the most important force undermining the difficult post-communist transition is *nationalism*. The transition to democracy requires freedom of debate and a variety of parties to put forward alternative programs. In the Balkans, where collective rights usually had priority over individual rights, there is a pronounced tendency to switch from one brand of collectivism to another: from communism to nationalism. Both leave limited room for political differentiation and therefore for effective democracy.

149

Civil Society

The prospects for democracy in the region will depend on the development of a vibrant civil society with organizations and associations independent of state power—on the capacity to create bonds of trust and cooperation essential for the emergence of a culture of pluralism and for the peaceful settlement of disputes. For historical reasons, civil society has been weak in the Balkans. Since the late nineteenth century, the state has always been the main agent of economic development, and political goals have always had precedence over economic goals. Most Balkan countries lack an economic class or social stratum with a strong interest in preserving or creating a larger economic space from which they could benefit. The predominance of political over economic elites means there are few agents to counterbalance nationalistic and disintegrative tendencies. The existing elites expect that they might benefit most from establishing their own, small, separate states.

Another integrative force might be expected to come from non-governmental organizations. Throughout Southeastern Europe, there is a multitude of new civil initiatives, groups, and associations: peace groups, women's associations, human-rights organizations, trade unions, and ecological organizations. Most of these, however, are still relatively weak or marginalized and suffer from similar problems—such as poor working conditions (lack of skills, material, equipment and funds), and political problems (pressure and obstruction by the local or central government authorities, including open threats and repression). Some have not yet evolved beyond a formal existence, and they could be drowned out by far more popular and powerful populist and nationalist organizations. One of the problems lies in the nature of these NGOs. The majority are weak and isolated, which is partly due to their uneven regional distribution. They are rarely able to grow from a spontaneous initiative to a real movement. They have poor organizational infrastructure. There is, moreover, a manifest lack of information, coordination, and cooperation. In talking about rebuilding civil society, these deficiencies need to be addressed directly.

37 **The Commission recommends that public and private Western institutions establish, as a long-term priority, the development and revival of the institutions of civil society, including independent cultural or professional associations, independent judiciaries, and free media.**

Support for NGOs should give priority to projects that help to establish mutual communication, coordination, and cooperation on a regional level. This might include creating networks or coalitions of movements and associations such as the Helsinki Citizens Assembly. Western NGOs can establish partnerships and provide expertise, equipment, and financial assistance.

This is a long-term process that will require the persistent involvement and support of Western NGOs and foundations. A problem with the major Western NGOs is that they sometimes focus on *their* priorities and agendas, and not always on where most of the effort is needed. This problem suggests a further recommendation:

38 A coordinating mechanism, an institute based in the Balkans, should be created to help international NGOs identify the priorities of their local partners and avoid too much duplication or working at cross-purposes. So far, only the Soros Foundations in the region tend to work on that basis. There is a case for extending the approach to other NGOs.

39 We would also support the creation of a region-based center for encouraging the building of democracy. It should be an independent, non-governmental institution, controlled by a body of representatives from the area in association with Western European and American partners. It should help undertake and disseminate research as well as initiate concrete steps in the following areas:

—Independent judiciaries and the rule of law;

—Parliamentary practice (joint seminars for MPs from the region and MPs from Western democracies);

—The high school and university system (including educational exchanges at high school and university level, with summer schools held both in the area and in Western European countries);

—The role of the media (see also pp. 152–57).

The aim would be to develop networks among individuals and groups committed to the democratic process. The target groups for such an effort should be academics, journalists, MPs, businessmen, environmentalists, etc.—i.e., the professional and political elites that will shape the future of democratic development in the Balkans.

151

40 Priority should be given to reviewing the curricula, and in particular textbooks, which are written from nationalist perspectives. History has been used and abused for nationalist purposes. This concerns the education system—from high school to university level in all states in the region. The long experience of the Franco-German and German-Polish commissions of historians in working out joint guidelines for school textbooks could be of relevance. Similar joint commissions could be organized on a bilateral or multilateral basis (e.g., Greek-Bulgarian-Macedonian-Albanian). This can only be a long-term process; a series of seminars for joint commissions of historians and for the preparation of textbooks should be promoted.

41 Consideration should be given in this context, too, to the establishment of a Southeast European University (recommendation 29, p. 130) on the lines of (or as an extension of) the Central European University.

42 Attention should be given to the development of local government in the Balkan states and the fostering of intra-regional cooperation at the local level.

Independent Media

This is a problem of vital importance to the prospects for democracy in the whole region. The countries of former Yugoslavia highlight this general problem in the most dramatic fashion.

Before war started in Yugoslavia, the media of mass communication were used by the individual republic regimes to prepare public support for their policies. The same media were then used to sustain public tolerance of the war, despite its terrible costs. It can be argued, indeed, that these regimes would never have been able to begin a war if they had not abused media unscrupulously, at times illegally. Campaigns of intense propaganda were used to mobilize the population—to make war thinkable in Yugoslavia at the end of the twentieth century.

The most dramatic element of this propaganda was the incitement of popular fear and hatred against specific national groups. However, the resort to hate-speech and hate-images was only the logical climax of a more insidious process: the transfer of the media to nationalist groups, which used them to define and champion new, post-Titoist political agendas. This process occurred at varying speeds and with varying intensities in the republics of Yugoslavia—beginning in Serbia—during the 1980s. After the first multi-party elections in 1990, the process accelerated as new (or not-so-new) governments swiftly moved to control the most influential media in their republics. In Serbia and Croatia, the regimes in power took effective control over broadcast news and the leading newspapers. Some early experiments in privatization and pluralization of media, dating from the late 1980s, were even reversed.

This is how the "media war" in former Yugoslavia—in which the regime-controlled or -influenced media in Serbia, Slovenia, Croatia, and Bosnia-Herzegovina traded blows—came to *anticipate* the military campaigns that began in summer 1991. Like the peoples of Yugoslavia, the media had been intermixed. After armed conflict started, however, the media were manipulated to sustain support for the republic regimes.

The media space in Croatia, Serbia, and Bosnia has been carved into self-sufficient zones of distribution and influence. These zones are coextensive with military control by different armed forces. Their borders are guarded with almost equal vigilance against both 'enemy' media and enemy armies. The relationship between media organizations and political authorities in most parts of the former Yugoslavia shows a pattern of contrasts. At the center are the major electronic and print media, closely controlled by the ruling parties. At one remove are the semi-official news media, nominally independent from the authorities, but in reality subject to their informal influence. In some cases, there are media owned by opposition political parties. Lastly, at the margins and in the background, there are some independent media—operating in an environment of constraint and numbering only a few daily newspapers (one each in Croatia and Serbia), weekly newspapers and news magazines, and a scattering of private local radio stations and television stations.

The current situation of the media—in all republics of the former Yugoslavia except Slovenia—presents a threat to the prospects for peace and democracy in the region. The public is not able to inform itself about the actions of government. Lacking elementary information about the motives and intentions of its leaders, it has been kept blindfolded and disoriented. In authoritarian political cultures such as those of Balkan countries, the state-controlled media offer a model of social obedience to the party-state—a daily confirmation of the tyranny of nationalism as defined by the ruling party. The rights of citizens

153

to know, to seek out, to receive or impart information, and to discuss issues of importance—rights repeatedly upheld by the United Nations—are essential to democracy.

The regimes in Serbia, Croatia, and Bosnia have shown skill at preempting or deterring uncontrolled participation by simulating it. Media have been an essential tool in perpetrating this deceit. If the main news media were not subject to direct political control, media would become more responsive to public opinion, assuming more of the role of watchdogs for society. Exposed to public opinion, the regimes would be vulnerable to higher expectations of accountability and pluralism.

Support for media with a professional attitude toward facts and news values in the Balkan countries also means support for the broadening of democratic accountability and participation in these societies. Independent news media, committed to professional values and standards, are an institution that strengthens civil society. This is of course why pro-democratic independent media in the former Yugoslavia have received considerable support from Western NGOs. Foremost among them have been the Open Society Institutes and Foundations, established in post-communist countries across the region by the Hungarian-American financier George Soros. In 1994, for example, almost $12 million were given to media and communications projects in the Balkans, particularly in Serbia, Romania, and Macedonia. The International Federation of Journalists and the *Federation Internationale des Editeurs de Journaux* have also given financial assistance to independent media in Serbia, Croatia, Bosnia, and Montenegro—some of which owe their very existence to this support.

The media situation has deteriorated in Serbia and Croatia (for the situation in Bosnia, see above, p. 92ff). On January 9, 1996, the Serbian government initiated a purge of management at the state broadcasting network, RTS. On January 19, the Serbian Minister of Information threatened to deny frequencies to independent broadcasters who, in his view, have been guilty of anti-government, inaccurate, one-sided reporting. On February 15, a Belgrade court revoked the status of the **Studio B** radio and television station as a registered private company. On February 17, some twenty journalists at the station were dismissed for refusing to cooperate with the new editorial board, appointed by the Serbian government. The content of Studio B's news programs reflected these developments. Serbia now has no television news produced independently of the regime. The

Soros Foundation, too, was banned from working in Serbia and Montenegro in February. (It was allowed to recommence its work in June.)

Developments in Croatia are also a matter for serious concern. In March 1996, a new editor-in-chief was appointed to *Vjesnik*, Croatia's principal daily newspaper. Following this change, the paper drew even closer to the regime. The new editor-in-chief dismissed a number of staff and penned a front-page accusation that Ivan Zvonimir Cicak, president of the Croatian Helsinki Committee for Human Rights and an outspoken critic of the regime, had been an informer for the Yugoslav state security service. No evidence was adduced. Meanwhile, on April 6, Croatian tax authorities presented the newspaper *Novi List*—Croatia's only independently owned daily newspaper—with a bill for US$ 2.5 million allegedly due in evaded taxes.

On March 29, 1996, the Croatian Parliament adopted two amendments to the Criminal Code that clearly are intended to intimidate journalists. One amendment obliges the public prosecutor to take legal action against anyone who offends or slanders the president of the republic, the speaker of parliament, the prime minister, or the presidents of the supreme court and the constitutional court. The other amendment prosecutes persons who reveal state secrets. The amendments do not define the meaning of "offense," "slander," or "state secrets." On June 17, the editor-in-chief of the weekly newspaper *Feral Tribune* and a senior columnist went on trial—accused of "rudely and falsely slandering" the president of the republic. If found guilty, they face fines or prison sentences.

Looking beyond the 1996 election campaign in Bosnia, it seems evident that an enduring, stable peace cannot be built without substantial changes in the media situation, and that, for political and economic reasons, these changes will not be achieved without external pressure and assistance. A coordinated effort toward media in the Balkans, pooling international and local resources, would greatly enhance the prospects for peace and democracy in the region. Long-term approaches are needed, both to support independent media and to pressure the regimes to eliminate state control of media.

43 **Western governments and international institutions should place a high priority on freedom of the media in their dealings with the countries of the region.** Such an effort would be implemented by international and non-governmental organizations. International organizations (such as the Council of Europe, the OSCE, UNESCO, and the European Union) should mainly assume the following tasks:

—Applying significant pressure upon governments in the region to respect international norms of media freedom, responsibility, and legislation. This pressure should not eschew retaliatory measures—e.g., within the framework of the Council of Europe and the OSCE, but also denial of satellite access via the European Broadcasting Union and boycotts of program sales to state broadcasting. (However, United Nations sanctions against particular states should not obstruct the flow of information);

—Establishing early warning systems, so that media campaigns to incite fear and hatred, which were so devastating in the republics of former Yugoslavia, would be noted, reviewed, and acted upon at an early stage;

—Ensuring that, during election campaigns in the countries concerned, media are monitored and reviewed by the OSCE as part of the assessment of the overall validity of the election results;

—Initiating a process of consultation among international bodies (such as the Council of Europe, the International Federation of Journalists, and the International Press Institute) and representatives from the governments, judiciaries and main media in the countries in question—with a view to helping these countries establish ground-rules for media legislation and codes of practice that are acceptable to all sides;

—Implementing, in the case of Bosnia and Herzegovina, a strategy to develop the conditions for a common media market (communications, access, sales, distribution, bureaus, etc.);

—Supporting the publicly stated intention of the International Criminal Tribunal in the Hague to investigate the role of media in the war;

—Translating and publishing basic texts on media freedom, including cases from the European Court of Human Rights and the Johannesburg Principles on National Security, Freedom of Expression, and Access to Information;

—Encouraging projects in the region (some already exist) to

compile media archives, databases, and libraries as resources against the manipulation of history; and

—Assisting the overall effort with funding.

Non-governmental organizations—such as Press Now (Netherlands), the Institute for War and Peace Reporting (United Kingdom), the International Federation of Journalists (Belgium), the Index on Censorship (U.K.), the Association for Independent Media (France), and the European Institute on the Media (Germany)—have a wealth of experience in working with independent media in the Balkans and elsewhere. As part of a coordinated strategy, they could be particularly responsible for:

—Working with local media and human rights groups to monitor the political, legal, and commercial conditions for media and the content of media;

—Devising programs to disseminate information throughout the countries of the region about international norms of media freedom, responsibility, and legislation;

—Devising programs to train and support independent media and journalists through exchange-programs with Western media, fundraising, subsidized access to information, and technical and legal assistance;

—Establishing an international professional commission to examine the role of journalists in fomenting war in Yugoslavia;

—Liaising between international organizations, local and international media, and local non-governmental organizations.

ETHNIC RELATIONS AND THE TREATMENT OF MINORITIES

This is one of the most important issues for security and stability in the Balkans. Prospects for peace in the area will to a large extent depend on the capacity of the states to provide solutions to the problem of national minorities.[12]

---

[12] The Roma (Gypsies) represent a special case, since they are a minority without a claim to separate territory and statehood. That has not made them any less vulnerable to discrimination and xenophobia. By too many people and for too long a time, the Roma have been seen either as irrelevant or as a local menace. It is high time they were taken seriously in the Balkans and elsewhere. They are estimated to

The notion of one state corresponding with one nation, one culture, one religion, one language is not only undesirable but indeed impossible if one rejects the two methods that have since the nineteenth century prevailed in much of the Balkans: 'ethnic cleansing' and forced 'assimilation.' Hence the need to seek solutions to assure respect for minorities without challenging the borders of existing states, and to reconcile the respect for diversity with respect for the sovereignty of existing states. The prime challenge for all nation-states is the integration of the population in a common public space in which rules of coexistence and civic culture are respected by all.

One school of thought argues that, to achieve this goal, it is important to defuse the political charge of ethno-nationalism by separating culture from politics—by granting minorities all the main cultural rights (linguistic, religious etc.) in order to avoid ethnicity's domination of politics. Cultural autonomy should pre-empt demands for territorial autonomy. The problem with this liberal approach is that it is sometimes difficult to draw the line between the two: it is only one step from the use of language for education and cultural activities to its use in the administration or the police. (In moving from one to the other, there is also potential for conflict). And what might well work in liberal democracies is less likely to function in the Balkans, where minorities tend to consider the civic concept of the state granting equal rights for all citizens to be a cover for supremacy by the dominant national group, while the dominant group in turn tends to see ethnic minorities as a potential "fifth column" of neighboring states. This element of "ethnoparanoia" means that minorities do not trust legal guarantees as long as collective rights are not accompanied by territorial autonomy, while the major national groups refuse to grant such territorial autonomy because they fear possible disintegration and irredentism.

---

number over 2 million in the Balkans. Sometimes their numbers are wildly exaggerated, but the following figures are probably less unreliable than most: former Yugoslavia, 750,000; Romania, 800,000 to one million; Turkey, 500,000; Bulgaria, 500,000; Albania, 65,000; Greece, 90,000. Despite popular opinion, only a fraction of them are criminal or anti-social. Despite the efforts of some of their number, they are still disorganized, disunited, and politically powerless, discriminated against, and despised. It may need revolutions to make them and their persecutors change. But the chances are that it is they who will change before their persecutors do, that they will become better organized, and better led. Then, as well as being aware of their grievances, they will become aware of their power. At present they are a footnote; early in the next century, they could well be making headlines.

A different approach involves giving the minority a stake in the state by granting it "constituent nation" status, collective rights with territorial autonomy in areas where it is in a majority, and veto power over legislation directly affecting it. This, the argument goes, is not without risks—but lesser risks than that presented by the majority nation's assumption that state control will be enough to preserve the status quo in the long run. What might well endanger a state might become the only means of saving it.

The policies of Western democracies represent an attempt to blur this distinction between the civic concept of individual rights and the concept of collective rights by defining national minority rights as *individual rights exercised collectively*. This has been the approach in particular of the Council of Europe, which has gone further than any other international institution in making the question of minority rights one of its central concerns, particularly in its relationship with the post-communist countries aspiring to a rapprochement with European institutions.

In Europe, the internationalization of national minority rights has two main channels related to two institutions: the Council of Europe and the OSCE.

The Council of Europe approach to minority rights, derived from human rights, gives a member of a minority who has exhausted domestic means of legal procedure the opportunity to appeal to the European Court of Human Rights in Strasbourg (the applications go through the European Commission on Human Rights). The decisions of the European Court are binding for member states and can force them to modify their internal legislation on minorities.

At its Vienna summit in October 1993, the Council of Europe decided on the elaboration of a Framework Convention for the Protection of National Minorities, which was adopted in November 1994 by the Committee of Ministers and has so far been signed by 30 countries. The Convention states that: "The protection of national minorities and of the rights of persons belonging to these minorities is an integral part of the protection of human rights and as such represents an area of international cooperation." The document also makes clear that the violation of minority rights by a given state will affect its relationship with other signatories. For countries that have made the joining of Western institutions their foreign policy priority, this is not without importance. Under Annex I of the

Constitution of Bosnia and Herzegovina, it is one of the human rights agreements to be applied in Bosnia.

The Council of Europe's Recommendation 1201, paragraph 11, states: " in the regions where they are a majority, persons belonging to national minorities have the right to dispose of local authorities and autonomy or to enjoy a special status in conformity with the specific historical and territorial situation and with the internal legislation of the state." This Recommendation is finding its way into the bilateral relations of member states. It has been explicitly referred to in the treaty between Hungary and Slovakia and remains the most controversial issue in the preparation of a Hungarian-Romanian treaty.

The OSCE document on national minorities adopted in Copenhagen in 1990 provides a second and more directly political approach. Unlike the Council of Europe Convention, it has been signed by all heads of state belonging to the OSCE and thus entails a political commitment to respect minority rights, starting with the most elementary one: self-ascription, or the right of a person to declare that he or she belongs to a particular minority. In some Balkan countries, this right is by no means self-evident (e.g., Macedonians in Greece and Bulgaria).

How then should the rights of persons belonging to a national minority be defined? Most of the international recommendations on this matter (as devised by the Council of Europe and the OSCE) include protection against discrimination and spell out positive rights. The list of these varies but generally includes the following main items (most of which are applicable when the minority represents a specified minimum percentage of the total population):

—Right to use one's mother tongue in public as well as in private;

—Right to use the minority language in dealing with the administration and judiciary;

—Right to education in the minority language;

—Right to freedom of association;

—Right to freedom of contact with citizens of other countries;

—Right to use bilingual names for towns and streets.

44 The Commission considers that, in order to create conditions for the effective participation of members of national minorities in cultural, social, and economic as well as political life, the following measures are important:

—Provisions for the protection of minorities should be embedded in the state constitution and not solely in laws that can fairly easily be modified or reversed.

—Minority rights should be spelled out as specifically as possible, not left in general terms for the interpretation of local officials from the majority national group.

—The electoral system should include proportional representation with a reasonable minimum threshold. Although this has well-known potential drawbacks (fragmentation), it is probably the only way to guarantee the political representation of minorities in parliamentary institutions (e.g., the Turkish minority in Bulgaria, the Hungarian minority in Romania, etc.)

—Decentralization: regional and municipal autonomy is essential in mixed territories (particularly where the minority is in a local majority).

Further recommendations could be derived from the experience of Western democracies in dealing with minority regional issues—experience that deserves to be better known in the Balkans. Relevant examples include: The Spanish Constitution, granting different degrees of autonomy to regions (Catalonia, Basque country); Finland's handling of the status of the Swedish minority there; the status of the German minority in Belgium (Eupen) and of the Danish minority in Germany. Italy and Austria have also worked out a satisfactory arrangement concerning the autonomous status of South Tyrol/Alto Adige. And Switzerland's canton system provides considerable linguistic autonomy in education and administration. Even when boundaries between cantons have been challenged, it has been done peacefully: The separation of the canton of Jura from the canton of Berne has been achieved through a legal and democratic process. These cases are specific to their own societies and cannot necessarily be transposed to other situations, but they can provide inspiration.

The point here is not to offer specific formulas to be applied in the Balkans, but a more general one. Ethno-linguistic tensions in some Western countries are no less acute than in the Balkans. The main difference is that in liberal democracies they are not in most cases considered a "security" risk because they take place in a civil society with a rule of law, where there are institutional mechanisms to manage and defuse them. Three elements—*a civil society* (where ethnicity is not the exclusive organizing principle), *the rule of law* (guaranteeing human

161

rights and minority rights), and ***institutional means of mediation and arbitration***—are central features in the creation of a "community of security." Such a community cannot be reduced to a set of legal measures or policies, but it represents an environment from which the use of force to deal with inter-ethnic differences is excluded (except as a last resort to ensure law and order). And that is also a central message for the Balkans: Legislation on minorities that observes international standards is a prerequisite; but no amount of legislation will be effective without democracy, civil society, and the rule of law—in other words, without the creation of a community of security.

One of the main lessons from the recent conflict in former Yugoslavia is the need for prevention by conciliation and arbitration. A first attempt was made with the creation in the summer of 1991 of the European Commission of Arbitration for former Yugoslavia (including five Chairmen of Constitutional Courts from Western European countries). But as Robert Badinter, Chairman of the Arbitration Commission, has observed: "Arbitration works best *before* or *after* a conflict—not during. Once you start exchanging bullets, it becomes difficult to exchange words."

45 **The Commission recommends the development of an international judicial institution to elaborate on the meaning of the right to "self-determination" of "peoples," as expressed in the U.N. Charter. There is an inherent tension between that principle and the no less important international commitment to the inviolability of borders. All the Balkan protagonists have different interpretations on these matters. There is a clear need for a tribunal on the limits to self-determination. This need not be a new institution. One obvious candidate would be the present World Court; another could be the European Commission and Court on Human Rights.**

Another step in the direction of a *preventive* approach has now been taken with the creation—under OSCE auspices in Geneva—of a Court of Conciliation and Arbitration, which has so far received the backing of 35 states (including Slovenia, Croatia, Bosnia-Herzegovina, and Macedonia, but, significantly, not by Turkey and Greece). The central idea is to create a procedure for conciliation and arbitration in order to defuse controversial issues between states (the building of a dam, border crossings, etc.) before they poison the bilateral relationship or escalate into conflict. But here again: The effectiveness of arbitration will depend on the political will of Balkan states and on the development of a legal culture that so far has been lacking.

No doubt international efforts to help resolve minority problems will be needed. But in many instances, more flexible political instruments rather than juridical processes may be more effective: for example, recommendations from the OSCE High Commissioner for National Minorities, or the kind of diplomacy the United States practiced to help defuse the Greek-Macedonian dispute.

The general rule in attempts to alleviate minority problems should be reciprocity: Treat your minorities the way you would want your own ethnic group to be treated as a minority in a neighboring state. More specific recommendations follow from that principle:

46 **All Balkan states should recognize the right of individuals to define their identity.** This includes, for instance, Macedonians in Greece and Bulgaria; Turks in Greece (the latter are recognized only as Muslims); and Greeks in Turkey (only recognized as Rum, i.e., Orthodox minority). People who claim minority status should not have to thereby risk being deprived of their citizenship (as has been the case with a number of ethnic Turks and Macedonians in Greece).

47 **Domestic legislation and domestic constitutions should be adapted to conform to international agreements concerning the protection of minority rights.**

48 **State tolerance toward all religious communities should be ensured (even where there exists an established creed).**

49 **Civil servants, particularly those working in the field of education and the judiciary, should be trained to implement the minority protections of the law.**

50 **An independent ombudsman should be installed to deal with complaints concerning the violation of rights in order to facilitate the relationship between the minorities and the legal system.**

51 **Institutions should be established to monitor incitement to ethnic, racial, or religious hatred in the media, which has been a major factor in all cases of ethnic**

tension or conflict in the Balkans. Awareness of this problem and a sense of responsibility (rather than the introduction of restrictive legislation) should be developed among editors, journalists, and politicians. Workshops and seminars should be organized in cooperation with major Western media institutions.

52 In ethnically divided areas, such as Cyprus or Bosnia and Herzegovina, consideration should be given to introducing a system of cross-voting as part of a broader power-sharing system.[13]

SECURITY

In late 1995, the Western Alliance finally refused to tolerate the war in Bosnia any longer. The Commission hopes that this collective refusal can help to establish, as a more general principle of transatlantic policy, that war in Europe remains intolerable. But the principle cannot be taken for granted. There is a significant risk that within a year of the publication of this Report, there could be another war in the Balkans.

1996 is not 1914. The danger that a Balkans conflict would set off a new *world* war can be safely excluded. Yet the Commission found disturbing evidence in Southeastern Europe of much greater potential for conflict than any found to exist elsewhere in Europe outside the former Soviet Union. The risks are most acute in former Yugoslavia: in Bosnia, if the NATO

---

[13] Cross-voting is an elaborately weighted voting system that is a politically important attempt to build bridges across communities. Such a system has been proposed as a feature of a Cyprus settlement, but the principle may be of relevance elsewhere in the Balkans: Bosnia and Herzegovina would be an obvious case. In essence, cross-voting would mean that, in countries divided along community lines, members of one community would also have a vote, albeit weighted downward, in the elections of the other community. Thus, for example, Bosniaks would have a limited influence over the results of elections in Republika Srpska and vice versa. Votes cast in the election of the 'other' community would then be adjusted so as to achieve the "desired percentage" strength of each community in the elections of the other; this "desired percentage" would of course have to be agreed and included in the constitution.

The likely effects of cross-voting would be: (1) to give an incentive to politicians to develop policies that would appeal to members of the other community; and (2) to enhance in the federal legislature the bridge-building presence of elected officials who depend on the votes of the other community (and therefore would be more likely to take into account the wishes of these voters).

presence is terminated too soon, and in the intolerable situation in Kosovo. The troubles in Eastern Slavonia still are not settled, and there is potential for ethnic conflict in Macedonia. There are also significant risks of conflict elsewhere in the Balkans: the Greek-Turkish disputes in the Aegean Sea; the unresolved situation in Cyprus; Greek-Macedonian tensions; Bulgarian-Turkish problems; and simmering difficulties between Albania and its neighbors.

In the preceding recommendations—concerning treatment of minorities, democracy-building, Balkan cooperation, and the roles and responsibilities of individual states—we have outlined some of the preconditions for lasting peace and stability. Yet it is also true that ethnic relations, democracy, and Balkan cooperation will all be at risk unless and until a framework for peace and military security can be established. Such a framework would require two dimensions: an *intra-regional* dimension of arms control, confidence-building, and collective security measures; but also—and probably more critically in the medium term—the *extra-regional* dimension of a continuing and coherent military engagement by NATO. Both dimensions are discussed below.

Arms Control and Collective Security

Except for Turkey's continued anxiety about Russia, most of the security threats perceived by Balkan countries arise from within the region rather than from outside. The need is therefore not so much for the collective defense guarantees that the Visegrad countries and the Baltic states seek from NATO, but for mechanisms of intra-regional stabilization that could develop into a sub-regional collective security structure.

Dayton offers a good start. Annex 1-B of the Dayton Agreement—the *Agreement on Regional Stability*—commits Serbia and Croatia as well as Bosnia and Herzegovina and its two constituent entities to "devising new forms of cooperation in the field of security aimed at building transparency and confidence and achieving balanced and stable defense force levels at the lowest numbers consistent with the Parties' respective security and the need to avoid an arms race in the region."[14] The annex

---

[14] Because of its non-aligned status during the Cold War, former Yugoslavia, like Albania, was not involved in any of the negotiations for Confidence Building or Arms Control measures in the 1980s.

then set out three sets of measures: (1) for confidence- and security-building in Bosnia and Herzegovina; (2) for sub-regional arms control covering all three republics; and (3) for the longer-term objective of a regional arms-control agreement involving the area in and around former Yugoslavia. All three sets of measures are to be taken up under the auspices of OSCE, whose Forum on Security Cooperation now has a general responsibility for these matters throughout Europe.

Agreement on the first set of measures was reached at the end of January 1996, and the Commission during its visit to Sarajevo was able to learn from Brigadier Per Skov-Christensen of the useful work that his team of officers already has undertaken "to enhance mutual confidence" through measures such as restrictions on military deployments, withdrawal of forces, notification of planned military activities, and monitoring of weapons-manufacturing capabilities.

The second set of measures, the arms control negotiations, were completed by early June 1996. Dayton includes figures requiring the Federal Republic of Yugoslavia (Serbia and Montenegro) to reduce its holdings of five major types of armaments specified—tanks, artillery, armored combat vehicles, combat aircraft, and attack helicopters—to 75 percent of those held in January 1996; and requiring Croatia and Bosnia and Herzegovina to reduce their holdings to 30 percent each—with the Bosnia quotas distributed according to a ratio of 2:1 between the Bosniak-Croat Federation and Republika Srpska. According to the agreement reached on June 14, 1996, the five parties have 16 months, starting on July 1, 1996, to reduce weapons to pre-arranged levels. Within these limits, the countries can import heavy weapons, military aircraft, and helicopters to reach parity with the other parties. For reasons already discussed (see p. 89) this poses the potential for reigniting a serious transatlantic disagreement over whether to equip and train the Bosnian forces. This Commission is itself divided on the issue, but it is unanimous in urging that the arms-control agreement be rigorously enforced. The credibility of the whole Dayton process will depend on it.

The third component of Dayton Annex 1-B seeks to go beyond the three republics and to establish, with the assistance of a special representative from the OSCE, a regional balance in and around the former Yugoslavia. This should start by including Slovenia, Macedonia, and Albania in confidence-building measures and arms control regimes, from which they are at present excluded. Such a regional arrangement should then involve the other Balkan countries—although some of them have said they do not wish to be subject to lower limits than those which already apply to them under the CFE Treaty (the existing European arms control treaty)—and could become the basis for a regional collective security system.

Proposals for a regional security organization inevitably run into resistance and mutual distrust similar to that raised by proposals for regional economic cooperation. Just as most Balkan countries see their political and economic future in EU membership, they aspire to NATO membership for reasons of security. These aspirations have obvious positive implications: They offer the Western Alliance significant leverage to influence the region for the better. Moreover, some of the Commission's interlocutors in the region made a distinction between American power and European "norms." In terms of the evolution of their own states and societies, they spoke of a process of 'Europeanization.' But wherever there is conflict to be settled or protection to be requested, they look to NATO.

The aspiration to join NATO raises at least two problems. First, the lure of NATO might discourage necessary regional cooperation (just as the lure of EU membership sometimes discourages regional political-economic cooperation). Second, pervasive naivete about the real prospects for membership poses the danger of bitter disappointment once it is recognized that NATO membership, if it comes at all, will be ten years or even a generation away. (Slovenia is a possible exception, and Greece and Turkey are of course already members.)

The Western Alliance should not underestimate the damage that such disappointment can do. It needs to deliberate carefully about regional arrangements that would draw on NATO's prestige and credibility without raising false expectations. Happily, one such half-way house—NATO's Partnership for Peace—already has proven more successful than many skeptics originally predicted. Initially regarded as either an anteroom to NATO membership, or a meager consolation prize for countries unlikely ever to become members, Partnership for Peace has proven to be a successful institution in its own right: promoting cross-border transparency, joint maneuvers, and general cooperation that has helped to professionalize post-communist armies and has further educated them in Western notions of democracy and subordination to civilian control. Most of the Balkan countries (other than Greece and Turkey, which are members) have an association with NATO through Partnership for Peace, and those that do not could be expected to obtain it.

53 The Commission recommends the creation of a "Balkan Association of Partnership for Peace," linked to NATO's wider structures, which could ensure—through a coordination office at NATO—that all the members of NATO keep a continuing active interest in the security of the region. The Association would try to anticipate some of the benefits of integration for this region. The goal would be to make use of the various existing structures in which there is confidence, but also to be imaginative in thinking of new models for the twenty-first century. Under this general rubric, there could be other partnerships for peacekeeping in the region similar to the Baltic Battalion, the Polish-Lithuanian and Polish-Ukrainian peacekeeping units. There are plenty of possibilities for more or less realistic proposals in which Italy, Hungary, and Austria could perhaps play a constructive part alongside one or more of the eleven countries of the Balkans. A regional "Open Skies" arrangement could be a practical proposal, and a common regional air traffic control regime could add to transparency. Such practical measures would be concrete confidence- and security-building measures for the region.[15] The military dimensions of security have to be seen alongside wider aspects of regional cooperation. The European Union has talked of the need for cooperation both within the region and with the Union. Together, they can create a culture of confidence and cooperation.

---

[15] Some small but important initiatives to foster closer regional defense cooperation have recently been undertaken. In April 1996, for instance, a meeting of the Southern Balkan defense ministers was held in Tirana. The meeting was the first of its kind in the Balkans and was attended by the Defense Ministers of Albania, Bulgaria, and Macedonia. The defense ministers of Turkey, Italy, and the United States participated. (Greece was invited but declined to attend). At the Tirana meeting, U.S. Secretary of Defense William Perry proposed a number of initiatives designed to foster closer defense cooperation among the countries of the region. These included: opening each nation's peacekeeping forces to troops from neighboring countries; creating military "rapid response teams" that could work together in search and rescue missions, civilian emergencies, and disaster relief; exchanging detailed information about military budgets, plans, and policies; setting up hot lines between the region's defense ministries; or withdrawing military units from border areas.

The Continuing Commitment of NATO

For the foreseeable future, such modest proposals are probably the most that can be achieved in the way of Balkan security cooperation. They will not be enough. There will remain the need for a NATO commitment that goes beyond Partnership for Peace and beyond mere containment of any future conflict.

A current irony of transatlantic politics is that as NATO debates enlargement to Central Europe, it is already massively present in the Balkans. It should not leave without the most careful consideration of the consequences. We have already emphasized the need to maintain a post-IFOR military force in Bosnia and Herzegovina, and it should be based on NATO rather than the United Nations. An important lesson of the recent Balkan war is that the West failed in Bosnia as long as Europe and the United States were divided, but succeeded when their diagnoses and strategies finally converged. Another lesson concerns the need for constructive engagement with Russia vis-a-vis Balkan problems.

From these conclusions, the Commission draws four general recommendations:

54 **Maintain the Contact Group as a mechanism for common decision-making. (This applies to Bosnia and Herzegovina, but may be useful for Balkans policy in general.) The Contact Group might be expanded to include Italy— first, because of its geographic proximity and many interests in the region; and second, because future uses of force would most likely originate from bases on Italian soil.**

Another virtue of the Contact Group is that it brings Russia into the consultative process. Indeed, when the Commission was in Moscow, it heard proposals for converting the Contact Group into something like a European Security Council under the auspices of the OSCE. Such proposals are premature, not least because the evolution of Russian democracy and foreign policy remains uncertain. For the time being, the Contact Group should remain an important but informal institution.

55 **Maintain the United States' military presence and engagement.** The main issue is not so much the level of military presence as its visibility, because American military power has special credibility in the region. The need for U.S. participation in a post-IFOR arrangement for Bosnia and Herzegovina already has been discussed—as has the advisability

169

of keeping roughly 500 American troops in Macedonia as part of the UNPREDEP deployment until substantial progress is made in resolving the Kosovo crisis. The U.S. military relationship with Albania should also be maintained and strengthened. We would repeat the caveat, already mentioned above, that the Berisha regime should not be allowed to interpret its strategic relationship with Washington as license for the kind of authoritarian behavior it has recently demonstrated. On the other hand, neighboring Macedonia sees the U.S. role in Albania as a reassuring factor, as Macedonian Foreign Minister Ljubomir Frckovski has emphasized. This reassurance factor would certainly apply to U.S. military presence elsewhere in the Balkans.

56 Foster transatlantic unity and a European defense identity. Some see the two as contradictory. We do not.

A major cause of transatlantic tension throughout the war in former Yugoslavia was not Europe's attempting to go it alone, but the fact that its aspirations exceeded its capabilities. The self-proclaimed "hour of Europe" was followed by tragic inadequacy, feeding suspicion and mutual recriminations among the major European capitals and Washington. Europe, present in warring Yugoslavia not as "Europe" but as individual nations, made by far the largest sacrifice: in money, in troops, and in lives. But it was not sufficient. The whole experience seemed to confirm the absolute primacy of American power. Yet this is also largely an illusion, if it is understood to mean that the United States can manage such problems without its European partners. Dayton became possible when the Americans and the Europeans worked together; it has a chance of success only if they continue to do so.

This challenge comes at a time when the European Union, in its Intergovernmental Conference to follow up on the Maastricht Treaty, is trying to agree on more effective mechanisms for a common foreign policy. It also comes at a time when the Americans expect Europe to take on more and more of the burden in Bosnia. In this context, the question of a post-IFOR deployment is becoming a test-case both for a European CFSP and for a new division of roles within NATO. Inevitably, the Bosnia crisis as a whole will be seen as a defining moment, for good or for ill, for the Atlantic Alliance.

Heartening in this regard was NATO's agreement at the June 1996 Ministerial Meeting to establish "combined joint task forces," allowing the Europeans to use NATO assets for special missions without the participation of the United States. This agreement is open to different interpretations. It is certainly true that many of NATO's key assets are really American assets, so that there are constraints on the idea of an "independent" European operation within NATO. But that should not obscure the fact of a fundamental philosophical rapprochement. The U.S. Administration of President Clinton has abandoned America's traditionally dogmatic opposition to a European defense identity, while the French government under President Chirac has moved back into Alliance institutions and has given up the position that the Western European Union rather than NATO should be the only vehicle for common European defense actions. Put simply, the Americans have recognized that an independent and coherent European foreign policy is in *their* interest, while the Europeans have reaffirmed that American engagement, and to some extent American leadership, as embodied in the continuing primacy of NATO, is in *their* interest.

57 **NATO members should recognize the need to demonstrate their will with military force when necessary.** This is perhaps the single most important lesson of the international response to the war in Bosnia. Sadly, it is a lesson that loses none of its relevance as the guarantor powers try to keep the fragile peace in Bosnia and Herzegovina. And it is a lesson that may have to be applied elsewhere in the Balkans.[16] Another war in the Balkans, or in Bosnia itself, might not directly threaten the West, but it would again have a corrosive effect on its sense of unity and progress. And, as was the experience of the early 1990s, intervention probably would take place—sooner or later.

We are not calling for military adventurism to replace the cautious restraint of recent years. Neither Europe nor the United States should or could intervene everywhere in the world where war breaks out. But they have a special responsibility on the European continent. And if war can be banned *there*, the twenty-first century may look more promising even in global terms.

---

[16] Washington will need to modify the prevailing military doctrine that contemplates the use of American power only where overwhelming force can be applied. This so-called "Powell Doctrine" was partly a legacy of the Vietnam war, in which incremental escalations progressively drew the United States into a quagmire.

EPILOGUE

The twentieth century began in Sarajevo, with war. Might it end in Sarajevo, with peace?

The guns have fallen silent in former Yugoslavia. But the precarious truce concluded at Dayton has yet to become a lasting peace. Large parts of the war-torn area are destroyed and depopulated. The task of reconstruction is compounded by the fact that the transition from communism to democracy and to free market economies has nowhere been completed. But the way to peace lies through reconstruction. Breaking the cycle of destitution and hopelessness is arguably the only way to break the cycle of violence.

In their final chapter, the authors of the first Carnegie Report on the Balkans, writing in 1913-14, observed that, for the region in general, the future seemed "well nigh hopeless." Such pessimism, we know, was warranted. Shortly after publication of the Report, mankind was engulfed by World War I.

In 1996, no comparable catastrophe looms on the horizon. This much, at least, the members of the international community have learned: They will not allow the regional actors, many of them imbued with their own exclusivist ethnic ideals, to set the outside powers against each other. Yet it would be very wrong to conclude that the world as a whole could safely ignore renewed savagery there. Another war would deliver yet another blow to hopes for constructing a just and stable international community in the next century. This is doubly true for the idea of Europe as embodied in the European Union. The Balkans are on the edge of this project and want to be a part of it. If they go awry, Europe's progress will be badly tarnished.

The outside powers committed grievous mistakes in the early 1990s. Their diplomatic interventions, well-meant but for the most part ineffective, lacked credibility because they were not backed by readiness to use military force when events demanded it. The Western powers vastly overestimated the fighting-strength of the Serb military machine; they therefore tarried and stalled far too long before committing troops to back up the protracted sequence of negotiations. Even after Dayton, they often continued to mistake words for deeds. If before they underrated the usefulness of the military instrument, now they were in danger of underestimating the need for the civilian underpinning of the peace process.

The lessons of the past, laid out in this Report, are clear. So is the task before us: to defuse the confrontation; to guarantee—and if need be enforce—both the process and the framework for peace; and to facilitate reconciliation by helping to pave the way from poverty to prosperity in the war-stricken region.

The atrocities perpetrated during the third Balkan war of this century would seem to bear out harsh judgments about the readiness of Balkan countries to join Europe. Yet most European states have gone through similar periods of upheaval, horror, and cruelty in their history—and have ultimately worked their way out of the darkness. In this sense, the Balkan predicament cannot be considered distinct from the European predicament.

The Balkans should not be seen solely through the prism of the Bosnian tragedy. Today they stand at the crossroads, confronted with the prospect of being marginalized once again, or overcoming the present crisis and creating the conditions for their integration into the European mainstream. The ultimate challenge for both the West and the Balkan peoples themselves is, we would suggest, to create a framework that gives everyone a stake in peace. This applies especially to the former warring parties of ex-Yugoslavia. To avoid a new nationalistic eruption, it is not enough to propose technical solutions. Each side must feel it is gaining something in exchange for sacrificing something. The Western powers are unlikely to maintain their forces in the Balkans forever. Thus each side must come to see the cost of resuming war as higher than the cost of maintaining peace.

The peoples of the Balkans deserve the chance to leave their tragic past behind. The European nations that have succeeded in moving beyond the painful burdens of their own history owe it to their sense of humanity, their dignity, and their peace of conscience to help the fragile nations in this region overcome their present predicament and transform the bloody Balkans of yesteryear into the Southeastern Europe of the future.

THE BALKAN 'POWDER KEG'

[1] Yugoslavia census of 1991. [2] Data for 1991. [3] Data for 1992. [4] Macedonian census, June-July 1994.

Source : The Military Balance 1995-1996, (London: Brassey's 1995).

★ **PRINCIPAL ZONES OF TENSION**

1 - Occupation of the north of the Republic of Cyprus by the Turkish Army.

2 - Delimitation of the territorial waters and air space of the Aegean Sea.

3 - Installation of military forces on the Greek islands of the Aegean.

4 - Status of the Greek minority in Istanbul.

5 - Status of the Turkish minority in Western Thrace.

6 - Status of the Turkish minority in Bulgaria.

7 - Territorial dispute over northern Epirus and the status of the Greek minority in Albania.

8 - Tensions following the proclamation of independence by the former Yugoslav Republic of Macedonia.

9 - Demands of the Kosovo Albanians.

10 - War in Bosnia-Herzegovina, and implementation of the peace agreement elaborated in the Dayton Accords.

11 - War in Croatia (the Krajina and Eastern Slavonia).

12 - Hungarian minority in Vojvodina.

13 - Hungarian minority in Romania.

© Philippe Rekacewicz. Reproduced with gratefully acknowledged permission (translated and adapted from color to black and white) from *Le Monde Diplomatique, dossier* "Maniere de Voir," February 29, 1996.

175

YUGOSLAVIA ON THE EVE OF ITS DISSOLUTION

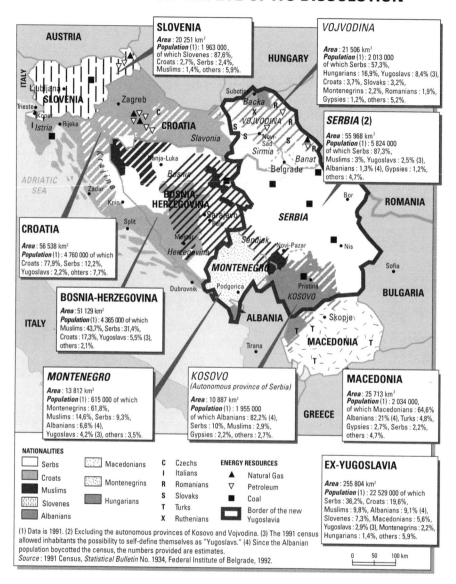

SLOVENIA
Area : 20 251 km²
Population (1): 1 963 000,
of which Slovenes : 87,6%,
Croats : 2,7%, Serbs : 2,4%,
Muslims : 1,4%, others : 5,9%.

VOJVODINA
Area : 21 506 km²
Population (1): 2 013 000
of which Serbs : 57,3%,
Hungarians : 16,9%, Yugoslavs : 8,4% (3),
Croats : 3,7%, Slovaks : 3,2%,
Montenegrins : 2,2%, Romanians : 1,9%,
Gypsies : 1,2%, others : 5,2%.

SERBIA (2)
Area : 55 968 km²
Population (1): 5 824 000
of which Serbs : 87,3%,
Muslims : 3%, Yugoslavs : 2,5% (3),
Albanians : 1,3% (4), Gypsies : 1,2%,
others : 4,7%.

CROATIA
Area : 56 538 km²
Population (1): 4 760 000 of which
Croats : 77,9%, Serbs : 12,2%,
Yugoslavs : 2,2%, ohters : 7,7%.

BOSNIA-HERZEGOVINA
Area : 51 129 km²
Population (1): 4 365 000 of which
Muslims : 43,7%, Serbs : 31,4%,
Croats : 17,3%, Yugoslavs : 5,5% (3),
others : 2,1%.

MONTENEGRO
Area : 13 812 km²
Population (1): 615 000 of which
Montenegrins : 61,8%,
Muslims : 14,6%, Serbs : 9,3%,
Albanians : 6,6% (4),
Yugoslavs : 4,2% (3), others : 3,5%.

KOSOVO
(Autonomous province of Serbia)
Area : 10 887 km²
Population (1): 1 955 000
of which Albanians : 82,2% (4),
Serbs : 10%, Muslims : 2,9%,
Gypsies : 2,2%, others : 2,7%.

MACEDONIA
Area : 25 713 km²
Population (1): 2 034 000,
of which Macedonians : 64,6%
Albanians : 21% (4), Turks : 4,8%,
Gypsies : 2,7%, Serbs : 2,2%,
others : 4,7%.

Map labels: AUSTRIA, HUNGARY, ITALY, Ljubljana, SLOVENIA, Trieste, Kopet, Istria, Rijeka, Zagreb, CROATIA, Slavonia, Banja-Luka, Bosnia, ADRIATIC SEA, Zadar, Knin, Split, BOSNIA-HERZEGOVINA, Sarajevo, Mostar, Herzegovina, Krajina, Subotica, Backa, VOJVODINA, Novi-Sad, Sirmia, Banat, Belgrade, SERBIA, Bor, ROMANIA, Sendjak, Novi-Pazar, Nis, Sofia, MONTENEGRO, Dubrovnik, Podgorica, Pristina, KOSOVO, BULGARIA, ALBANIA, Skopje, MACEDONIA, Tirana, GREECE

NATIONALITIES

Serbs	Macedonians
Croats	Montenegrins
Muslims	Hungarians
Slovenes	
Albanians	

C Czechs
I Italians
R Romanians
S Slovaks
T Turks
X Ruthenians

ENERGY RESOURCES
▲ Natural Gas
▽ Petroleum
■ Coal
▭ Border of the new Yugoslavia

EX-YUGOSLAVIA
Area : 255 804 km²
Population (1): 22 529 000 of which
Serbs : 36,2%, Croats : 19,6%,
Muslims : 9,8%, Albanians : 9,1% (4),
Slovenes : 7,3%, Macedonians : 5,6%,
Yugoslavs : 2,9% (3), Montenegrins : 2,2%,
Hungarians : 1,4%, others : 5,9%.

(1) Data is 1991. (2) Excluding the autonomous provinces of Kosovo and Vojvodina. (3) The 1991 census allowed inhabitants the possibility to self-define themselves as "Yugoslavs." (4) Since the Albanian population boycotted the census, the numbers provided are estimates.
Source : 1991 Census, *Statistical Bulletin* No. 1934, Federal Institute of Belgrade, 1992.

0   50   100 km

© Philippe Rekacewicz. Reproduced with gratefully acknowledged permission (translated and adapted from color to black and white) from *Le Monde Diplomatique, dossier* "Maniere de Voir," February 29, 1996.

EX-YUGOSLAVIA: THE MARK OF HISTORY

Bold line represents the border of Yugoslavia in January 1991.

Serbia (and the independent principality of Montenegro) gradually acquire automomy—but remain under Ottoman domination until 1987.

The Congress of Berlin grants complete independence to Serbia (and Montenegro), the territory of which is enlarged.

Bosnia-Herzegovina is annexed by Austria-Hungary while the Sandjak is returned to Turkish rule.

The Balkan Wars of 1912 and 1913 complete the dismantling of Ottoman rule in Europe (with the exception of eastern Thrace). Serbia acquires part of Macedonia and shares control over the Sandjak with Montenegro.

The creation of the "Kingdom of the Serbs, Croats, and Slovenes" Yugoslavia) encompasses Serbia and Montenegro as well as former territory of the Habsburg Empire: Croatia, Slovenia, Bosnia-Herzegovina, and Dalmatia.

Under King Alexander I, the Kingdom is renamed "Yugoslavia" and the historical regions are replaced by nine *banovina* (provinces).

© Philippe Rekacewicz. Reproduced with gratefully acknowledged permission (translated and adapted from color to black and white) from *Le Monde Diplomatique, dossier* "Maniere de Voir," February 29, 1996.

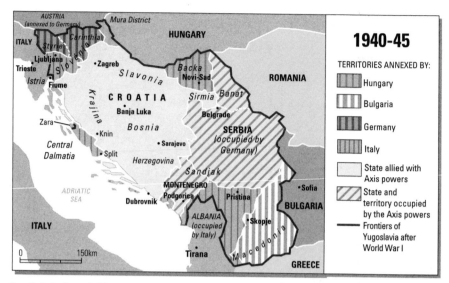

Yugoslavia is dismantled (creation of a Croat state; Serbia and Montenegro under German occupation) and divided among its neighbors allied with Germany.

Yugoslavia is restored as a federation of six republics and two autonomous regions (Kosovo, Vojvodina).

© Philippe Rekacewicz. Reproduced with gratefully acknowledged permission (translated and adapted from color to black and white) from *Le Monde Diplomatique, dossier* "Maniere de Voir," February 29, 1996.

COMMISSION STUDY MISSIONS AND MEETINGS
SEPTEMBER 1995–APRIL 1996

Note: In the course of its study missions, the Commission had an opportunity to exchange views with the individuals listed below, whose time is gratefully acknowledged. The Commission emphasizes, however, that the views expressed in this Report are its own and in no sense attributable to those here listed; names and affiliations are shown here solely to provide a sense of the diversity of views represented in its discussions.

STUDY MISSION TO TURKEY (October 1995)

ANKARA

Suleyman Demirel, *President of the Republic*

Deniz Baykal, *Foreign Minister*

Naci Akinci, *Deputy Director General of Relations with the EU, Ministry of Foreign Affairs*

Ali Dincer, *Minister of State (MP from CHP Party)*

Ibrahim Efendioglu, *President of the Association of Turks from Bulgaria*

Celal Gole, *Dean of the Political Science Faculty, Siyasal Bilgiler Fakultesi*

Emre Gonensay, *Chief Counsellor to the Prime Minister*

Hasan Gurel, *Assistant Professor, Bilkent University*

Ali Karaosmanoglu, *Professor, Bilkent University*

Omer Kurkcuoglu, *Professor of Political Science, Siyasal Bilgiler Fakultesi*

Baskin Oran, *Professor of Political Science, Siyasal Bilgiler Fakultesi*

Turel Ozkarol, *Deputy Director General for Relations with the Council of Europe and for Human Rights, Ministry of Foreign Affairs*

Ambassador Nabi Sensoy, *Director General of Policy Planning, Ministry of Foreign Affairs*

Ambassador Ali Tuygan, *Deputy Undersecretary of State, Ministry of Foreign Affairs*

ISTANBUL

Bulant Akarcali, *Member of Parliament (Motherland Party)*

Mensur Akgun, *Marmara University, International Relations Department, and Member, Helsinki Citizens Assembly*

Sadik Albayrak, *Journalist,* **Milli Gazete**

Zeynep Atikkan, *Journalist,* **Hurriyet Gazetesi**

Hamit Batu, *Retired Ambassador*

Murat Belge, *Journalist, Assistant Professor, Bogazici University, and Member, Helsinki Citizens Assembly*

Cengiz Candar, *Journalist,* **Sabah Gazetesi**

Abdurrahman Drlipak, *Journalist,* **Akit, Aksam** newspapers

Zeynep Duruhal, *Researcher, IRCICA*

Ethem Eldem, *Historian, Bogazici University*

Kerim Erden, *President of the Association of Bosnians*

Halit Eren, *Former President of Association of Western Thrace Turks*

Mehmet Gok, *Professor, Bogazici University*

Nilufer Golet, *Professor of Sociology, Bogazici University*

Halil Ibisoglu, *Secretary General, Association for Balkan Turks*

Ekmeleddin Ihsanoglu, *Director, Research Center for Islamic History, Art and Culture (IRCICA)*

Burhanettin Ismail, *Secretary General of Association of Western Thrace Turks*

Ersin Kalaycioglu, *Professor, Bogazici University*

Altemur Kilic, *Advisor to Tugrul Turkes*

Sami Kohen, *Journalist,* **Milliyet Gazetesi**

Orhan Kologlu, *Press Counsellor to Bulent Ecevit, Leader of Democratic Left Party*

Gun Kut, *Assistant Professor, Bogazici University*

Sule Kut, *Assistant Professor, Marmara University,*

Nilufer Kuyas, *Journalist,* **Milliyet Gazetesi**

Ahmet Lacin, *Researcher, IRCICA*

Yasemin Dobra Manca, *Journalist,* **Turkish Daily News**

Hidayet Nuhoglu, *Deputy Director, IRCICA*

Mehmet Oaktan, *Journalist,* **Yeni Safak**

Necati Ozfatura, *Journalist,* **Turkiye Gazetesi**

Amir Pasic, *Researcher, IRCICA*

Kemali Saybasili, *Professor, Marmara University*

Ismail Sever, *President of Association of Balkan Turks*

Ismail Soysal, *Retired Ambassador, Director, Foundation for Middle East and Balkan Studies*

Acar Tanlak, *Researcher, IRCICA*

Turgut Tarhanli, *Istanbul University Law Faculty, and Member,* Helsinki Citizens Assembly

Zafer Toprak, *Professor, Bogazici University*

Haluk Tukel, *Secretary General, TUSIAD (Association of Turkish Industrialists and Businessmen)*

Mete Tuncay, *Journalist and Historian, and Member,* Helsinki Citizens Assembly

Tugrul Turkes, *Executive Board, Nationalist Action Party (MHP)*

Stephane Yerasimos, *Director, IFEA (Institut Francais d'Etudes Anatoliennes)*

STUDY MISSIONS TO GREECE (November 1995 and January 1996)

ATHENS

Gerasimos Arsenis, *Defense Minister*

Admiral Christos Lymberis, *Defense Ministry*

George Georgiou, *Secretary General of Foreign Ministry*

Admiral Antonio S. Filipou, *Defense Ministry*

Ino Afentouli, *Journalist,* **Ependitis**

Savvas Agouridis, *Professor Emeritus of Theology*

Babis Andreopoulos, *Jehovah's Witnesses Representative*

Bjorn Barth, *Ambassador of Norway*

Philippe Bastelicu, *Charge d'Affaires of the French Republic*

Georg Calice, *Ambassador of Austria*

Costa Carras, *Businessman, Head of Porto Carras*

Panayote Elias Dimitras, *Spokesperson, Greek Helsinki Monitor*

Nikos Dimou, *Writer*

Derek Fraser, *Ambassador of Canada*

Nikos Gasparakis, *Catholic lawyer*

Prof. P. C. Iokamidis, *Professor of European Studies, Athens University and Advisor to ELIAMEP*

Georges Kapopoulos, *Journalist,* **Ependitis**

Dimitris Levantis, *Catholic lawyer, Secretary General of SOS-Racisme Greece, and Legal Advisor of Minorities' Representatives*

Alec Mally, *First Secretary, Embassy of the United States*

Takis Mihas, *Journalist*

Thomas Niles, *United States Ambassador*

Michalis Papakonstantinou, *Former Foreign Minister, Leader of New Democratic Party*

George Patsaouras, *Protestant lawyer*

Enrico Pietromarchi, *Ambassador of Italy*

Antonis Samaras, *Former Foreign Minister, Leader of Political Spring Party*

Prof. Yannis Valinakis, *Director General of ELIAMEP (Hellenic Foundation for European and Foreign Policy)*

Thanos Veremis, *President of ELIAMEP*

THESSALONIKI

Konstantinos Triaridis, *Minister of Macedonia and Thrace*

Gabriel Gziovas, *Director for Political Affairs, Ministry of Macedonia and Thrace*

Veniam Karakostanoglou, *Research Associate of IMXA*

Veniam Karakostanoglu, *Former CSCE monitor to Pristina, and designated OSCE team leader in Visegrad*

Kyriakos D. Kentrotis, *Research Associate of IMXA*

Basil Kontis, *Director of the Institute for Balkan Studies (IMXA)*

Ibram Onsounoglou, *Minority Scientists Association and Advisor to the Mufti of Komotini–Turkish Minority*

Christos Pritskas, *Rainbow–Macedonian Minority*

Leonidas Rokanas, *Counsellor of the Ministry of Foreign Affairs*

Anthony-Emil N. Tachiaos, *President of the Institute for Balkan Studies (IMXA)*

Pavlos Voskopoulos, *Rainbow–Macedonian Minority*

STUDY MISSION TO BULGARIA (November 1995)

SOFIA

Zhelyu Zhelev, *President of Bulgaria*

Georgi Pirinski, *Foreign Minister*

Stefan Agov, *UDF, Deputy Chairman of Foreign Affairs Committee*

Ivan Danilov, *Sofia Representative of the Foundation for Freedom and Democracy in Bulgaria*

Philip Dimitrov, *Former Prime Minister*

Ivan Gaitandjiev, *Democratic Left, Member of Foreign Affairs Committee*

Prof. Nikolai Genchev, *University of Sofia*

Vassil Gotsev, *Vice-President, UDF*

Ivo Indjev, *Vice-President, Association of European Journalists*

Mihail Ivanov, *Presidential Advisor on Ethnic and Minority Questions*

Nikolai Kamov, *Democratic Left, Chairman of Foreign Affairs Committee*

Nikola Kitzevski, *Journalist,* **Trud**

Deyan Kiuranov, *Center for Liberal Strategies*

Yordan Kojouharov, *Ministry of Foreign Affairs*

Ivan Kostov, *President of UDF*

Prof. Ivan Lalkov, *University of Sofia*

Veselin Metodiev, *People's Union, Vice-President of Democratic Party*

William Montgomery, *Ambassador of the United States*

Anastasia Dimitrova Moser, *People's Union, Deputy in National Assembly*

Ivan Pirovski, *Director, Center for International Relations*

Valery Russanov, *Association for Contacts and Cooperation: East European Self-Support*

Stefan Savov, *People's Union, Co-President, and Ex-President of National Assembly*

Yordan Sokolov, *Chairman of UDF Parliamentary Group*

Ilona Tomova, *Presidential Consultant on Ethnic and Religious Issues*

Luchezar Toshev, *UDF Parliamentary Group*

Tatiana Vaksberg, *Journalist,* **Standart**

Antonina Zheliazkova, *International Centre for Minority Studies*

STUDY MISSIONS TO ALBANIA (September and November 1995)

TIRANA

Sali Berisha, *President of Albania*

Alfred Serreqi, *Foreign Minister*

Ali Spahia, *Chairman of Albanian Parliament*

Arion Starova, *Deputy Foreign Minister*

Dimiter Anagostis, *Member of Parliament, Member of Foreign Affairs Committee, and Former Minister of Culture*

Ambassador Paolo Foresti, *Ambassador of Italy*

Rushen Golemi, *Member of Parliament, and Member of Foreign Affairs Committee*

Ismail Kadare, *Writer*

Joseph E. Lake, *Ambassador of the United States*

Halil Lalaj, *Member of Parliament, and Member of Foreign Affairs Committee*

Rudolf Marku, *Member of Parliament, and Member of Foreign Affairs Committee*

Briseida Mema, *Journalist*

Prof. Paskal Milo, *Chairman, Social Democratic Party, and Balkans Historian*

Piro Misha, *Director of Open Society Foundation of Albania*

Genz Pollo, *Advisor to the President*

Arbenz Puto, *Professor of Law, Tirana University, and Executive Director, Albanian Helsinki Watch Committee*

Ilaz Ramajli, *'Representative of the Prime Minister of the Republic of Kosovo'*

Eduard Selami, *Member of Parliament, Senior Member of the Foreign Affairs Committee, and President of Democratic Party*

Izet Shehu, *Member of Parliament, and Member of Foreign Affairs Committee*

Doug Smith, *U.S. Deputy Chief of Mission*

Isa Zymberi, *Director of Kosovo Information Center*

STUDY MISSIONS TO MACEDONIA (November 1995 and January 1996)

SKOPJE

Stojan Andov, *President of the Assembly of the Republic of Macedonia*

Branko Crvenkovski, *Prime Minister of the Republic of Macedonia*

Stevo Crvenkovski, *Minister of Foreign Affairs*

Blagoj Handjiski, *Minister of Defense*

Ljubomir Frckovski, *Minister of Interior*

Emilija Simovska, *Minister of Education and Physical Culture*

Tore Bøgh, *Head of Mission, OSCE*

General Juha Engstrom, *Commander-in-Chief*

Ljupcho Georgievski, *Chairman of VMRO-DPNME*

Branko Geroski, *Journalist, **Vecher** (daily)*

Petar Goshev, *Chairman of the Democratic Party*

Sami Ibrahimi, *Independent Albanian Member of Parliament, and former Professor of English at Pristina University*

Eleonora Karanfilovska, *Journalist, **Puls** (weekly)*

Ambassador Tony Millson, *Embassy of the United Kingdom*

Mirjana Najcevska, *Center of Inter-Ethnic Relations*

Sascho Ordanoski, *President, Macedonian TV*

Dietrich Pohl, *Charge d'Affaires of the Federal Republic of Germany*

Erol Rizaov, *Journalist, **Nova Makedonija** (daily)*

Henryk J. Sokalski, *Assistant Secretary-General, UNPREDEP*

Bob Sorenson, *First Secretary, Embassy of the United States*

Yuri Trushin, *Charge d'Affaires of the Russian Federation*

Abdilhadi Zilfiquari, *Journalist, **Flake Vllazrimit***

TETOVO

Abdurahman Aliti, *Party Chairman, PDP*

Eten Aziri, *Vice-President, NDP*

Alaydin Demiri, *Foreign Affairs Spokesman PDP-A*

Shakir Haliti, *PDP, Mayor of Tetovo*

Bedredin Ibrahimi, *General Secretary, NDP*

Dragche Kuzmanovski, *VMRO-DPMNE, Deputy Mayor of Tetovo*

Menduh Thaci, *Party Vice Chairman, PDP-A*

GOSTIVAR

Zare Apostoloski, *Chairman of the All-Macedonian Committee (MAAK), Gostivar branch*

Miljaim Feiziu, *Chairman of the Democratic Forum for Protection of Human Rights and Freedoms and 'President of the Senate of the Albanian University at Tetovo'*

Ismet Ferai, *Secretary of the Executive City Council*

Jakov Jakovlevski, *Deputy of Nikola Kukoski*

Kiro Kiprovski, *Correspondent, **Nova Makedonija***

Nikola Kukoski, *Chairman, VMRO-DPMNE, Gostivar branch*

Nasir Selimi, *PDP, Deputy Mayor of Gostivar*

STUDY MISSIONS TO CROATIA (December 1995 and April 1996)

ZAGREB

Franjo Tudjman, *President of the Republic of Croatia*

Mate Granic, *Minister for Foreign Affairs*

Vladimir Seks, *Parliament Deputy Speaker*

Josip Manolic, *Former Speaker of the Second Chamber of the Croatian Parliament*

Mark Baskin, *Member, Analysis Assessment Unit, U.N. Headquarters*

Ambassador Zoran Bosniak, *Advisor to the Minister of Foreign Affairs*

Ivan Zvonimir Cicak, *Chairman, Croatian Helsinki Committee for Human Rights*

Peter Galbraith, *Ambassador of the United States*

Slavko Goldstein, *Historian, and Editor of* **Erasmus**

Vlado Gotovac, *Chairman, Liberal Party and Matica Hrvatska*

Jaque Greenberg, *Head, Analysis Assessment Unit, U.N. Headquarters*

Danijel Ivin, *Journalist*

Ivan Jakovcic, *Head of the Istrian Democratic Forum*

Zlato Kramaric, *Mayor of Osijek*

Cardinal Kuharic, *Roman Catholic Primate of Croatia*

Mira Ljubic Lorger, *President, Dalmatian Action Party*

Boris Maruna, *Editor,* **Vijenac**

Ambassador Vladimir Matek, *Chief of Cabinet*

Stipe Mesic, *First Prime Minister of Croatia*

Slobodan P. Novak, *President, PEN Center*

Zarko Puhovski, *Professor of Political Philosophy, University of Zagreb*

Milorad Pupovac, *Representative of Serbs from Coatia*

Ivica Racan, *President of the Social Democratic Party*

Ambassador Fernando Sanchez-Rau, *European Union Monitoring Mission*

Prof. Ivan Supek, *President of Croatian Academy of Science and Arts*

Nikica Valentic, *Former Prime Minister*

Radovan Vukadinovic, *Professor, University of Zagreb*

Jagoda Vukosic, *Editor,* **Novi List**

STUDY MISSION TO SERBIA (January 1996)

BELGRADE

Slobodan Milosevic, *President, Republic of Serbia*

Momir Bulatovic, *President, Republic of Montenegro*

Milan Milutinovic, *Foreign Minister*

Ljubivoje Acimovic, *Researcher, Institute for International Politics and Economics*

Branka Alendar, *Researcher, Institute for International Politics and Economics*

Dragoslav Avramovic, *Governor, Yugoslav National Bank*

Milan Babic, *Former 'President of the Serbian Republic of Krajina'*

Francesco Bascone, *Charge d'Affaires ad interim of Italy*

Milan Bozic, *Serbian Renewal Movement, Member of the Serbian Parliament, Member of the Federal Parliament*

Misa Brkic, *Editor-in-chief,* **Nasa Borba**

Stojan Cerovic, *Vreme*

Zoran Dindic, *President, Democratic Party*

Aleksa Djilas, *Independent Researcher and Writer*

Veselin Djuretic, *Historian, and Member of Balkanology Institute of the Serbian Academy*

Vuk Draskovic, *President, Serbian Renewal Movement*

Milorad Ekmecic, *Historian*

Vladeta Jankovic, *Leader of the Democratic Party of Serbia*

Gabriel Keller, *Charge d'Affaires ad interim of the Embassy of France*

Vojislav Kostunica, *President of the Democratic Party of Serbia*

Ivan Kovacevic, *Serbian Renewal Movement*

Sonia Licht, *Soros Foundation, Belgrade*

183

Gordana Logar, *Former Editor-in-chief,* **Nasa Borba**

Mihajlo Markovic, *Member of Serbian Academy of Sciences and Arts, and former ideologue of the SPS*

Mirjana Markovic, *Leader, United Yugoslav Left (JUL)*

Zoran Matic, *Editor-in-Chief, Studio B*

Jan Matthysen, *Charge d'Affaires ad interim of Belgium*

Dragoljub Micunovic, *Director of the Democratic Center Foundation, and former leader of the Democratic Party (DS)*

Patriarch Pavle, *Patriarch of the Serbian Orthodox Church*

Goran Percevic, *Vice President, Socialist Party of Serbia (SPS)*

Rudolf V. Perina, *Charge d'Affaires of the United States*

Vesna Pesic, *President, Civil Alliance of Serbia*

Ranko Petkovic, *Researcher, Institute for International Politics and Economics*

Nebojsa Popov, *Professor of Philosophy, and Editor,* **Republika**

Dejan Popovic, *Dean of the Faculty of Law*

Dragoljub Popovic, *Member of the Democratic Party of Serbia*

Ivor Roberts, *Charge d'Affaires ad interim of the United Kingdom*

Milorad Roganovic, *Director, Studio B*

Gerhard Enver Schroembgens, *Charge d'Affaires ad interim of the Federal Republic of Germany*

Predrag Simic, *Director, Institute for International Politics and Economics*

Vladimir Stambuk, *JUL*

Svetozar Stojanovic, *Former Advisor to the Federal President*

Mirko Stojcevic, *Researcher, Institute for International Politics and Economics*

Julian Sutor, *Charge d'Affaires ad interim of Poland*

Milos Vasic, *Vreme*

STUDY MISSION TO KOSOVO (January 1996)

PRISTINA

Fehmi Agani, *Vice-Chairman of the LDK*

Xhavit Ahmeti, *LDK Educational Specialist*

Jusuf Bajraktari, *Vice-Chairman of the Peasant Party*

Mahmut Bakalli, *Former Chairman of the Kosovo Party Organization of the League of Communists of Yugoslavia*

Mehmet Bardhi, *Chairman of the Democratic League of Montenegro*

Ismet Berdynja, *Vice-Chairman of the Council for Defence of Human Rights and Freedoms*

Gjergj Dedaj, *Chairman of the Liberal Party of Kosovo*

Adem Demaci, *Chairman of the Council for Defence of Human Rights and Freedoms*

Bosko Drobnjak, *Head of the Secreatariat for Information of the District of Kosovo*

Fatmir Fehmiu, *Constitutional lawyer*

Alush Gashi, *Advisor to Ibrahim Rugova*

Dukagjin Gorani, *Political affairs editor of Pristina weekly,* **Koha**

Vasvija Gusinac, *Coordinator, Muslim National Council of Sanjak*

Harun Hadzic, *Vice-President, Muslim National Council of Sanjak*

Riza Halimi, *Chairman, Party for Democratic Action*

Bardh Hamza, *Editor-in-chief of Pristina weekly,* **Zeri**

O. Terry Heselius, *Country Director of Mercy Corps International*

Skender Hyseini, *Advisor to Ibrahim Rugova*

Agim Hysejni, *Chairman of the Union of Education, Science and Culture of Kosovo*

Rexhep Isamili, *Dean of the Philosophical Faculty of the parallel Albanian university*

Hivzi Islami, *Demographer*

Aleksa Jokic, *Governor of the District of Kosovo and Minister of Traffic and Communications of the Republic of Serbia*

Bajram Kelmendi, *Constitutional lawyer*

Nekibe Kelmendi, *Constitutional lawyer*

Zejnel Kelmendi, *'Dean of Medical Faculty'*

Bajram Kosumi, *Chairman of the Parliamentary Party*

Mark Krasniqi, *Chairman of the Albanian Christian-Democratic Party*

Sami Kurteshi, *Executive Secretary of the Council for Defense of Human Rights and Freedoms*

Zulfikar Kurtesi, *Office of the Governor of the Autonomous Province of Kosovo-Metohija*

Adem Limani, *Chief of the Mother Teresa Gynecological Clinic*

Rasim Ljajic, *Chairman, Party for Democratic Action (SDA) of the Sanjak*

Nike Lumezi, *Constitutional lawyer*

Shkelzen Maliqi, *Commentator for the weekly,* **Zeri***, and representative of the Soros Foundation in Pristina*

Enver Maloku, *Editor-in-chief of the Kosovo Information Center*

Mirijana Marijanovic, *Office of the Governor of the Autonomous Province of Kosovo-Metohija*

Ramush Mavriqi, *Vice-Chairman of the Social-Democratic Party (faction Besim Bokshi)*

Lulezim Mjeku, *Political Commentator,* **Bujku**

Bejlul Nasufi, *Member of the Serbian Parliament*

Milos Nesovic, *Vice-Governor of the District of Kosovo*

Rexhep Osmani, *Chairman of the Albanian Teachers' Association*

Tahir Pereziqi, *Member of the Presidency of the Democratic League of Montenegro*

Luljeta Pula-Beqiri, *Chairwoman of the Social-Democratic Party (faction Pula-Beqiri)*

Bardhyl Qaushi, *Constitutional lawyer*

Rexhep Qosja, *Leader of the political movement Levizija Popullore*

Abdyl Ramaj, *'Head of the Parliamentary Commission on Education'*

Blerim Reka, *Political Commentator for* **Bujku**

Tadej Rodiqi, *Constitutional lawyer*

Ibrahim Rugova, *Chairman of the Democratic League of Kosovo (LDK) and leader of Albanians in Kosovo*

Valentina Saracini, *Kosovo Correspondent of the Albanian program of* **Deutsche Welle***, Cologne*

Blerim Shala, *Political affairs editor of the Kosovo Albanian weekly,* **Zeri**

Avni Spahiu, *Editor-in-chief of the Pristina daily,* **Bujku**

Ejup Staovci, *'Rector of the Albanian University of Pristina'*

Esat Stavilevci, *Constitutional lawyer*

Dzemail Suljevic, *Vice-Chairman, Muslim National Council of Sanjak*

Veton Surroi, *Editor-in-chief,* **Koha**

Izudin Susevic, *Chairman, Reform-Democratic Party of Sanjak*

Edita Tahiri, *LDK Foreign Affairs Secretary*

Radovan Urosevic, *Secretariat of Information, Office of the Governor of the Autonomous Province of Kosovo-Metohija*

Naip Zeka, *Member of the LDK Steering Committee*

Agim Zogaj, *Editor,* **Zeri**

Kasim Zoranic, *Liberal Bosniak Organization of Sanjak*

AJVALIJA

Shaban Shkodra, *Mining Engineer and Village Leader of the Democratic League of Kosovo*

GRACANICA

Sister Fotina, *Serbian Orthodox Monastery*

Sister Katerina, *Serbian Orthodox Monastery*

STUDY MISSIONS TO NEW YORK AND WASHINGTON, D.C. (February 1996)

NEW YORK

Boutros Boutros-Ghali, *United Nations Secretary General*

Madeleine Albright, *U.S. Permanent Representative to the United Nations*

Marrack Goulding, *Under-Secretary General for Political Affairs, Department of Political Affairs, United Nations*

Fouad Ajami, *Professor of Middle Eastern Studies, Paul Nitze School of Advanced Internatiuonal Studies, Johns Hopkins University*

Gilles Kepel, *Professor of Islamic Studies, Centre National de la Recherche Scientifique*

Aryeh Neier, *President, Open Society Fund*

Herbert Okun, *Former ICFY Deputy to Cyrus Vance*

David Phillips, *Consultant to the Council of Foreign Relations, European Center for Common Ground*

Barnett Rubin, *Council of Foreign Relations Center for Preventive Action, South Balkans Project*

Anya Schmemann, *Program Associate, Council on Foreign Relations*

George Soros, *President, The Soros Foundation*

Shashi Tharoor, *Special Assistant to the Under-Secretary-General for Peace-Keeping Operations, United Nations*

Cyrus Vance, *Former U.S. Secretary of State, and Former Co-Chairman of ICFY Steering Committee*

WASHINGTON, D.C.

Samuel Berger, *Deputy Assistant to the President for National Security Affairs, National Security Council*

Robert Gallucci, *Bosnia Coordinator, U.S. State Department*

Daniel Hamilton, *Associate Director of Policy Planning Staff, Department of State*

Lee Hamilton, *Congressman*

John C. Kornblum, *Principal Deputy Assistant Secretary for European & Canadian Affairs, Department of State*

Joseph Lieberman, *Senator*

William J. Perry, *U.S. Secretary of Defense*

Miriam Sapiro, *Member, Policy Planning Staff, Department of State*

James Steinberg, *Director of Policy Planning Staff, Department of State*

Peter Tarnoff, *Undersecretary of State for Political Affairs*

Alexander Vershbow, *Special Assistant to the President, Senior Director for European Affairs, National Security Council*

Morton I. Abramowitz, *President, Carnegie Endowment for International Peace*

Sheppie Abramowitz, *International Rescue Committee*

Paul Balaran, *Vice-President, Carnegie Endowment for International Peace*

David P. Calleo, *Professor of European Studies, Paul H. Nitze School of Advanced International Studies, Johns Hopkins University*

Lynne Davidson, *Carnegie Endowment for International Peace*

Kemal Dervis, *Head of Central European Division, World Bank*

John Fox, *Open Society Institute*

Misha Glenny, *Woodrow Wilson Center*

Patrick Glynn, *Fellow, American Enterprise Institute*

Jane Holl, *Carnegie Commission on Preventing Deadly Conflicts*

John Lampe, *Woodrow Wilson Center*

Anthony Lewis, *Columnist, **New York Times***

Charles W. Maynes, *Editor, **Foreign Policy***

Martin Peretz, *Publisher, **The New Republic***

Lionel Rosenblatt, *Refugees International*

James Schear, *Carnegie Endowment for International Peace*

Helmut Sonnenfeldt, *The Brookings Institution*

Ronald L. Steel, *University of California, School of International Relations*

Paul Wolfowitz, *Dean, Paul H. Nitze School of Advanced International Studies, Johns Hopkins University, former Undersecretary of Defense*

Susan Woodward, *The Brookings Institution*

Ambassador Warren Zimmerman, *Former U.S. Ambassador to Yugoslavia*

Leon Wieseltier, *Literary Editor, **The New Republic***

STUDY MISSION TO BRUSSELS (February, 1996)

Ambassador Gebhardt von Moltke, *Assistant Secretary General for Political Affairs, NATO*

Anthony Cragg, *Assistant Secretary General for Defense Planning and Policy, NATO*

Stefano Sannino, *Political and Economic Advisor to Carl Bildt*

José Maria Meniluce Pereiro, *Member of the European Parliament*

Hans van den Broek, *Member of the European Commission*

Hans-Jorge Kretschmer, *Head Department for ex-Yugoslavia, European Commission*

STUDY MISSION TO PARIS (February 1996)

Hervé de Charette, *Minister for Foreign Affairs*

General Jean Cot, *Former French Commander, UNPROFOR*

Paul Garde, *Professor of History, University of Aix-en-Provence*

Nicole Gnesoto, *IFRI*

Jean Marie Guehenno, *Former Head of Policy Planning*

Dominique Moisi, *Deputy Director of IFRI*

General Philippe Morillon, *Former Commander of U.N. troops in Bosnia*

Christian Rouyer, *Deputy Head of European Department, Foreign Ministry*

Hans Stark, *Secretary General of Committee for Franco-German Studies*

STUDY MISSION TO LONDON (February 1996)

Douglas Hurd, *Member of Parliament, and Former Foreign Secretary of the United Kingdom*

Paddy Ashdown, *Liberal Party Leader, Member of Parliament*

Mats Berdal, *International Institute for Strategic Studies (IISS)*

Jonathan Eyal, *Director of Studies, Royal United Services Institute for Defence Studies*

Lawrence Freedman, *Professor, King's College, London*

Philip H. Gordon, *Editor, **Survival**, IISS*

James Gow, *Department of War Studies, King's College London*

Charles Grant, ***The Economist***

Kirsty Hughes, *Head, European Programme, Chatham House*

Charles King, *IISS*

Calum Macdonald, *Member of Parliament*

Noel Malcolm, *St. Antony's College, Oxford*

James Sherr, *IISS*

Michael Williams, *IISS*

STUDY MISSION TO BONN (February 1996)

Hans-Dietrich Genscher, *FDP, Former Foreign Minister, Member of the Bundestag*

Klaus-Peter Klaiber, *Head of the Planning Staff, Foreign Ministry*

Wolfgang Ischinger, *Political Director, Foreign Ministry*

Freimut Duve, *SPD, Member of the Bundestag*

Joschka Fischer, *Speaker Bundnis 90/Die Gruenen, Member of the Bundestag*

Prof. Karl-Heinz Hornhues, *CDU, Chairman Foreign Committee*

Karl Lamers, *Speaker on Foreign Policy CDU/CSU*

STUDY MISSION TO MOSCOW (March 1996)

Aleksandr Andreyev, *Foreign Affairs Committee, Our Home is Russia Party (NDR)*

Aleksei Arbatov, *Deputy State Duma*

Vladimir Averchev, *Foreign Affairs Committee, Yavlinsky Bloc (Yabloko)*

Djamil D. Bashirov, *Counsellor, Policy Planning Directorate, Ministry of Foreign Affairs*

Yuri Baturin, *National Security Advisor to the President*

Sergei Blagovolin, *Presidential Assistant, Chairman of Russian Channel 1-TV, and President of Institute of Strategic Studies in Moscow*

Yakov Borovoi, *Journalist,* **New Times**

Nikolai Gonchar, *State Duma*

Aleksandr S. Gorelik, *Head of U.N. Affairs, Ministry of Foreign Affairs*

Vladimir Gussinsky, *Head of the MOST Bank and NTV*

Igor Ivanov, *Deputy Minister of Foreign Affairs*

Vladimir E. Ivanovski, *Head of Balkan Affairs, Ministry of Foreign Affairs*

Lev. N. Klepatsky, *Policy Planning Directorate, Ministry of Foreign Affairs*

Yevgeni Michailovich Kozhokin, *Director, Institute for Strategic Studies*

Vladimir Lukin, *Chairman, Foreign Affairs Committee, State Duma*

Vadim B. Lukov, *Director of Policy Planning, Ministry of Foreign Affairs*

Aleksandr Paradis, *NDR*

Marina Pavlova-Silvanskaya, *Political Scientist*

Vladimir Plechko, *Senior Counsellor, Policy Planning Directorate, Ministry of Foreign Affairs*

Aleksei Podberyozkin, *Foreign Affairs Committee, Communist Party*

Vladimir N. Podoprigora, *Senator, and Former Chairman of the International Committee Upper Chamber*

Yuri V. Ushakov, *Head of European Security, Ministry of Foreign Affairs*

Vladimir K. Abarinov, *Foreign Editor,* **Sevodnya**

Stanislaw Ciosek, *Ambassador of Poland*

Dimitri A. Danilov, *Senior Fellow, Institute of Slavic and Balkan Studies, Russian Academy of Science*

Tofik M. Islamov, *Institute of Slavic and Balkan Studies*

Gen. Gennady Ivanov, *Deputy of Col.-Gen. Karchenko*

Pavel E. Kandel, *Institute of Europe, Russian Academy of Science*

Col.-Gen. Dimitri Karchenko, *Senior Staff Officer, International Security Planning*

Irina Kobrinskaya, *Institute of USA and Canada, Russian Academy of Science, and Carnegie Endowment Moscow Center*

Metropolitan Kyrill, *Moscow Patriarch*

Aleksei Mitrofanov, *Chairman of Geopolitics Committee, State Duma, Member, Liberal Democratic Party*

Pierre Morel, *Ambassador of France*

Sergei A. Romanenko, *Institute of Slavic and Balkan Studies*

Sergei P. Tsekhmistrenko, *Journalist,* **Delovye Liudi**

Bakhtiar R. Tuzmukhaedov, *Department of International Law, Constitutional Court of the Russian Federation*

Alla Yazhkova, *USA-Canada Institute, Russian Academy of Science*

Maksim A. Yusin, *Journalist,* **Izvestia**

Col-Gen. Nikolai N. Zlenko

STUDY MISSIONS TO BOSNIA (December 1995 and April 1996)

SARAJEVO

Ejup Ganic, *Member of Presidency of Bosnia and Herzegovina, and Vice President of Federation of Bosnia and Herzegovina*

Stjepan Kljuic, *Member of Presidency of Bosnia and Herzegovina, and former head of HDZ-BH, and present head of Republican Party*

Ivo Komsic, *Member of Presidency of Bosnia and Herzegovina, and head of Croat Peasant Party in Bosnia and Herzegovina*

Mirko Pejanovic, *Member of Presidency of Bosnia and Herzegovina, head of Serb Civic Council*

Haris Silajdzic, *Former Foreign Minister and Former Prime Minister of Bosnia and Herzegovina*

Kresimir Zubak, *President of Federation of Bosnia and Herzegovina*

Bogic Bogicevic, *Former Member of the Yugoslav Presidency*

General Jovan Divjak, *Deputy Commander-in-Chief of Army of Bosnia-Herzegovina*

William Eagleton, *U.N. Representative for Reconstruction and Development*

Robert Froick, *Chief of Mission, OSCE*

Zdravko Grebo, *Director of independent* **Radio ZID**

Hadzem Hajdarevic, *Editor-in-chief,* **Ljiljan**

Mehmeh Halilovic, *Editor-in-chief,* **Oslobodjenje**

Lt. Gen. Jean Heinrich, *French Commander, IFOR*

Rasim Kadic, *Leader of Liberal Party*

Ozren Kebo, *Deputy Editor,* **Dani**

Ademir Kenovic, *Film-maker, SaGA studios*

Adil Kulenovic, *Director and Editor-in-chief,* **Studio 99**, *independent radio and television in Sarajevo*

Goncalez Vargas Llosa, *UNHCR Spokesman*

Lt. General William L. Nash, *U.S. Commander IFOR Tuzla*

Soren Jessen Pedersen, *Chief of Mission, UNHCR*

Ambassador Erik Pierre, *Ambassador of Sweden*

Elizabeth Pryor, *Senior Advisor for Public Policy, OSCE Mission*

Cardinal Vinko Puljic

Brigadier General Per Skov-Christensen, *Senior Deputy for Regional Stabilization OSCE Mission to Bosnia and Herzegovina*

Faruk Smailbegovic, *Industrialist, Director of UNIS*

Students in the Faculty of Economics, Sarajevo University

William Stuebner, *Senior Deputy for Human Rights, OSCE Mission*

Boris Tihi, *Dean of the Economics Faculty, Sarajevo University*

Marko Vesovic, *Writer*

Lt. General Sir Michael Walker, *Commander ARRC (Allied Command Europe Rapid Reaction Corps), Commander Land Forces IFOR*

Michael Steiner, *Deputy to the High Representative Carl Bildt*

PALE

Momcilo Krajisnik, *'President of the Assembly of Republika Srpska'*

Nikola Koljevic, *'Deputy President of Republika Srpska'*

TUZLA

Klelija Balta, *Vice President, Liberal Party of Bosnia and Herzegovina*

Izet Hahzjc, *President of the Canton of Tuzla and Podringe*

Jasmin Imamovic, *Deputy Mayor of Tuzla*

MOSTAR

Ambassador Klaus Metscher, *EU Administration of Mostar*

Didier Fau, *Director for Economics and Transport, EU Administration of Mostar*

Mijo Brajkoviv, *Mayor West Mostar*

Safet Orucevic, *Mayor East Mostar*

189

ABOUT THE INTERNATIONAL
COMMISSION ON THE BALKANS

Based in Berlin and funded by donors on both sides of the Atlantic, the International Commission on the Balkans is an independent panel of leading figures from Europe and the United States who were asked to examine the interrelated conflicts and continuing problems of the region, and to propose a concerted, long-term approach to promoting regional stability. The Commission was established by the Aspen Institute Berlin and the Carnegie Endowment for International Peace in 1995, and owes its inspiration to a Carnegie Endowment-sponsored 1914 Commission report on the origins and conduct of the Balkans wars of 1912 and 1913.

"Governments around the world are preoccupied with managing the Bosnian crisis, day-by-day and minute-by-minute," argued Chairman Leo Tindemans when the current Commission was established. "There is a real need for an independent effort that takes the long view, that looks at the area as a whole, that reflects upon the interrelationship of complex problems in many countries, and that can formulate a set of principles for a comprehensive international strategy."

This Report, prepared with the help of an expert staff, is the result of extensive study missions—conducted between September 1995 and April 1996—to major international capitals and throughout the Balkans, where the commissioners met with a wide range of government and opposition leaders, as well as intellectuals, business leaders, cultural and religious figures, and journalists (see pp. 179-189). The Commission was supported in its work by a staff of resident and consulting experts from ten countries.

MEMBERS OF THE COMMISSION

Leo Tindemans (Commission Chairman), a leading figure in the European integration movement, was Prime Minister of Belgium in 1974-78 and Minister of Foreign Affairs in 1981-89. He is the author of *European Union: Report to the European Council*, published in 1976 and better known as the *"Tindemans Report,"* which advocated the creation of a European political union and is one of the landmark documents in the literature of European integration. Mr. Tindemans has also devoted much of his political career to the search for constitutional solutions to the competing Walloon and Flemish demands for autonomy within Belgium. Since 1989, he has been a member of the European Parliament.

Lloyd N. Cutler, a prominent international lawyer, is a partner in the Washington firm of Wilmer, Cutler & Pickering. He was Counsel to the President of the United States (Carter) in 1979-80, and Special Counsel to the President (Clinton) in March-September 1994. He has also served as Special Counsel to the President on Ratification of the SALT II Treaty, 1979-80; as the President's Special Representative for Maritime Resource and Boundary Negotiations with Canada, 1977-79; and as Senior Consultant to the President's Commission on Strategic Forces, 1983-84.

Bronislaw Geremek, a professor of history, was one of the first leaders to emerge from the *Solidarity* movement. He resigned from the Polish United Workers Party following the 1968 invasion of Czechoslovakia. Mr. Geremek co-founded *Towarzysiwo Kursow Naukowych,* the independent opposition educational organization. From 1980 to 1990, he was an advisor to various *Solidarity* committees and to Lech Walesa. A member of the Polish Parliament (Sejm) since 1989, he is Chairman of its Foreign Affairs Committee and now chairs the Union for Freedom Parliamentary Caucus..

John Roper was a Member of the British Parliament, 1970-83; a Labour Party Spokesman on Defense, 1979-81; and Chief Whip of the Social Democratic Party, 1981-83. From 1983 to 1990, he was a senior staff member of the Royal Institute of International Affairs (Chatham House) and editor of its journal, *International Affairs.* In 1990, he was appointed the founding director of the Institute for Security Studies of the Western European Union. In 1995, he returned to Chatham House as Associate Fellow.

Theo Sommer, a leading German journalist and author of several books on international and strategic affairs, became foreign editor of the weekly, *Die Zeit,* in 1958 and its Deputy Editor in 1969. In 1969-70, he served as Chief of Planning Staff in the West German Ministry of Defense. He returned to *Die Zeit* as Editor-in-Chief in 1973. Since 1992, he has been Publisher of the paper.

Simone Veil, a leading French political figure, is a survivor of the Auschwitz-Birkenau concentration camp. She studied law and became a judge in France before entering politics. She was Minister of Health and Social Security in the French Government in 1974-76, and President of the European Parliament, 1979-82. She later chaired its Legal Affairs Committe and was an active member of its Human Rights Committee. From 1993 to 1995, Madame Veil was Minister of State for Health, Social Affairs and Urban Development in the French government.

David Anderson is Director of the Aspen Institute Berlin. A career U.S. Foreign Service Officer, he was the U.S. State Department's Director of Central European Affairs, 1975-77; Deputy Executive Secretary, 1977-78, U.S. Minister in Berlin, 1978-81, and U.S. Ambassador to Yugoslavia from 1981 until his retirement in 1985.

SENIOR STAFF

Jacques Rupnik (Commission Executive Director) is Director of Research at the Center for International Studies and Research of the National Foundation for Political Science and a professor at the Institute of Political Studies in Paris. He has been a Research Fellow at the Russian Research Center at Harvard University, a specialist on Eastern European Affairs for the BBC World Service, and an advisor to Vaclav Havel, President of the Czech Republic. His most recent book is *Le Dechirement des nations* (Paris: Seuil, 1995).

Dana H. Allin (Commission Deputy Director) is Deputy Director of the Aspen Institute Berlin. Previously a professorial lecturer at the Johns Hopkins University Bologna Center, he is the author of *Cold War Illusions: America, Europe and Soviet Power, 1969-1989* (New York: St. Martin's Press, 1995).

James F. Brown (Commission Senior Analyst) is former Director of Radio Free Europe (RFE) in Munich. Earlier, he was a Senior Member of St. Anthony's College, Oxford; taught at Berkeley and UCLA; and was a senior analyst at the RAND Corporation. His most recent book is *Hopes and Shadows: Eastern Europe After Communism* (Duke University Press, 1994).

Mark Thompson (Commission Senior Analyst) is an author and independent journalist who has written on the Balkans. He was also an analyst for the Analysis and Assessment Unit at UNPROFOR (later UNPF) in Zagreb. His most recent book is *Forging War: The Media in Serbia, Croatia and Bosnia and Herzegovina* (London 1994).

CONSULTANTS

Note: The Commission and its Staff drew on the expertise of the following consultants, who briefed commissioners and wrote background papers (some of the essays will be published in a separate volume). Consultants made their contributions in their personal capacity; institutional affiliations are shown for identification only. It should again be noted, however, that the views expressed in this Report are those of the Commission alone.

Pierre Hassner (Paris), Centre d'Etudes et de Recherche Internationales—International Institutions and the Balkan Crisis

Hanns Maull (Bonn), Trier University—Germany's Policy

Jane Sharpe (London), Kings College—Britain's Policy

Patrice Canivez (Lille), University of Lille—France's Policy

Nadia Arbatova (Moscow), Russian Academy of Sciences—Russia's Policy

Pavel Kandel (Moscow), Russian Academy of Sciences—Russia and the Balkans

Duygu Sezer (Ankara), Bilkent University—Turkey's Policy

Sherif Mardin (Washington), American University—Islam in the Balkans: The Case of Bosnia

Fouad Ajami (Washington) Johns Hopkins School of Advanced International Studies—The Balkans Between Islam and the West

Costa Carras (Athens)—The Orthodox Church and Politics in the Post-Communist World

Marie Janine Calic (Ebenhausen), Stiftung Wissenschaft und Politik Research Institute for International Affairs)—The International Community and Post-War Reconstruction

Morgane Labbe (Paris), Institut National d'Etudes Demographiques—The Uses and Abuses of Demography in the Balkans

Stefan Troebst (Berlin), Free University, Berlin—The Macedonian Question

Jasna Dragovic (Geneva), Graduate School of International Studies—Serb Nationalism

Panayote Dimitras (Athens), Greek Helsinki Committee—Rewriting History in the Context of Balkan Nationalisms

James Gow (London), Kings College, London University—The Role of the Military and the Specific Nature of Warfare in the Balkans

William Pfaff (Paris), International Herald Tribune—Judging War Crimes

George Schoepflin (London), London University—Minorities in the Age of Ethnic Cleansing

John Lampe (Washington, D.C.), Woodrow Wilson Center—Economy and Communications in Southeastern Europe

Jonas Wildgren (Vienna), International Center for Migration Policy—Refugee Problems and Migrations

Stephen Larrabee (Santa Monica, California), The Rand Corporation—A Regional Security Framework for the Balkans

ADMINISTRATIVE STAFF

Diana Kendall
Isabella Clough
Julia Henze

THE ASPEN INSTITUTE BERLIN

The Aspen Institute Berlin is a private, non-profit, non-partisan institute that organizes international conferences, study groups, and workshops on major contemporary issues. During the more than twenty years of the Berlin Institute's existence, it has regularly brought together members of elites from both sides of the Atlantic as well as Eastern and Western Europe to exchange ideas and perspectives on the pressing transatlantic and East-West issues of the time.

The Aspen Institute Berlin is part of the international Aspen Institute network, headquartered in Washington, D.C. The Aspen Institute was founded in 1949 in Aspen Colorado, at the initiative of Walter Paepcke, Chairman of the Container Corporation of America. Following the opening of the first Aspen Institute outside the United States in Berlin in 1974, the network was extended at the beginning of the 1980s to include Aspen Italia and Aspen France, and in the mid-1990s to include the Aspen Japan Council.

The mission of The Aspen Institute is to enhance the quality of leadership through informed dialogue about the timeless ideas and values of the world's great cultures and traditions as they relate to the foremost challenges facing societies, organizations, and individuals. The Seminar Programs enable leaders to draw on these values to enrich their understanding of contemporary issues. The Policy Programs frame the choices that democratic societies face in terms of the enduring ideas and values derived from those traditions.

ASPEN INSTITUTE BERLIN

Edzard Reuter, *Chairman of the Board*
David Anderson, *Director*
Dana H. Allin, *Deputy Director*
Steffen Sachs, *Deputy Director*

HONORARY MEMBERS OF THE BOARD

Willy Brandt †
Former Chancellor,
Federal Republic of Germany

Eberhard Diepgen
Governing Mayor of Berlin

David T. McLaughlin
President and CEO,
The Aspen Institute U.S.A.,
Queenstown, MD

Walter Momper
Former Governing Mayor of Berlin

Paul Doty
Professor,
Harvard University,
Cambridge, MA

Joseph E. Slater
President Emeritus,
The Aspen Institute U.S.A.,
Salk Institute, New York

Helmut Schmidt
Former Chancellor,
Federal Republic of Germany

Lothar Spath
Former Minister President,
Baden-Wurttemberg

Dietrich Stobbe
Former Governing Mayor of Berlin;
European Director,
Arthur D. Little International, Inc.

Shepard Stone †
Former Director,
Aspen Institute Berlin

MEMBERS OF THE BOARD

David Anderson
Director,
Aspen Institute Berlin

Evan Bayh
Governor of Indiana,
Indianapolis, IN

Georges Berthoin
Honorary European Chairman,
The Trilateral Commission, Paris

Kurt Biedenkopf
Minister President of Saxony, Dresden

Bill Bradley
U.S. Senator,
Washington, DC

Lord Alan Bullock
Historian, Former Vice-Chancellor,
Oxford University, Oxford

Marion Grafin Donhoff
Publisher,
Die Zeit, Hamburg

Lawrence Eagleburger
Former U.S. Secretary of State,
Washington, DC

Hans-Dietrich Genscher
Former Foreign Minister,
Federal Republic of Germany, Bonn

Bronislaw Geremek
MP, Chairman of Foreign Affairs Committee
of the Polish Parliament, Warsaw

Francois Heisbourg
Senior Vice-President,
Matra Defense, Velizy Villacoublay

Hans-Olaf Henkel
Chairman of the Supervisory Group,
IBM Deutschland GmbH,
President, Federation of German
Industry, Dusseldorf

Georg Krupp
Member of the Board,
Deutsche Bank AG, Frankfurt/M.

Alexander A. Kwapong
Former Director, African Programmes,
Commonwealth of Learning,
Accra, Ghana

Wolf Lepenies
Rector,
Institute for Advanced Study,
Berlin

David Marquand
Professor,
Sheffield University, Sheffield

Ann McLaughlin
Former U.S. Secretary of Labor,
Washington, DC

Dominique Moisi
Deputy Director, French Institute
for International Relations,
Editor-in-Chief,
Politique Etrangere, Paris

Horst Niemeyer
Secretary General, Doners Association
for the Promotion of Science and
Humanities in Germany, Essen

Jurgen Reuning
Managing Director,
OTIS GmbH, Berlin

Edzard Reuter
Former Chairman of the Board,
Daimler Benz AG, Stuttgart;
Chairman of the Board,
Aspen Institute Berlin

Harald J. Schroeder
Vice-Chairman,
Board of Management,
Merck KGaA, Darmstadt

Klaus Schutz
Former Governing Mayor of Berlin

Carlo Scognamiglio
President,
Aspen Institute Italia, Rome

Fritz Stern
Seth Low Professor of History,
Columbia University,
New York, NY

Rita Sussmuth
President,
Federal German Parliament,
Bonn

Richard von Weizsacker
Former President,
Federal Republic of Germany,
Berlin

195

THE CARNEGIE ENDOWMENT
FOR INTERNATIONAL PEACE

The Carnegie Endowment for International Peace was established in 1910 in Washington, D.C., with a gift from Andrew Carnegie. As a tax-exempt operating (not grant-making) foundation, the Endowment conducts programs of research, discussion, publication, and education in international affairs and U.S. foreign policy. The Endowment publishes the quarterly magazine, *Foreign Policy*.

Carnegie's senior associates—whose backgrounds include government, journalism, law, academia, and public affairs—bring to their work substantial first-hand experience in foreign policy through writing, public and media appearances, study groups, and conferences. Carnegie associates seek to invigorate and extend both expert and public discussion on a wide range of international issues, including worldwide migration, nuclear nonproliferation, regional conflicts, multilateralism, democracy-building, and the use of force. The Endowment also engages in and encourages projects designed to foster innovative contributions in international affairs.

In 1993, the Carnegie Endowment committed its resources to the establishment of a public policy research center in Moscow designed to promote intellectual collaboration among scholars and specialists in the United States, Russia, and other post-Soviet states. Together with the Endowment's associates in Washington, the center's staff of Russian and American specialists conduct programs on a broad range of major policy issues ranging from economic reform to civil-military relations. The Carnegie Moscow Center holds seminars, workshops, and study groups at which international participants from academia, government, journalism, the private sector, and nongovernmental institutions gather to exchange views. It also provides a forum for prominent international figures to present their views to informed Moscow audiences. Associates of the center also host seminars in Kiev on an equally broad set of topics.

The Endowment normally does not take institutional positions on public policy issues. It supports its activities principally from its own resources, supplemented by nongovernmental, philanthropic grants.

CARNEGIE ENDOWMENT FOR INTERNATIONAL PEACE
OFFICERS AND BOARD OF TRUSTEES

Robert Carswell, *Chairman of the Board*
James C. Gaither, *Vice Chairman of the Board*
Morton I. Abramowitz, *President*
Paul Balaran, *Vice President*
Stephen Sestanovich, *Vice President for Russian and Eurasian Affairs*
Michael V. O'Hare, *Secretary & Director of Finance and Administration*

Morton I. Abramowitz
President,
Carnegie Endowment

Charles W. Bailey II
Journalist

Harry G. Barnes Jr.
Director,
Conflict Resolution and
Human Rights Program,
The Carter Center

Derek H. Burney
Chairman, President, and CEO,
Bell Canada International, Inc.

Robert Carswell
Of Counsel,
Shearman & Sterling

Gregory B. Craig
Partner,
Williams & Connolly

Richard A. Debs
Advisory Director,
Morgan Stanley International

William H. Donaldson
Donaldson, Lufkin, Jenrette

Marion R. Fremont-Smith
Partner,
Choate, Hall & Stewart

James C. Gaither
Partner,
Cooley, Godward, Castro,
Huddleson & Tatum

Leslie H. Gelb
President,
Council on Foreign Relations

Stephen D. Harlan
President,
H. G. Smithy Co.

James A. Johnson
Chairman of the Board & CEO,
FannieMae

Donald Kennedy
President Emeritus and
Bing Professor of Environmental Science,
Stanford University,
Institute for International Studies

Robert Legvold
Professor of Political Science,
The Harriman Institute,
Columbia University

Wilbert J. LeMelle
President,
The Phelps Stokes Fund

Stephen R. Lewis, Jr.
President,
Carleton College

George C. Lodge
Professor,
Harvard University,
Graduate School of
Business Administration

Jessica Tuchman Mathews
Senior Fellow,
Council on Foreign Relations

Barbara W. Newell
Regents Professor,
Florida State University

Olara A. Otunnu
President,
International Peace Academy

Geneva Overholser
Ombudsman,
The Washington Post

Edson W. Spencer
Spencer Associates

Charles J. Zwick
Retired Chairman,
Southeast Banking Corporation

THE OTHER BALKAN WARS

A 1913 Carnegie Endowment Inquiry in Retrospect, with a New Introduction by George F. Kennan

Eight decades ago, the then young Carnegie Endowment for International Peace, established in 1911, launched an International Commission to conduct an on-the-scene investigation of the causes and conduct of the Balkan Wars of 1912 and 1913—short, sharp, and largely forgotten conflicts inflamed by virulent nationalism all too familiar to readers of today's headlines.

By reissuing the Commission's report, together with a new introduction by the eminent historian and former diplomat George F. Kennan, the Endowment seeks to provide a historical perspective to deepen contemporary understanding of the current war and tragedy in the former Yugoslavia.

In his introductory essay, Professor Kennan writes: "The importance of this report for the world of 1993 lies primarily in the light it casts on the excruciating situation prevailing today . . . to reveal to people of this age how much of today's problem has deep roots and how much does not. It will be easier to think of solutions when such realities are kept in mind." He judges, as will many readers, that this report "may stand, in its entirety, as one of the most eloquent and compelling pleas for recognition of the folly of war and the essentiality of international peace, not just in the Balkans but everywhere in the civilized world."

CONTENTS OF THE REPORT: Introduction by the Commission Chairman. The Origins of the Two Balkan Wars. The War and the Noncombatant Population. Bulgarians, Turks, and Servians. The War and the Nationalities. The War and International Law. Economic Results of the Wars. The Moral and Social Consequences of the Wars and the Outlook for the Future of Macedonia.

MEMBERS OF THE 1913-14 COMMISSION: Baron d'Estournelles de Constant, Commission Chairman (France), French Senator; M. Justin Godart (France), Lawyer and Member of Chamber of Deputies; Dr. Josef Redlich (Austria), Professor of Public Law, University of Vienna; Dr. Walther Schucking (Germany), Professor of Law, University of Marburg; Francis W. Hirst (Great Britain), Editor of *The Economist*; Dr. H.N. Brailsford (Great Britain), Journalist; Professor Paul Milioukov (Russia), Member of the Douma; Dr. Samuel T. Dutton (United States), Professor, Columbia University.

424 pp. ISBN: 0-87003-032-9 Price: $16.95/£13.25

To order (by charge card), please call Carnegie's distributor, The Brookings Institution, toll-free at 1-800-275-1447; in Washington, D.C., call 202-797-6258. Fax: 202-797-6004. When ordering, please refer to code SBW.

If ordering from U.K. or Europe, call or fax Plymbridge Distributors (U.K.). Tel: 44-1752-202301. Fax: 44-1752-202331.